THE INNER
MYSTERIES

PROGRESSIVE WITCHCRAFT AND
CONNECTING WITH THE DIVINE

Janet Farrar & Gavin Bone

THE INNER
MYSTERIES

PROGRESSIVE WITCHCRAFT AND
CONNECTING WITH THE DIVINE

ROBERT HALE

First published in 2003 by Acorn Guild Press

This edition published in 2024 by Robert Hale, an imprint of
The Crowood Press Ltd, Ramsbury, Marlborough Wiltshire SN8 2HR

enquiries@crowood.com
www.crowood.com

British Library Cataloguing-in-Publication Data
A catalogue record for this book is available from the British Library.

ISBN 978 0 7198 3160 7

Figures and illustrations by Corbin

Cover design by Sergey Tsvetkov

Printed and bound in India by Parksons Graphics Pvt Ltd.

Contents

Figures vi

Photographs vii

Preface ix

Introduction xvi

Acknowledgments xxi

Chapter 1   In the Beginning: From Witchcraft to Wicca 1

Chapter 2   Into the New Millennium:
Progressive Witchcraft Evolves 22

Chapter 3   At the Heart: Spirituality and the Mysteries 44

Chapter 4   God and Goddess: Deity-Centered Witchcraft 60

Chapter 5   The Progressive Coven: The Witch's "Family" 76

Chapter 6   Making the Witch: Training within Witchcraft 92

Chapter 7   Spiritual Cosmology: Walking Between the Worlds 111

Chapter 8   Sorcery: The Magical Art of the Witch 131

Chapter 9   The Wheel: Cycles of Time and Fate 153

Chapter 10   Priesthood: Connecting with and Serving Deity 170

Chapter 11   First Steps on the Path:
Finding a Progressive Teacher or Coven 186

Liber Actios: A Training Manual 199

Appendix A Occult/Spiritual Laws 219

Appendix B Goddesses and Gods of Witchcraft 223

Appendix C Correspondence Tables 235

Appendix D Contacts and Useful Addresses 238

Bibliography 240

Index 244

Figures

Figure 1	Polytheism, Duotheism, and the Lightning Flash	page 36 (chapter 2)
Figure 2	Maslow's Triangle	page 96 (chapter 6)
Figure 3	The Lady's Star	page 116 (chapter 7)
Figure 4	A Wiccan Cosmology	page 118 (chapter 7)
Figure 5	The Chakras and Aura	page 143 (chapter 8)
Figure 6	The Wheel of the Year and the Power Tides	page 157 (chapter 9)
Figure 7	Pentagram Ritual: Invoking and Banishing Pentagram	page 206 (chapter 11)
Figure 8	Invoking and Banishing Celtic Cross	page 206 (chapter 11)
Figure 9	Ritual Stance: Invoking and Banishing	page 207 (chapter 11)

(All figures by Corbin.)

Photographs

Photograph 1 Doreen Valiente (1922–1999)—Regarded as page xiii
"the mother of modern Witchcraft." She was
responsible for much of the prose and ritual
within the Wiccan Book of Shadows (photo by
Stewart Farrar).

Photograph 2 Mithras—The Cult of Mithras was predominant page 5
amongst the Roman officer and merchant
classes at the time of the rise of Christianity
and the cult of Diana of Ephesus (photo
courtesy British Museum).

Photograph 3 Diana or Artemis of Ephesus—Diana/Artemis page 6
took on the major attributes of all the major
goddesses of the Mediterranean as part of
her cult. Unable to ignore her influence,
Christianity revived her as Mary Theotokos
at the Council of Ephesus in 431 AD. (Photo
courtesy Turkish Department of Antiquities.)

Photograph 4 Hermanubis—In the later Graeco-Egyptian page 53
Mysteries, Hermes and Anubis became
combined as Hermanubis the Psychopompos
(photo courtesy Vatican Museum).

Photograph 5 Shrine to Bast—The creation of permanent page 61
shrines and altars helps the Witch to connect
spiritually with individual deities on a personal
level (photo by author).

Photograph 6 Coven Training—Teaching within Circle is an page 105
important aspect of training. Here one of the
authors teaches the mysteries through the use
of the tarot (photo by author).

Photograph 7 Perron, Rathkenny, County Meath, Ireland— page 115
The perron (a stone pillar found in villages
in England, Scotland, and Ireland) supplanted
the earlier pagan maypole as the community's
axis mundi (photo by author).

Photograph 8 Two-Person Energy Exercise—This form of page 149
              visualization exercise teaches student Witches
              how to control the magical energy that
              emanates from the aura and chakras (photo
              by author).

Photograph 9 Group   Energy   Exercise—Using   energy page 150
              exercises as a form of coven training helps
              to reinforce the gestalt or coven mind, while
              teaching how to create the cone of power
              (photo by author).

Photograph 10 The Use of Masks and Veils—Covering the page 183
              face helps to sublimate the priest or priestess'
              persona during the Rite of Drawing Down the
              Moon or Sun (photo by author).

Photograph 11 Connecting with the element of Earth—This page 210
              is the element of physicality and the material
              world, represented by the pentacle (photo by
              author).

Photograph 12 Connecting with the element of Air—High page 211
              places such as mountains or hilltops are good
              places to use to connect with this element.
              Governing the intellect, its magical tool is the
              wand (photo by author).

Photograph 13 Connecting with the element of Fire— page 213
              Meditation on this element helps the Witch
              to understand the nature of the will and its
              connection with its magical tool, the sword
              (photo by author).

Photograph 14 Connecting with the element of Water—Wells page 214
              have traditionally been seen in Northern
              Europe as access points to the underworld
              because of Water's associations with the
              emotions. Its magical tool is the chalice (photo
              by author).

Preface to the Second Edition

This book was first published as *Progressive Witchcraft: Spirituality, Mysteries & Training in Modern Wicca*. It received mixed reviews when it was released in 2003, but as time has passed, many have recognized the work's groundbreaking qualities. To quote one author who read the book when it first came out, "Sometimes a book can be ahead of its time, and can be released too early." We now believe this was the case with *Progressive Witchcraft*. Not only are there increasing numbers of Witches who define themselves as "progressive" in their attitudes to Wicca, but a network also developed made up of like-minded covens of mixed origins who also define themselves as progressive. (See footnotes on page 22.)

One of the markers of an advanced spiritual practice is that it is never static but is always evolving. We have been teaching the material within this book (*The Inner Mysteries*) for the past ten years. During that time, we've developed a method of teaching energy work in combination with a more coherent spiritual cosmology. We have found this to have great usefulness in practical magical work. We began an online course in Progressive Witchcraft, using the book as the basic text, while continuing to teach our Inner Mysteries workshops. Over time, we supplemented the written material with another workshop: Inner Mysteries 2: Progressive Magic. As of the new publication of this book, we have taught these workshops in more than nine countries both inside and outside Europe. These workshops have increased interest in this book and fueled the decision to change the title to *The Inner Mysteries: Progressive Witchcraft and Connection with the Divine*.

Our writing team has been at the forefront of the modern Witchcraft revival since its beginnings in the mid-twentieth century in Great Britain. As we move into the twenty-first century, we are happy to see that Wiccans are maturing into more advanced spiritual practices. Wiccans and other modern Witches are no longer content to simply "drive the magical car," but also want to "look under the hood and learn how the engine works," to quote from our workshops. Our idea that Wiccans need a firmer basis in training, and a stronger focus on relationship with Deity, is coming to fruition with the establishment of several covens in both Europe and the United States. These covens reject the assertion that lineage and traditions are primary, and instead put magical training, personal gnosis, and direct revelation at the forefront of their efforts.

We live in a time in which Pagan and Wiccan practices are becoming more and more mainstream. Best-selling women's magazines found at any newsstand have "resident Witches" and feature beginning spells for readers to try. A best-selling book recently drew on magical teachings that all modern Witches learn as a basic skill when they come into the Craft. Now that magic is becoming commonplace in the media, what should our role as modern Witches be? We believe Witches need to move into being the magical experts, the "fixers" that are consulted when things go awry. To follow up on the magical car metaphor, it's time for us Witches to become the magical "mechanics" rather than mere magical "drivers." This is the reason we originally published *Progressive Witchcraft*—to fill in the expertise gap, particularly in terms of relationship with the divine and the personal gnosis that is so sadly lacking in many established Craft traditions.

The modern Witchcraft revival can be compared to a child growing to maturity. The child Wicca was born in the 1940s, and started to crawl in the 1950s. Still very influenced by monotheism, Wicca began to totter to its feet in the 1960s, when it began to explore the world for the first time. By the 1970s, Wicca was at school, beginning to learn about its lengthy and inspiring history. In the 1980s, Wicca entered its rebellious adolescence and challenged all of its previously established sacred cows and shibboleths. By the 1990s and into the new millennium, Wicca is finally looking up to the stars in the night sky in wonder, and asking the question "Why am I here?"

Janet came into Wicca in the early 1970s, when Wicca was in its learning phase. Gavin came in the 1980s, when many were challenging the doctrines of the past and throwing out those aspects that (at the time)

seemed irrelevant to the spiritual connection that Wicca seemed to promise. It was during this time that the established duotheistic view of Divinity in Wicca was first challenged. And that was the root of what we see
as a positive new trend that is now coming to fruition. In the past, many
writers emphasized the psychological aspects of Deity and used phrases
like "numinous archetype," drawn from Jung's writings. Many Witches
saw their gods and goddesses as part of their own internal psychological
makeup rather than as spiritual entities with their own existence. This
view is now changing. While most Witches still believe that Deity is an
immanent part of them, many have now realized that each deity is a
separate divinity it its own right, with a character, personality, likes and
dislikes, and its own individuation (another Jungian term). And so the
famous quote from Dion Fortune that "all gods are one god, all goddesses
are one goddess" is being placed in a more truly polytheistic context.

Another major change in Wicca, which we foreshadowed in *Progressive Witchcraft*, is the rise of priests and priestesses devoted to one specific deity. Devotion to a single deity was the norm in most polytheistic
traditions in ancient times and still is in modern polytheistic traditions.
As more initiates devote themselves to single deities in Wicca, we are
seeing the rise of larger groups devoted to a single divinity. There have
also been more books written recently about a single divinity, as compared to encyclopedias with short entries on many deities. We first wrote
about this trend in chapter 4 of this book. For example, there is a large,
international group on Facebook dedicated to Hekate that draws inspiration from a book by Sorita d'Este. They have been planning rituals on
a regular basis, a fascinating intersection of ancient-style devotion using
entirely modern means.

As we move into the twenty-first century, it seems to us that Wicca is
moving more and more into the priestly patterns of the ancient polythe-
isms rather than being focused on the ritual structures, forms of Deity,
and styles of Witchcraft envisioned by Gardner and Sanders. It is not so
much a learning, as an unlearning, or perhaps a change in focus. Today's
Witches seem to be focusing more strongly on creativity and spirituality,
and less on strict duotheism and ritual structures drawn from Ceremonial
Magic. Many of the parts of Wicca that are being de-emphasized today are
patriarchal norms and values. Since it arose in the 1940s and 1950s, Wicca
couldn't altogether avoid the pervasive climate of patriarchy that charac-
terized that time. It is our hope, however, that those who have progressed
beyond needing patriarchal structures in their lives will appreciate this
work, especially its truly polytheistic approach to Divinity. We believe this

book offers a workable blueprint for training and coven structures that will benefit the modern Witchcraft movement.

At the time of this writing, Wicca has evolved into diverse vibrant traditions worldwide. This self-definition was driven by a sudden influx of many people calling themselves Witches or Wiccans in the late 1990s. The trend was driven by mass media, especially television and film. Publishers and authors were quick to respond, with often-exploitative books that jumped category from New Age to Witch with no change in content or style. In our communities, we were suddenly faced with many people calling themselves Wiccan or Witches who knew little of the history of modern Witchcraft or the neo-Pagan movement, and much less of the underlying philosophies. For these people, being a Witch was a fashion statement, and they were unkindly referred to as "fluffy bunnies." It is not surprising that the movement began polarizing at that time, in reaction to the sudden arrival of many people who only see Witchcraft as a magical practice, rather than one of devotion and worship of the divine through nature.

In reaction to this influx of people—who not only didn't know much about Witchcraft, but also in many cases were unwilling to learn—various new designations for traditions within Witchcraft were coined. British Traditional Witchcraft, or BTW, is an American term that first began to be used around this time. A corollary term: American Traditional Witchcraft, or ATW, also came into use. British Traditional Witchcraft is an umbrella term for the paths within Witchcraft that still adhere to the teachings of Gardner and Sanders. BTW Witches have strict beliefs, initiatory paths, and a traceable lineage from the founders of the traditions. ATW Witches instead follow traditions founded in America that were inspired by the modern Witchcraft revival in Great Britain. Examples of ATW traditions are the 1734 tradition; the Cabot tradition of Salem, Massachusetts; NROOGD in Northern California; and the Assembly of the Sacred Wheel in the mid-Atlantic region.

We believe that BTW and ATW came into the terminology of Wicca to define the participants of those traditions as separate from the large numbers of people from other backgrounds who began calling themselves Witches and Wiccans in the 1990s, not to separate BTW and ATW from each other. And it is important to remember, from a purely British standpoint, that the two traditions that are considered BTW in America have developed in very distinct ways. At this point in time, we believe they are separate traditions from their British rootstock.

Some, though certainly not all, British Traditional Witchcraft covens in America have very rigid rules about secrecy, initiation, what can (and can't) be taught to initiates, and they also have very strict practices in Circle. This is a movement away from the practices of their British brethren. Some of this rigidity of practice is a result of fear that their tradition will be watered down by new ideas or practices. And the concept of "oral law"—doctrine passed down only through word of mouth—has also appeared in BTW covens as the Book of Shadows becomes more and more public. But no one has ever established what "oral law" means outside of individual covens and extended coven families.

Doreen Valiente (1922–1999)

We believe that most of these new rules fly in the face of what Gerald Gardner, Doreen Valiente, and later Alex Sanders actually taught. We believe that when Wicca is codified into a static format, it ceases to be the all-embracing magical tradition envisaged by these important figures. As Doreen Valiente put it, "The most important code of Witchcraft is, if it works, use it!" This statement by definition encourages the adoption of new ideas and practices. Gardner, Valiente, and Sanders did not believe in the codes of secrecy or the rigid rules that are part of today's Wicca. They would have seen such static practices as restricting their practice of Witchcraft. If they had followed such as rigid code of secrecy when they were practicing, Wicca would not be so widespread, nor would there be so many different versions of the Book of Shadows.

All of the original practitioners of Wicca adapted and evolved their practices over time. They also believed that "a Witch is a Witch" regardless of the type of initiation the individual went through. All of them accepted individuals on their individual merits. Both Alex Sanders and Doreen Valiente believed that formal initiation was not always necessary to accept someone as a Witch. Sanders in particular was well-known to turn to people and say, "I don't need to initiate you; you are already a Witch." And Doreen Valiente would say, "You can tell a Witch by the look in her eyes." There is wisdom in both of these approaches to who is and is not a Witch.

We believe that the founders of Wicca would not approve of the emerging trends toward dogma, and in fact would see them as a step backwards. There has emerged an intolerance of other Wiccan paths on the part of those who consider themselves BTW. This fundamentalist approach to Wicca has now brought us to a real danger: that Wicca will lose its soul and go down the road that orthodox religion took two millennia ago. We believe these attitudes stem from people's ideas about religion being formed in a monotheistic culture. When such people come to polytheism, they get a form of spiritual agoraphobia and seek to cling to the comfortingly rigid structures found in their original religions. Of course, this is a form of insecurity, a type of Shadow that most of us who have gone through the initiatory process work through at the second-degree level. Unfortunately, it seems that for some, the Shadow-need for rigid control never loosens, and these people apply their old concepts of religion to Wicca. They become concerned with the form of the religion rather than the spirit. They glorify the system of lineage initiations, the coven structure and laws, and they ignore the spiritual and magical practice.

In doing so, many lose the meaning of one of the most important writings in Wiccan literature, the Charge of the Goddess—"If you do not find it within thee, you will never find it without!" In other words, the external structure of your religion is not more important than the inner mysteries of your spiritual path. The outer structure of your practice should aid your quest for connection with the divine, in the best manner to facilitate that connection.

In contrast with some BTW Wiccans, we believe in tolerance—and even enthusiasm—for the diversity of Wicca we see today. There is much to recognize and respect in the less mainstream paths of Wicca these days. We write this from the viewpoint of us both having our origins in the Alexandrian Tradition and then deciding to move on to our own path. If a BTW Witch were to attend one of our ceremonies, they would be familiar with the Circle casting, the coven structure, and many of the words. But our real attention is not on the Circle casting or the coven structure. We think what goes on above and beyond the Circle casting and the coven structure is the most important part of modern Wicca.

What we hope to convey to our readers in this volume is the Deity-centered cosmology and energy work that we believe are at the core of all magical and spiritual traditions. A focus on the energy work and the direct connection to the divine provides a rich vein of spiritual nurturance. Initiation comes directly from the divine, as quoted often in British Traditional Wicca: "There is only one true initiator," a statement that derives from Dion Fortune. Because of the tremendous variety and quality of training systems, initiations in Wicca are currently only valid within their group of origin. In this book, we are presenting a system of Witchcraft that places psychic training and connection to the divine at the center of a Witchcraft practice rather than doctrine, dogma, and codified rituals.

We hope the reader will take this book for what it is: not a system but a philosophy. That it is completely acceptable to embrace new ideas, and that in any magico-spiritual tradition such as Wicca it is important not to forget why we practice it—to serve the divine in its myriad faces.

Introduction

God[dess], grant me the serenity to accept the things I cannot change, the courage to change the things I can, and the wisdom to know the difference.
　—REINHOLD NIEBUHR

It has been over fifty years—bridging two centuries and a millennium—since the Witchcraft revival began. This is quite an achievement for a new religious movement, especially when one of its founders believed it would only manage to survive another decade. Doreen Valiente related how Gerald Gardner, the "father" of modern Witchcraft, said to her in the early 1960s that "the problem with this religion, Doreen, is that it has too many chiefs and not enough Indians." He strongly believed this would be its downfall as a religious path, and that it would not survive beyond the 1970s. Luckily for many of us, he was wrong. Gardner failed to take into account one of the most important factors that has allowed Witchcraft to survive: its ability to change with the times: to change and adapt culturally and socially. There is, of course, a scientific word for this type of change—*evolution.*

This is why we used the words *Progressive Witchcraft* in the subtitle of this book. We know we are not the only ones within Wicca who have used the term *progressive* to describe themselves. The term *progressive Wicca* was used for the first time in the 1980s, as far as we know, to describe a diverse and eclectic movement originating in the United Kingdom (see footnotes on page 22). Others may think of "eclectic" disparagingly, but it is the nature of evolution to encourage diversity and variety. A look at Wicca's history shows there is nothing more eclectic than Traditional Wicca, with its blend of Italian-Etruscan lore, ceremonial magic, Freemasonry, and possibly even Sufi teachings! For us, the use of the term *progressive* does not indicate a specific tradition, but rather a way of seeing the spiritual truths that underlie all nature-based religions—especially the truth that they must be able to adapt if they wish to satisfy the spiritual needs of the individual.

Wicca is a religious movement with its roots in nature and in natural law. Evolution is at the core of its philosophy whether its practitioners realize it. It is important to note that evolution affects not only physical and social development, but also spiritual growth. Nearly all practices in Witchcraft have changed over time. This is mainly due to a better understanding of the origins of such practices and their true meaning. Generally, most Wiccans now have a better understanding of such things as magical practice and the Wheel of the Year than the practitioners of Wicca did in the 1950s and '60s; and (of specific importance with reference to this book) of change within the self—that is, initiation and the mechanisms that cause it. In the spiritual cultures of the ancient past, these changes and their causative actions came to be called the *mysteries*.

In the last few decades, we have seen many changes in the way Wicca has been viewed, both publicly and internally. What was once a small group of individuals secretly trying to recreate the past has now become a large movement trying to embrace the future. Because of this, it has become more noticeable. All Witchcraft was once viewed by the public with suspicion; the word *Wicca* was unknown and rarely appeared in the lurid stories of Witchcraft in the tabloid press. Now the word *Wicca* appears regularly in all the media as a modern, fashionable kind of Witchcraft, and has become one of the fastest growing spiritual practices in the Western world.

Witches embrace positive change, and when this change does not occur, they create it. Witches are, and probably always have been, irrepressible rebels by nature. They challenge the status quo, not just within their own sphere of practices, but also in the wider world. It may be for this reason that witchcraft was seen to be a challenge to established authority in the past, particularly by the Christian church. In the twenty-first century, corporations and governments have become the authority challenged by the Witch. These institutions put materialism over spirituality, while threatening the environment. Witches know that both materialism and spirituality need to be in balance if there is to be a positive future for ourselves and the planet we live on.

Materialism has seen a market in Witchcraft, and herein lies the paradox of this book. The market has been flooded with books on Witchcraft due to the increasing need and desire for a spirituality that challenges the doctrines of consumer society. The paradox is that now spirituality can be purchased from your nearest bookshop, just as fast food can be purchased from your nearest fast-food chain. Or this is what modern society would like to have us believe. Many of these books contain substantially the same information, rewritten and regurgitated for mass consumption. But Witches, being rebels, know differently; they know that true spiritual connection comes from the soul, and that books can only give us ideas—and, of course, the experiences of the author. This is a book about the quest for the spiritual experience that is the path of Witchcraft, but it is *not* the quest itself, only a guide to help the seeker along this path.

Witchcraft has reinvented itself several times since the 1950s because of the need by those within it to revolt against the dogmatic practices that seeped into it. Such dogmas and doctrines go against the true nature of the Witch: there are and always have been rebels, and there always will be. This was the factor that Gardner, himself a rebel of his time, did not pencil into the equation when he made that statement to Doreen Valiente about Wicca not lasting beyond the 1970s. Without the rebels, Gardner's prophecy would have come to pass: for change, evolution, and revolution would not have happened.

We were both part of this process: Janet, in a more direct way, by being involved with the king of Wiccan rebels—Alex Sanders, and Gavin by being part of an organization that rebelled against the doctrine that you could only be a Witch if you were part of a traditional lineage. We were both rebels, as was Janet's late husband, Stewart. Likewise, the need to rebel against dogma encouraged other authors such as Starhawk, Ray Buckland, Phyllis Curott, and Raven Grimassi to put pen to paper to cause change and to cause Wiccan evolution to take a leap forward.

How people face the evolution of new ideas is very different from person to person, but generally people either embrace or reject it. Witches are no different. As we try to show in this book, Witchcraft has never been slow to accept the inevitabilities of time. Evolution and the will of the Goddess eventually win through. Modern Witches know that time, evolution, and spirituality are indivisible, so Witchcraft as a spiritual path will always embrace changes as they occur. Unfortunately, there will always be those who feel differently. These are the people who are comfortable where they are, or who are scared of the effect change might have on the personal power that they have obtained for themselves. For them, the leap across the void of the mysteries is too large a journey to contemplate. They sit in spiritual stagnation. They are—regardless of a string of initiations with validated lineage and heritage—not what we would consider true Witches.

The mysteries, the central theme of this book, are about change. They are about the transformation of the self for the benefit of all. When you change the self, you change the world. This is inevitable, for the macrocosm (the whole of the world) and the microcosm (the individual self) are intertwined like the two snakes on the staff of Hermes. This is a book about shaping Witchcraft into a spiritual path for this new millennium. Microcosmically, this is done by first changing the individuals who call themselves Witches. This can only occur when change is first accepted as inevitable, and then the strength for change is found in spiritual connection.

The need for spiritual union is at the core of all living spiritual paths. This was forgotten somewhere along the line by many within Wicca. The form of ritual became more important than its actual purpose; words became more important than intent. It is time to right this; it is time for Wicca to take its rightful place alongside the other contemporary spiritual paths that encourage connection and union with the Divine—alongside Santeria, Vodoun, Hinduism, Buddhism, and Shinto.

The authors have also changed over the years. We have embraced the need to look at new philosophies as part of our spiritual growth. We have looked into the past for inspiration—into the ancient Celtic, Norse/Anglo-Saxon, and Greek worlds. We have drawn what we can from them, but in recent years have found more inspiration from living religions than from the fragmented remains of dead ones. Others feel the same. We have noticed that many Witches have become drawn to contemporary spiritualities that are alive and vibrant and offer one-on-one spiritual connection—particularly Vodoun and Santeria. This is because some Wiccan practice has become lacking in such connection. It is our hope that we can encourage Witches to take their experiences of such living religions and infuse them into Wicca, thus boosting its next evolutionary leap forward. Wicca can become a vehicle for the return of the old gods and goddesses—not just into Circle, but into the everyday personal life of the Witch.

When you approach Wicca from this direction, you come to a realization—an epiphany, if you will. As Wiccans, we like to say that "all religions are paths to the same truth." If we truly believe this, we must accept that many of the ceremonial aspects in Wicca are simply "icing on the cake," a way of enticing us to experience the truth of the spiritual experience. The ritual and the systems associated with it are nothing more than tools to connect you to God/Goddess. They are thereby tools to change you and the way you view the world you live in.

There is no right or wrong in the way you do things, or in the way you think, so long as you seek the guidance of Spirit in the quest for the experience of the Mystery. What we wish to do here is help the reader to access the mystery in the term *mystery tradition*. The irony is that no one can write about the individual spiritual experience in an objective way, as there are no words to convey the impact such experiences have. We believe that the purpose of any true priestess or priest of Witchcraft in the modern age is to encourage, inspire, and guide the individual to experience the mysteries for themselves.

If Wicca is to survive the next millennium, it must now come of age and accept the importance of its core spiritual beliefs in the scheme of things; beliefs that can unite true religions of healing in understanding and tolerance. It must also accept the truth of its origins as a new religion based on old wisdoms rather than a surviving remnant from the Middle Ages, if it is to truly become a spiritual path for a modern world. This is not a book telling you what to do or what to think; it is a book telling you that it is okay to do what you are already doing so long as it is done with the guidance of Spirit.

There are some points that we need to emphasize regarding our use of the words *Wicca* and *witchcraft*. We use the capitalized terms *Wicca* and *Witchcraft* to describe modern traditions of Witchcraft stemming from Gerald Gardner, Alex Sanders, and their contemporaries. The word *witchcraft* is used to describe general practice, and may also apply to older, more historical practices, such as Strega—the Italian practice of witchcraft that still survives today.

We have attempted in this book to create aspects of a philosophy of Witchcraft useable by all, regardless of whether they are solitary or in a coven that can easily be applied to already existing traditional practices. We could just have easily subtitled this work "A Modern Coven Handbook" or something similar, but the reality is that many Wiccan practitioners are solitary. At the end of the day, individual Witches have the task of teaching themselves. It is not our intention that the practices within this book should be dogmatic or even doctrinal. This book simply offers ideas to guide the reader.

For the above reasons, we do not claim within this work to be publishing ancient knowledge, secrets, or archaic occult techniques, although much of what we have written has its origins in past occult practices that we have synthesized for the modern world. All of the practical exercises are ones we have created ourselves and have used successfully; they were not created purely for this book, as some writers have done in their works. The exercises are drawn from our work with our magical training group and from a series of intensive workshops called *The Inner Mysteries*, which we started back in early 2002 and have since held in Europe, the United Kingdom, the United States, and Australia. This work inspired the title of this book.

Acknowledgments

Our thanks go to those who attended these workshops, encouraging and inspiring us to write this book. Our experiences with you have changed us—just as they should. We would also like to thank several others for their assistance in creating this book: Adam for his graphical professionalism and Cathbad for his philosophical insight; and, of course, the members of our coven for being patient guinea pigs for many of the magical exercises. Special thanks to Corvia, Kel, and Jim for their patience in proofreading and their insights and additions to the manuscript.

Dedicated to:

Novices of the Old Ways, The Star and Crescent Moon Coven,
Teampall Na Callaighe, and The Italian Wiccan Study Group

And in remembrance of a passing generation of
Witches and trailblazers:

Doreen Valiente, Eleanor Bone, Leo Louis Martello, Jesse Belle,
Chris Gosselin, Ellen Cannon Reed, and our beloved Stewart.
May they meet and laugh in the Summerlands.

1

In the Beginning:
from Witchcraft to Wicca

Study the past if you would define the future.
—CONFUCIUS*

irst we must look at the true origins of witchcraft, those hidden in the mists of time. This is a subject that has been written about many times by many authors. This, of course, may be quite repetitive to those who have been involved in the modern Witchcraft movement for several years, but they must bear with us, as this book is just as likely to be picked up by those who are making the first steps in the sometimes confusing world of the neo-Pagan movement. It is our hope though, that we have given some different viewpoints to its origins that have not been covered before in our own, or other literary works.

Witchcraft's Origins in Shamanism

Looking at cave art and archaeological artifacts, we can theorize that the earliest magical practices came about when Homo sapiens began to migrate east and west from Africa. Their magic revolved around the most basic instinct of mankind, survival. Imagine the following scene: In a firelit cave, a man dresses in deerskin and dons an antlered headdress. He begins to chant; the chant grows into a grunt; the grunt into the recognizable *hurnnn* call of the rutting stag. As he slowly circles the fire, the

---

* Kung Fu-tse (Latinized as Confucius) was born in the state of Lu in 551 BC and died in 479. He was a Chinese philosopher and reformer; his teachings are known as Confucianism and compiled as "Analects."

1

other male members of the tribe come out of the darkness. Each tightly grasps a stick as though it were a spear. At a given moment, they lunge on the costumed figure. In a frenzy, they symbolically kill the stag. By doing this form of magic, they see themselves as successfully procuring meat for the tribe on the following day's hunt.

A division of sexual roles was often noticeable in hunter-gatherer societies. This was not sexism, but arose from the reality that men were better capable of defending the group and hunting large game due to their physical build and strength. We think men were, therefore, responsible for defending their communities and providing meat, while women cared for the young and the old. During the hunt, the women of the tribe gathered berries, nuts, and tubers to supplement the tribe's diet and, more importantly from a magical perspective, had the opportunity to gather herbs for the sick. As we have seen, the male mysteries probably revolved around their role in the preparation for the hunt. Here we see the female mysteries in the treatment of the sick, and in caring for other women during pregnancy. As they were healing the sick, they also found themselves dealing with the spirits that caused the illness. We still see this division between the sexes today in hunter-gather communities, such as the aboriginal peoples of Australia. Within this culture, there is a strict division between "men's business" and "women's business" when it comes to the mysteries. This division was probably responsible for mistrust of the old feminine magical ways during the period and the development of the feminine descriptive word *witch*.

It is in both male and female forms of magic that we see the roots of what we now call shamanism and its development into what we now call witchcraft. As humanity developed and settled into an agricultural way of life, the role of the tribal magic-worker evolved. It became a family affair, with the skills of one generation being passed down to the next. Here we see the idea of "hereditary witchcraft" first appearing, but it should be remembered that at this time *all* trades and skills were passed down through the family. Within the tribe/village, specific families would have been responsible for passing down specific skills, such as metalworking, torch making, farming, et cetera. This is the origin of such descriptive surnames as "Baker" and "Smith." In a harsh world, specialization is more conducive to survival than a strategy in which everyone is "a jack-of-all-trades, but a master of none." The magical worker became a priest or priestess in the village; although they were not considered more important than any other trade, they were respected. Their roles might have included being responsible for keeping a track of the seasons and performing the seasonal rites. This could have involved making offerings to the local gods and spirits for good crops and good hunts. These are important rites in an agricultural society, and the priesthood had to understand the cyclical nature of the seasons to do them. They were most likely the keepers of the mysteries of birth, death, and rebirth. They looked after the sick with the herb lore they had accumulated over generations; they were responsible for the banishment of malign spirits, which caused disease. Here again, we can see the underlying reason for the existence of the magical practitioner was survival, but now the individual need was more important. The roles within the tribe/village were more specialized, and the death of one of its members would threaten the well-being of the whole tribe/village. Here we see the idea of the witch at its purest, without any of the preconceptions put on it by Christianity and the twentieth century.

Origins of the Word *Witch*, and the Mediterranean Cults

With the spread of several different cultures across Europe—Celtic, Germanic, Italian/Etruscan, Greek, et cetera—we see the next development within witchcraft, that of taking on cultural symbolism, including language. We see the origins of the word *witch* in Anglo-Saxon culture, and we see other words evolved in other cultures to describe the tribal magical worker. The word *witch* in old English has its origins in the word *wicce*. It would be wrong to say that witchcraft is of purely Anglo-Saxon origin just because *witch* is an Anglo-Saxon word. *Witch* is a modern descriptive word that crosses cultural barriers, and this is important to remember. It has several interpretations: it can mean "to bend and shape" (as in the forces of nature); others say it means "wise." Of course, this is the feminine declension of the word, the male being *wicca,* which was the word adopted by the modern Witchcraft movement in the early 1950s. Intrinsically, the meaning of *wicca* is no different than the word *witch*. This is important to remember, because in recent years some in the neo-Pagan community have felt it necessary to define these words differently, but more on this later in the chapter. Christianity turned the word *wicce* into *wych,* then *wytch,* and finally into our modern word *witch*. The use of the feminine word rather than the masculine form came about because of the underlying misogyny of the early Christian church. Women were seen as the root of all evil—ever since Eve took the fruit of the tree of knowledge. The idea of women being in prominent, responsible positions and dealing with spiritual forces was repugnant to the church. Not surprisingly, they adopted the feminine rather than the masculine word, as they considered all female mysteries to be inherently evil.

Similar words for "witch" exist in other cultures. The Old Norse used the word *vitki*, a word that obviously has similar etymological roots as the words *wicce* and *wicca*. The Italians use the word *strega*. According to Raven Grimassi, a noted author on the subject of Italian witchcraft, its origins are very different to that of the word *witch*:

> The word Strega is derived from both lore and language. The cultural roots extend back to the Latin word *strix*, which indicates an owl (and particularly a screech owl). In archaic Roman religion there was a mythological creature called a striga. The striga was a type of vampire woman that could transform into an owl. The death of infants in their sleep (as well as the disappearance of babies) was blamed on the striga. This brought a supernatural connection to both words, and so *strix* and *striga* came to be interchangeable. In time the Latin word *striga* evolved into the Italian word *stregare*, which means to enchant. Then, over the course of time a female witch came to be called a *Strega*, literally an enchantress.[1]

Grimassi has also recently discovered that there is a relationship between the earliest known word for a witch, the Greek word *pharmakis*[2] (an herbalist who prepares potions), and the Italian word *strigare*, which means "to extract." He believes that the word *strega* may, in fact, have had its origins from this word rather than the word *strix*. This, of course, seems to link Italian witchcraft directly back with the origins we mentioned earlier in this chapter.

We once believed that there was no such thing as hereditary witchcraft, as we had seen no proof, but our contact with members of the Strega tradition has convinced us otherwise. The survivals of witchcraft, in hereditary form, into the modern era are very much linked to the early days of Christianity and its absorption of three other cults in the Mediterranean. Within the Roman Empire, during the early part of the first millennium, a new cult appeared in Rome—Mithraism. It had its origins in Persia and, ultimately, in Zoroastrianism.

Mithraism was a mystery religion whose followers believed in an entity of Good and an entity of Evil in conflict with each other on the spiritual plane. These manifest as the personalities of Mithras and Ahriman. Mithraism was widely adopted by Roman military officers and spread throughout the empire—a Mithraic temple has even been found and excavated in London. As the Roman officers settled in the new provinces of the far-flung empire, they became traders and the cult changed from having a militaristic focus to having one of business. The new, young, and open Christianity absorbed the idea of dualism from the older cult. This occurred because many of the converts in Britain and mainland

Mithras

Europe were settled Roman officers who already practiced Mithraism.* But the biggest challenge to early Christianity was from another cult, one which would be difficult to absorb.

The cult of Isis/Artemis was centered in Ephesus in Asia Minor, which is now Turkey. Its rituals and practices are some of the best-recorded ceremonies of ancient times. Visitors described a haze of incense permanently settled as fog above the city. It was truly the pagan Vatican of its time, with pilgrims coming from all over the known world to worship and pay homage to the "Great Goddess." The cult had begun to develop into a more structured multinational religion that absorbed many of the other principle national goddesses existing around the Mediterranean basin: the Egyptian Isis, the Assyro-Babylonian Ishtar, the Roman Diana, the Greek Selene, and others became identified as this one Great Goddess who absorbed symbolism from them all.[3]

This cult remained a thorn in the side of Christianity for four centuries. Women in Greek, Roman, and European culture generally refused to give up worship of the Great Goddess, and there was no replacement within Christianity. The misogynistic views and teachings of St. Paul of Tarsus made it difficult for Christianity to absorb the Goddess. The problem was finally resolved in 431 AD at the Council of Ephesus when the doctrine of Panagia Theotokos—the All-Holy Virgin Mother

---

* Some have suggested that modern Freemasonry has its origins in the practices of Mithraism, which is why there are similarities in practice.

Diana or Artemis of Ephesus

of God—was declared, thereby incorporating the Great Goddess into Roman Catholicism and the Orthodox Christian religions, both Greek and Russian. Unknowingly, they had planted a seed that allowed the survivals of goddess and pagan practices to grow under the very eyes of the Christian hierarchy right up until today, and allowed the survival of hereditary witchcraft. Some authors and historians have suggested that witchcraft has its origins in the Goddess cult of Isis/Artemis, and we would not argue this point.

Witchcraft Survivals in Christianity and Their Similarities with African Diaspora Religions

The first act of established Christianity was to discredit the existing pagan religions. They destroyed the temples and statues dedicated to the old gods, while at the same time absorbing pagan symbolism into their practices, just as they had absorbed some of the philosophy of Mithraism earlier. The old gods became saints; their festivals became feast or holy days. The placing of churches on sacred pagan sites was encouraged to bring the existing pagans into Holy Mother Church. It was these very acts that allowed the village witch to survive. The old pagan priesthood of the community actively adopted these changes for their own survival while teaching those they trusted the pagan symbolism hidden within the new Christian practices. As time went by, many of the origins of these magical practices were diluted and became lost, particularly by the time of the Protestant Reformation.

In Roman Catholic Ireland we have seen folk magic continuing to be practiced under the guise of Christianity. We once discovered a "prayer" attached to a fairy tree at a holy well close to where we live. It was a piece of paper folded up in plastic and attached by twine to one of the boughs of the tree. The contents read, as closely as we can remember, as follows:

> Blessed Holy Saint Martha, I ask of you to intercede on my behalf to Holy Mary Mother of God, and her Son Jesus Christ. Bring wealth, health, and prosperity to my family. If such blessings are not forthcoming, I will refuse to light candles to our Lady in the Chapel, and will not pray for the soul of ——. I ask this in the name of Holy Mary and her Son Jesus Christ.

I doubt very much that the person placing this in the tree would consider herself a Witch, and being a good Christian soul, would have little knowledge about the fact that the tree is of pagan symbolic origin and that the holy well was originally dedicated to the pagan god Lugh!* Raven Grimassi told us that such practices are still common throughout Italy, much as they are in Ireland. He recounts practices that involve the threatening and cajoling of saints, including the practice of turning statues of the Madonna on her head if the petitioner did not get her way. From traveling in Greek Orthodox Crete we can also report that the survivals of pagan magical practice are common there, too. We have in our collection a small beaten brass plate depicting a leg used as an offering for healing. It is obvious that magic is far from being just a Roman Catholic phenomenon, although it is, in fact, more common in non-Protestant countries. There are also interesting similarities with Afro-American magic.

When slaves were brought from the west coast of Africa to the Americas during the sixteenth and seventeenth centuries, they brought with them their own spiritual and magical practices. These practices continue today with several names. The pure forms are still practiced in West Africa where they are known as Ifa and Vodoun, but in the Caribbean, Central and South America, and in the southern United States they have developed into distinctly separate forms. When the slaves were brought to the colonies they were, of course, converted to Christianity. Like early Christian Europe, they refused to give up their Pagan practices easily and hid their magical practices and beliefs behind the culture that had enslaved them. In French colonies, such as Haiti and New Orleans, this was less of a problem, as the French had a much more laissez-faire attitude to religion. Here we

---

* Saint Kieran's Well, Castle Kieran, Kells, Co. Meath, is a Lughnasadha site. One myth related to the site is that the evening before the annual Lughnasadha festival held there, a salmon (the symbol of the god Lugh) swims up the river alongside the site.

see the development of what is known as Voodoo, or as it is more correctly known, Vodoun, which has always been linked in the popular imagination with witchcraft. The old ancestral spirits, the loas of the West Africans, were quickly absorbed into existing French culture; a good example of this is Baron Samedi (Lord of Saturday), popularized by the James Bond film *Live and Let Die*.* He was originally the West African spirit of death, Ghede—and his black and white, top-hatted face remains one of the popular icons of Voodoo in people's minds. Saturday is, of course, the last day of the week, and is ruled by Saturn, the planet and classical god who rules death.

In the Spanish colonies, Christianity was less forgiving. It became necessary for the slaves to hide their deities behind saints, just as the pagans did in Europe. This practice is commonly known as Santeria and its mystical practices bear striking similarities to the Catholic folk magic practices we have found in found in Ireland. There is one major difference though: the practitioners of Santeria are still very aware of its pagan origins and know whom the saints represent. One should bear in mind that only three hundred years have passed since the Christianization of their practices, as opposed to over a thousand years within Europe, but by looking at Santeria and Vodoun we can possibly see hints of what hereditary witchcraft—minus the cultural overlays—would have looked like up until the twelfth and thirteenth centuries. What is also interesting is that hereditary practitioners still consider themselves priests and priestesses, just as we do in modern Witchcraft. This seems to confirm the idea that magical practitioners were always considered to be priesthood. Within Vodoun and Santeria, the idea of the spirit of the deity or loa possessing ("riding," as it is commonly known) the priest or priestess seems to be reflected in the process known in modern Wiccan ritual as "Drawing Down the Moon," in which the priestess allows a deity to speak through her. Again we see that Vodoun, Santeria, and the other African diaspora religions survived within prominently non-Protestant areas of the world, but we see few survivals in areas of the Americas that were strongly Protestant, such as Georgia or Virginia, but we do see an evolution of it into southern hoodoo or conjure practices among the large West African slave population.

---

*   A surprisingly accurate portrayal of Caribbean Vodoun ritual is shown. This is due mainly to the fact that Ian Fleming spent many years working in this area of the world for British Intelligence. He also had strong occult connections, being friends with occult writer Dennis Wheatley.

Catholicism, Protestantism, and the Witch Hunts

It is the rivalry between Catholicism and Protestantism that is the key to understanding the nature of hereditary witchcraft in Western Europe, because Protestants systematically went about trying to destroy pagan survivals. From the writings of the time of the Reformation, it is clear that their main aim was to remove the remains of pagan practices from Christianity. Martin Luther's main argument with Catholicism was that such survivals existed within its system of indulgences, relics, and saints, and that these were unholy and against the Christian god. The result was that many a Catholic went to the fire or was hung as a witch by Protestant inquisitors. It also goaded the Catholic Church into having its own witch hunt to try to clear its name, as well as seek out Protestant heretics. But of the estimated three hundred thousand witches who were executed during this period, it is probable that the majority were good Christians and hardly any would have practiced witchcraft, let alone considered themselves witches.

In Britain, the real witch hunts did not start until the Stewart king, James the First of England, the Sixth of Scotland, came to the English throne, even though Britain had rejected Roman Catholicism two monarchs earlier in one of the bloodiest periods in English history. King James was paranoid about being poisoned by witches, and therefore commissioned the rewriting of the Bible to reflect his paranoia. For example, he changed "thou shalt not suffer a poisoner [of wells] to live" to "thou shalt not suffer a witch to live." Even though there were few witch trials in England, there appeared to be many in his home country, Calvinist Scotland. When the English Civil War erupted, Mathew Hopkins, the infamous Witchfinder General, set forth from Cambridge in England, and it was no coincidence that he headed toward the fen lands of East Anglia, an area known not only for witchcraft, but also for its Roman Catholic population. It must be remembered that Hopkins did this during a conflict very much fuelled by the antagonism between Roman Catholicism and English Puritan Protestantism that dated back to the Tudor king Henry VIII. In modern Witchcraft history, which we discuss later, East Anglia comes up again as one of the supposed birthplaces of Wicca. This is important to note.

It is here that an interesting paradox occurs in the modern history of witchcraft. Protestantism almost completely eradicated its survivals in the United Kingdom, Germany, and the other countries of that faith, or else they forced it so deep underground it almost disappeared completely.

In Catholic countries, it survived, but was slowly absorbed into Catholicism to the point that its origins became unknown, even though a few folk practices continued as part of that faith. We are not trying to say here that the neo-Pagan movement or even hereditary witchcraft has its origins in Roman Catholicism. We are saying quite the reverse: that from one perspective, the origin of many Catholic practices is witchcraft and paganism! So here is the paradox: if you look at the rise of the modern Witchcraft and neo-Pagan movement, they are most prominent in Protestant countries. Why has this happened?

The fact is, even though some Witches might dispute it, modern Witchcraft has its origins very much in *rebellion* against the established Protestant monotheistic culture rather than the Catholic. In the United Kingdom, many who come into Wicca and Paganism do so because they are looking for the magic in their spirituality—which they find in the ritual practices of Wicca. In Catholic countries such as Ireland, Spain, Italy, and Portugal, the situation is a bit different. Ever since childhood, members of this faith are brought up with the high ritual, mysticism, et cetera, which Protestantism rejected. The result is that when they reject the Catholic Church they reject these aspects too. While in Protestant countries, neo-Paganism is one of the fastest growing religious groups, in Catholic countries, we have found it to be traditions such as Zen Buddhism. Of course, this situation is now changing as the Roman Catholic Church loses social power, and Catholic countries are now starting to develop growing neo-Pagan communities.

Gerald Gardner and the Reconstruction of Witchcraft

It was in the early 1950s that we saw the rise of modern Witchcraft, or Wicca as it is known today. In most Witches' minds, this came about mainly because of one man, but it is not the only history. It is from the 1950s that we first see the first named traditions within Witchcraft. This is not only a modern idea, but also one that came out of acrimony between a self-professed hereditary witch and the followers of Gerald Gardner— the man often referred to as the father of modern Witchcraft. Of course, there are those who avoided such labels, and in recent years this has included us. To understand the argument, you have to understand some of the history of modern Witchcraft relating to Gerald Gardner and the New Forest coven.

In 1936, Gerald Gardner retired from his duties as a tea and rubber planter and customs official and moved back to England to be with his wife, Donna. His interest in folklore and the occult had been sparked while living in Malaya. This area of the world has always been a melting pot of cultures, and Gardner had already started to work prior to his retirement on his book *The Keris and Other Malay Weapons,* which was published in 1936. It is not surprising that he chose this time to move back to England. The Japanese had already invaded China and everyone was expecting a war in the Far East between the armies of the rising sun and the colonial nations. Of course, by the time Gerald and his wife settled in the New Forest, war with Germany was imminent.

Gardner was a well-read man on the subject of magic. His interest in Malaysian folk magic now made him look carefully into its European equivalent, witchcraft. After reading Margaret Murray's *The Witch Cult in Western Europe*, he became convinced that her central hypothesis that witchcraft had survived the Middle Ages was correct. It spurred him on to read more on the subject, including Charles Godfrey Leland's *Aradia, or the Gospel of the Witches,* which Leland claims in his introduction originated with a hereditary Italian witch, or strega, named Maddalena.

It was during this period that Gardner supposedly first made contact with what he claimed was the survivals of British witchcraft. He first met several people who were Rosicrucians through the Rosicrucian theatre in Christchurch. It soon became obvious to him that there was more here than met the eye. He was introduced to the members of the Fellowship of Crotona, formed under the guidance of one Brother Aurelius and Mrs. Besant-Scott—the daughter of Annie Besant, who had been an active figure in the Theosophy and Co-Freemasonry movements. According to Gardner's story, it was through them that he met several other people, including one Dorothy Clutterbuck, and it was she who was to initiate him into a surviving witch coven in England. Of course, there is much more to the story, which has been told, retold, and reinterpreted several times. It is, in fact, the most analyzed story of modern Witchcraft, but bear in mind that, as we said earlier, it is not the only history. More information of the history of modern Witchcraft and Gerald Gardner can be found in Doreen Valiente's *Witchcraft for Tomorrow* and *The Rebirth of Witchcraft,* as well as in our own books: *A Witches' Bible* and *What Witches Do.* The most complete work we have come across is *Wiccan Roots*[4] by Philip Heselton (where he argues that Gardner did in fact find a surviving coven in the New Forest). This is a subject that has been written about to the point of exhaustion and remains the central myth of the modern Witchcraft movement.

Gardner claimed right from the beginning that the origins of what he practiced were hereditary, although the material he produced in his Bok of Ye Art Magical and then Book of Shadows (the main liturgy of Wicca) was anything but! His story is that he was initiated into a coven that originated with an East Anglian gentleman known as George Pickingill. There are several problems with this story, the main one being that Pickingill never claimed to be a witch. He was often referred to as "the cunning man," but was a self-confessed Satanist. It is fascinating that East Anglia comes into the picture again, as an area renowned for its survivals of witchcraft.

We will probably never know whether Gardner really found a genuine surviving coven. We believe that those he referred to as "witches" probably never referred to themselves as such, or considered their working group to be called "a coven." There is plenty of evidence that the group he was talking about was, in fact, the Fellowship of Crotona, a Rosicrucian group whose ritual practices included those originating from the French Lodge of Masonry (Grande Loge Symbolique Ecossaise Mixte de France).[5] This was very different to English Freemasonry: it was Co-Masonic—allowing women members, and was also more gnostic in its approach—incorporating elements of Cabalistic ritual magic in its practices. We base this belief on two claims. The first of these being that the degree system used by Gardner is patently Masonic, even down to some of the ritual acts. The second is that the word *witchcraft* had a broader meaning at the time of Gardner than the way it is used today within the neo-Pagan movement. During this period, any form of magic was referred to as witchcraft, as was Spiritualism and even Theosophy. From this perspective, one could even argue that Co-Masonry is really a survival of witchcraft. But note that many hereditary practitioners stated that they never originally described themselves as witches, as we mentioned earlier regarding Pickingill. What we have here is a problem with the definition of the word *witch*.

Gerald Gardner wrote several books, including *High Magic's Aid* and *Witchcraft Today,* which were some of the first books on the subject of Wicca. He claims he was thrown out of the original coven for betraying their secrets in his books. He therefore became the first known *banished witch* in the history of modern Wicca. It is more than likely the real reason was that the group got fed up with being referred to by a term they very likely found insulting. Gardner went on to form a coven in the early 1950s and initiated several high priestesses over the years, including Doreen Valiente, Eleanor (Rae) Bone, Madge Worthington, Patricia Crowther, and Monique Wilson. All went on to initiate more modern Witches and to create more covens. This resulted in Wicca not only spreading through Britain but also into America.

It was Doreen Valiente who first pointed out some of the inconsistencies in Gardner's claims regarding the origins of the witchcraft he practiced or wrote about. The young Doreen was a well-read person when it came to the occult, and she quickly picked up on the fact that much of the material scribbled into Gardner's Book of Shadows was from published sources. When she challenged him about this, his reply was that this was necessary, as much of the material had been lost. Gardner had introduced large amounts of Western magical tradition into Ye Bok of Ye Art Magical* and his later Book of Shadows. Most obvious is the use of passages from Leland's *Aradia*,† but there are also passages from the *Carmina Gadelica*.‡ There are even claims that elements of the teachings of the infamous Aleister Crowley are present§ (see page 31). Regardless, it was a viable magical system for its time; it fulfilled the needs of those practicing it and, more importantly, it worked.

Gerald Gardner's absorption of material from several sources, but mainly published works, has been cited as proof of his creation of modern Witchcraft. Although this can be seen as an argument as to why Wicca is not an ancient tradition, there is one factor ignored in it: cross-culturally, witchcraft has always used magical techniques "to get the job done." Magical practice has been a tool for survival in the forms of tribal healing and sympathetic hunting magic rather than a method for the creation of religious doctrine. Like all crafts, it has always updated its methods and used what was around at the time. An exchange of ideas between craftsmen to update their skills is a common practice. After all, the aim at the end of the day is produce quality work. This is no different for the witch; the method of magical practice is only important in that it produces a

---

*   This was his second book. A ritual book predating even this exists in the care of Doreen Valiente's estate.

†   Doreen Valiente is responsible for converting "How Diana Gave Birth to Aradia" into "The Charge of the Goddess"—the central rite of any Wiccan ritual.

‡   The Carmina Gadelica is a collection of folk prayers from the Hebrides of Scotland gathered in the late nineteenth century by amateur folklorist Alexander Carmichael. "Queen of the moon, Queen of the sun ...," used in the consecration of the cakes at the end of ritual, derives from this source.

§   There is little doubt that there was communication between Crowley and Gardner; Gardner held the rank of Philosophus 4=7 in Crowley's Ordo Templi Orientis (OTO). Evidence can be found in the original copies of *High Magic's Aid*.

quality outcome for the person for whom it is done. The aim and intent has always been more important that the form that it takes. As a nurse, Gavin found there was no dogma in the nursing techniques that he used; members of his profession regularly updated, exchanged, and integrated new ideas into their skills for the benefit of their patients. Gardner and his followers integrated the magical technique of their time—ceremonial magic—rather than necessarily trying to historically recreate those of the past. By doing this, they unwittingly continued the *real* tradition of witchcraft—"if it works, use it."

Gardnerians did not initially describe themselves or their practice as "Gardnerian." There is actually no noted use of the term *Gardnerian* in any of Gardner's works or in the literature on witchcraft of the time; the term simply wasn't in use. We find the term first used in a rather condescending article in a March 1965 copy of *Pentagram* magazine called "'Ancients' and 'Moderns'" by an anonymous figure calling himself Taliesin. It reads as follows:

> The report of Mrs. Valiente's talk at the *Pentagram* dinner, together with Mr. Cochrane's article in the same issue, make fascinating reading, and could be said to represent the two extremes of the Craft—Witchcraft Ancient and Modern, so to speak. From the former one gets the Gardnerian atmosphere of sweetness and light coupled with good clean fun, all under the auspices of a Universal Auntie. (1)

Not surprisingly, Arnold Crowther, the husband of High Priestess Patricia Crowther, wrote a rebuff, particularly as a following article by Taliesin attacked Gardnerians for cloak-and-dagger initiations. In Taliesin's rather curt reply, he uses the term *Gardnerites*, not *Gardnerian*. It is likely that those who were initiated by Gardner originally thought they possessed the only survivals of witchcraft in England. To be rebuffed by others claiming hereditary origins would have been a shock.

In September of 1999, in the final interview prior to her death, Doreen pointed to Robert Cochrane as the originator of the label *Gardnerian,* and probably the real identity of the anonymous figure, Taliesin:*

> He [Cochrane] claimed to be an hereditary witch, and detested those whom he called "the Gardnerians." In fact, I believe he invented this word "Gardnerian"—originally as a term of abuse.[6]

---

*   Confusion remains over whether they are the same figure, as Cochrane never admitted to the deception. According to author and publisher Michael Howard, Taliesin was believed by some to be Tony Melacrino.

Prior to 1965, Gardnerians were referred to as "followers of Gardner." This division by Taliesin was meant to outline the difference between self-professed "hereditaries" (if their claims were even really true) and those following the modern tradition of Witchcraft embodied by Gardner's teachings. Inadvertently, Taliesin sowed the seeds of the idea of "tradition" in the Witchcraft movement by his attack on the new wave of Paganism. Even Cochrane—"the Magister," as he is often referred to— found it necessary to label his practices as those of the "Clan of Tubal Cain,"* to separate them from Gardner's. He also didn't use the term *witch* until the public use of it by Gardnerians, and stated that none of his family used it either. Prior to this, there is no evidence from the past that witches separated themselves into specific traditions (although some may have used coven names).

What does appear are natural traditions dictated by culture and language—for example, Strega or hereditary Italian witchcraft. The ancestral tribal magical worker may not have used the term *witch* to describe him or herself; it may have been a label put on them by the Christian culture around them. Its use today is most definitely a modern reclaiming of the word. More on this is covered by Margot Adler in *Drawing Down the Moon: Witches, Druids, Goddess-Worshippers and other Pagans in America Today*.† She dedicates a whole section of one chapter to "that vexing 'w' word," discussing whether it should be used by modern Witches at all. We feel that, whether we like it, we are stuck with the word and should therefore make the best of it. For many, the use of the term *Wiccan* was one of convenience, a way of avoiding the use of the word *witch*, which had too many overtones for people who were influenced by the Christian concept of the word. The use of the word *Wiccan* allowed people to reply with "What's a Wiccan?"—thereby creating dialogue.

Alex Sanders and the New Traditions

It is apparent that when the Gardnerian form of Witchcraft appeared, its practitioners were considered to be the "new-age fluffy bunnies" of their time (if you'll excuse the detestable term) by many of the hereditaries, as well as by Britain's general occult community. Ironically, this was something the Gardnerians themselves were to accuse others of in the future. This is important, as a pattern soon seems to appear within the tensions

---

*   What commonly became known as the "1734 Tradition" was to emerge from Cochrane's teachings and the "Clan of Tubal Cain."

†   This remains one of the most complete and scholarly books to date on the development of the Pagan movement in the United States.

of the mainstream Wiccan traditions that reaches its height with the appearance of Alex Sanders in the mid-to-late-sixties.

Pat Kopinsky, a renegade priestess of Patricia and Arnold Crowther, brought Alex Sanders into Wicca. She did not actually initiate him, but introduced him to Medea—her initiator—and passed the Gardnerian Book of Shadows (the liturgy of modern Witchcraft) to him. This was done without the Crowthers' permission, although recent letters show that Kopinsky was in contact with Gerald Gardner, and that it is likely that Gardner and Sanders had been in contact with each other, as evidenced by an abridged letter from Pat Kopinsky to Gerald Gardner, dated September 5, 1963:

> Dear Dr. Gerald,
>
> I have just had a letter from Alex Saunders who I gather has been writing to you . . . she [Medea] finally made her mind to initiate him [Saunders] on the 9th of March with me as his sponsor. . . . I have five members in my coven at the moment, counting Alex who comes now and again.[7]

Alex Sanders' claim that he was a hereditary witch initiated by his grandmother[8] to gain acceptance from the wider occult community was hardly surprising. Hereditary origins have been claimed by those wanting acceptance as witches ever since Gardner, and have included many false claims. The causes lie very much in the arguments we mentioned earlier between self-professed hereditaries and "moderns" as they called them, and the continuing desire for validity via the idea of lineage, something we examine more fully in chapter 2 (see pages 27–29). Sanders did not initially use the term *Alexandrian* to describe the way he worked. There are several stories surrounding how this description came into being. One is that the name was a creation of Janet's late husband, the renowned Pagan writer Stewart Farrar. It was suggested that Stewart coined the term *Alexandrian* during the writing of *What Witches Do*. During an interview with Alex in 1969, he asked him how many Witches recognized him as "king of the Witches." Alex's reply confirms the origins of the word *Alexandrian*: "Probably all of them, apart from Gardnerians. . . . Gardnerians, and those that don't want publicity, tend to refer to my witches as 'Alexandrians.'"[9]

So here we have it "from the horse's mouth," so to speak. Regardless of origins, *Alexandrian* soon became a name for the new tradition of Witchcraft created by Alex Sanders, and the concept of *tradition* was compounded even more.

It was into the Alexandrian Tradition of Wicca that Janet and Stewart were first initiated. To quote Stewart, Alex had a "scattergun" approach to initiation. The standing joke was that if the milkman were to hang around the front door too long he'd find himself initiated! His approach paid off: by the early seventies, the Alexandrian brand of Wicca had reached the United States and was gaining ground on the Gardnerians. The Gardnerians refused to accept the Alexandrians, and the literate battles in Pagan periodicals seemed to be at their most prevalent in the United States. This situation continued until the 1980s when finally the two groups realized they had more in common with each other, particularly as new traditions started to arise out of the United States from the early seventies onward. Alex Sanders' contribution to the modern Witchcraft movement was two-fold: he caused growth by initiating so many into Wicca; but more importantly, he introduced the idea of a *system of training* into Wicca (more on this in chapter 6)—certainly within the U.K.

Raymond Buckland* can be credited with the next stage of development within Wicca: the open creation of new traditions, often referred to as "reconstructionist" Wicca. In many ways, there was more honesty in these traditions, as they made no false claims of lineage. Ground was initially broken with Buckland's *The Tree: The Complete Book of Saxon Witchcraft*, which was the ritual liturgy for Seax-Wica—a whole new tradition. Buckland had lived in the United States since the early sixties and had become very much influenced by its more liberal occult culture. Seax-Wica was almost completely researched from the literature of the time, the most obvious work being Brian Branston's *Lost Gods of England*. Here, Ray Buckland explains his reasons for creating it:

> I started it at a time when I realized that Gardnerian [Witchcraft] was not totally satisfying for me—this after about twelve years of it! There were things about it—about the make-up of the rituals, specifically—that didn't work for me. . . . I decided to construct a tradition that was exactly right for me, as an individual. . . . I did not pretend, and never have pretended, that I was reconstructing anything ancient; this was new and I just wanted something right for me that had an ancient flavor to it. I most certainly did NOT start it as a joke, as has been erroneously reported. . . . I would hardly give up Gardnerian and devote my life to a joke![10]

---

* An ex-Royal Air Force officer, initiated by Monique Wilson in Perth, Scotland, before moving to the United States in the mid-1960s and initiating his ex-wife Rosemary. He is a highly regarded and prominent figure in the American Wiccan movement and a renowned author.

Seax-Wica also introduced another idea into print that was completely against the grain of the other main traditions. It was a tradition where it was acceptable to self-initiate. This concept was followed by the publication of Doreen Valiente's *Witchcraft for Tomorrow*, which also contains a self-initiation ritual, and by our own arguments for self-initiation in *The Witches' Way*.

Gardnerian and Alexandrian Wicca had maintained the dogma of "only a witch can make a witch," even though it seemed to contradict the Craft law that states "there is only one true initiator." The origins of the idea of lineage are not from hereditary witchcraft as one first might suppose. As mentioned earlier, Gardner had adopted rituals from the Co-Masonic-influenced Fellowship of Crotona, and one of these rituals was the passing of power at initiation. This rite was, in fact, of Christian Gnostic origin rather than of pagan, although some would argue that in Gnosticism it derived from Roman paganism, and was based on the idea of apostolic succession.* The same rite can in fact be still seen today in the modern Catholic and Protestant churches at ordination.

Original witchcraft teachings were passed down in a generational learning process (see chapter 6, first paragraph) from parent to child for reasons already given. They would happily adopt and train others if they showed promise, but this was not lineage. The reason it was kept "within the family" as a secret was purely a mechanism to survive what modern Witches often refer to as "the burning times"—the period of repression previously mentioned. If you couldn't trust your family, since your family would undoubtedly face the same fate as yourself, then whom could you trust? In recent years, many have challenged whether lineage has any place in modern Witchcraft. We count ourselves among this group.

Witchcraft, Feminism, and the New Age

The 1970s saw the rise of Dianic (women-only) forms of Witchcraft coming out of the feminist movement. These reached their height in the 1980s after the publication of Z. Budapest's *The Feminist Book of Lights and Shadows*. *The Spiral Dance* by Starhawk was also published, which has a strong feminist (although inclusive) tone to it. Starhawk's lineage is from Victor and Cora Anderson's Feri Tradition based in Northern California (although the Andersons often referred to it just as "the Craft"). Feminist Witches sought to reclaim the word *Witch*

---

* Apostolic succession traces its lineage back to St. Peter, physically touched by Christ; therefore, the power of Christ is passed on from one Pope to the next, and down through the hierarchy of the church.

as a word of feminine power. Their nonhierarchical, eclectic approach clashed with the English traditional (Alexandrian and Gardnerian) approach of a fixed doctrine. Feminist works and views heavily influenced the development of Wicca, both in the United States and in the United Kingdom. Feminist Wicca also assertively pushed the ideals of environmentalism as being an integral part of Pagan spirituality, as well as political involvement in the antiwar movement. This was considered not only desirable, but also necessary (many in Feminist Wicca had been activists at the time of the Vietnam War).

By the time Gavin joined the Craft in 1986, *The Spiral Dance*—with its idea of "power from within," rather than "power over" (see pages 132–133)—had become compulsory reading with those who'd had bad experiences with the more dogmatic covens. This resulted in one of the first Pagan contact networks in the United Kingdom: Pagan Link, which rejected Wicca as "old hat." Regardless, there were those who stayed true to the ideas of Wicca, but in a nontraditional way. They questioned the systems of training, the need for degrees, and the hierarchical structure, which had sneaked through the backdoor from Freemasonry into Witchcraft.

One of the most obvious things that stick out in this short history is the importance and influence of *books* in the growth of modern Wicca; Gardner would never have got the new movement off the ground without them. The main reason for this was that, even in U.S. culture up until the 1990s, information on Witchcraft was hard to come by. When Janet joined the Craft in the early seventies, there were less than a dozen books specifically about Wicca and modern Witchcraft. Some books claiming to be about the subject were in fact about ceremonial magic or even demonology. By the mid-1980s we see a change. A more liberal attitude toward religion meant more books were being published on the subject—but still, there were few. Gavin remembers having to specifically order books, and the mainstays were Gardner's, Valiente's, and the books by Janet and her late husband, Stewart Farrar. There were, of course, other works, such as *A Book of Pagan Rituals*[*] by Ed Fitch and, as previously mentioned, *The Spiral Dance* by Starhawk. Most other books were heavily Cabalistic in their influence. Technology was soon to change everything.

The rise of modern Witchcraft is noticeably riddled with paradoxes, but there is power in paradox (see Appendix A). The major influences on the neo-Pagan movement and Wicca in the 1990s was not only the

---

[*] This book is listed as "authorless." Fitch originally wanted it to be freely available to the Pagan community, and without copyright.

same film companies and media that had been portraying lurid images of witchcraft since the 1950s, but also something that had come out of the United States military-industrial complex, the very thing Feminist Witchcraft was aimed at bringing down. This was the Internet.* While books were available forms of information, the Internet—first through bulletin boards, then e-mail, mailing lists, chat rooms, and websites—offered a two-way, easily accessible form of communication and information for Witches that cost almost nothing. It was also completely anonymous if you wanted a free exchange of ideas without fear of reprisal, regardless of age, an important point we come to later. Very soon, the terms *cyber Witch* and *cyber coven* began to appear. This resulted in a boom of interest in Witchcraft, something quickly noticed and exploited by the producers and film moguls of Hollywood.

The growth of neo-Pagansim, with interest from a younger generation, combined with an ever-increasing number of books on the subject, caused the media to look at ways of exploiting this new trend. Initially, it was rather badly portrayed, in films such as *The Craft*, then represented on television with good witches such as *Sabrina, The Teenage Witch*, and was mentioned as a positive spiritual tradition in *The X-Files*. Unfortunately, the urge to turn the witch character Willow into something evil became irresistible to the producers of *Buffy the Vampire Slayer*. There had, of course, been positive portrayals prior to these, such as the film of John Updike's novel *The Witches of Eastwick*—which, if examined carefully, is a pro-feminist statement of the reclaiming of woman's power. But the link between witchcraft, rebellion, and teenage angst had been firmly made by the film and television producers. Witchcraft by the end of the 1990s had become the new outlet for teenage rebelliousness.

The result was a sudden growth of interest caused by media and the Internet. The interest from a younger generation, particularly from those under eighteen, caused Wicca to reel as it tried to cope with the influx of teenagers asking questions about Witchcraft. This became a difficult period for many of us in Wicca who were brought up with the idea that you had to be eighteen or older to be a Witch, particularly when encountering a sixteen-year-old running a coven from the school playground. It also begged the question: if Christianity can teach its young, why can't we? The issue is still being debated today as many Wiccans try to put into place mechanisms for dealing with these future Witches.

---

* The Internet was originally a network created in the 1970s between research universities, defense contractors, and the Pentagon.

Now that we are into the new millennium, Witchcraft has started to enter its own renaissance: it has moved from heath and backroom to the online communities of the World Wide Web. We are now seeing a new breed of Witch influenced not by the figures of the immediate past, but by the culture of the present. This has left Witchcraft facing several questions that need to be addressed before it moves on. Is it a religion or a craft? Is it old, or is it something new? Where is it going? And more importantly, why has it resurrected in this new technological age? We try to answer these questions in the next chapter as well as the question of why Wicca should realize its past failings if it is to evolve and survive into the new millennium. We will also show that the future of Wicca is already here, if we but look.

NOTES

1   Personal mail between ourselves and Raven Grimassi, 13 November 2003.
2   A more thorough explanation on this can be found in *The Witches' Craft* by Raven Grimassi, page 15.
3   R. E. Witt, *Isis in the Graeco-Roman World*.
4   Chapter 4, pp. 52–63.
5   This is according to *Wiccan Roots* by Philip Heselton, a book we would highly recommend.
6   Doreen Valiente's interview with Sally Griffyn, *Wiccan Wisdomkeepers* (Boston, MA: Red Wheel/Weiser, 2002).
7   Circulated copy of a letter originating from Gerald Gardner's Castletown collection.
8   This claim first appeared in June John's *King of the Witches*. It has since been refuted by Maxine, Alex's High Priestess and ex-wife.
9   From an unpublished interview between Stewart Farrar and Alex Sanders in 1970 (in the authors' collection).
10 Personal correspondence, following a discussion between Gavin Bone and Ray Buckland at Witchfest, 28 November 2002, in New Orleans in 2001.

2

Into the New Millennium:
Progressive Witchcraft Evolves

When we blindly adopt a religion, a political system, a literary
dogma, we become automatons. We cease to grow.
—ANAIS NIN,* THE DIARIES OF ANAIS NIN. VOL. IV

W hat is progressive Witchcraft? It is not our intention to create
yet another new tradition of Wicca claiming ancient roots—
quite the reverse. For us, the use of the term *progressive Witch-*
craft does not imply a tradition, but a way of thought, belief, and practice
related to being a Witch. During the writing of this book, we came across
Witches who had adopted the term *progressive Witchcraft* to describe
themselves and their method of working.† After this book is published,
others may, of course, adopt the term; this will not make us unhappy! We
understand it is in human nature to need collective labels, and we have
used such a label, but we hope we do so in a positive way.

---

* U.S. (French-born) author and diarist (1903–1977). Generally known for her works
of erotic fiction: *Delta of Venus*, *Tropic of Cancer*, et cetera.

† We discovered that Karen Rainbird and David Rankine published *Magic Without*
Peers: A Course in Progressive Witchcraft for the Solitary Practitioner (Capall Bann
Publishing), during the writing of this work. They had been using the term pro-
gressive Wicca since 1989: "Progressive Wicca is not an organization as such be-
cause of its considerable diversity but rather reflects an attitude towards the Craft.
A Progressive Witchcraft Foundation has been set up through the Cylch y Gwyllt
a'r Rhydd coven to provide information and training" (Michael Jordan, *Witches: An*
Encyclopedia of Paganism and Magic).

From a historical viewpoint, it would be easy to suggest that the origins of modern Wicca came from a group of misfits, desperate for recognition as Witches, not only editing published material and passing it off as proof of ancient survivals, but also creating their own material with the same intent. We would like to put forward the point of view that this is not the right approach to take. Instead, we see a growth process—just as when a child learns to walk—and modern Witchcraft has on many occasions fallen over and grazed its knees. Modern Witches need to look at the past and realize that its failings are in fact an evolutionary process at work, returning witchcraft to its original roots. A danger of "building a house on sand" comes about when the mistakes of the past are not recognized. This results in no evolution or growth, just as we have seen in the contemporary monotheistic religions that have replaced spirituality with dogma.

The Death of Dogma, and the Cult of Personality

It is important for people to realize that Gerald Gardner, Alex Sanders, and all those trailblazers who have gone before, have made positive contributions to the development of what we have today, but they were human beings with failings like everyone else. The way they worked and saw Witchcraft was appropriate for their time, but not necessarily for ours. If they had made any serious mistakes in their approach, Wicca would not have survived this long. It must be remembered that all added something new that was needed at the time and dropped out those things that were redundant and would therefore hinder its growth. We can see this beginning to occur in the United States from the seventies onward, but it didn't seem to happen in Britain until the 1980s.

Something also happened at the end of the 1970s and beginning of the 1980s within the modern Witchcraft revival: we saw the end of the cult of personality, which had played a dominant part in the development of Wicca. This cult is common in many new religions when they are beginning to establish themselves. A central figure becomes the focus of the movement and is responsible for its direction. We do, of course, see this in religious cults, and it is taken to extremes in the monotheistic religions where the founder is deified. Up until his death in 1964, Gerald Gardner fulfilled this role; this was taken over by Alex Sanders within years of Gardner's death. It is interesting to note that these were male figures rather than female ones—again this relates to the fact that Witchcraft had not really managed to discard the old Christian values of the culture in which it grew up.

When Alex Sanders died in 1988, the Elders of the Alexandrian Tradition in the United Kingdom issued the following document:

Statement of the Council of Elders of the Alexandrian Tradition

A meeting of the Elders of the Alexandrian Tradition was held on Thursday 12th May 1988.

The Law of the Craft has always been that a King is chosen by the Craft when the need arises. After due consideration, a unanimous motion was carried that there is no need for a King of the Witches.

This is fortunate, as there is no one properly prepared for the role.

Alex Sanders led the Hidden Children of the Goddess into the light. It was a task well done and it was his last and most earnest wish that they should continue their work into the light.

This officially ended the end of the idea of kings and queens of the Witches within the modern Witchcraft revival, which the majority of us were not sad to see go. It is important because it marked the end of this cult of personality within Witchcraft with its inherent risks. There were, of course, others who tried to wear the crown. Even today some have tried to claim to be the "king" or "queen," but they have generally been ignored or have had to face the ridicule of the majority of rational Witches. What replaced it was not one, but multiple leaders who surfaced within the Witchcraft community. They did not claim to be hereditary, or to be initiated by their grandmothers, nor have they courted the press, as both Sanders and Gardner did. Instead, they have attempted to pass their wisdom on by writing and by action. Instead of one, there are now many leaders of the movement to reestablish Witchcraft. They are mostly, but not exclusively, authors. It is interesting that this very much reflects the change within Wicca regarding traditions, and the move toward a truly polytheistic doctrine. Some examples are Raymond Buckland, Ed Fitch, Starhawk, Vivianne Crowley, and a host of new writers, such as Fiona Horne, Phyllis Curott, to name a few. But it is not just writers who are now shaping it. There are also those who are active in networking and in creating the idea of community, such as Fritz and Wren Jung, who run The Witches' Voice website. We would rate the work of the cyber Witches as equally important to that of print writers—if not more so—as they provide the anonymous individual Witch a voice. To this end, Wicca has become a "republic," as we like to put it, with individual Witches collectively giving a consensus of direction to the movement rather than a direction being set by one leader, as in the past.

Books have had much to do with the development of Wicca. We have given the principle reason toward the end of chapter 1 (see page 19), but there is also another reason: Monotheistic culture has its norms and values rooted in the religions "of the book": Christianity, Judaism, or Islam. In these religions, the book is "the Word," the book is always right or "righteous." It is inevitable that being brought up in such a culture, even if you reject the predominant religion, these influences will remain part of you. Therefore, books outlining sacred ritual practice were treated with similar reverence as the predominant sacred books of the culture, be it the Bible, the Torah, or the Koran. Initially, this caused problems with the way the main liturgy of Wicca (the Book of Shadows) was seen and treated. Many saw it as sacred, treating it on a par with the Christian Bible; its origins were therefore not to be questioned.

At the end of the day, the Book of Shadows was (and is) nothing more than a collection of rituals, rites, and information cobbled together by Gerald Gardner and Doreen Valiente. It was expanded as time went on with material from books whose ideas were not questioned. It must be remembered that most people in Britain in rural areas didn't learn to read until the late 1800s, so the idea that it was ancient is quite ludicrous from a historical viewpoint. Even the name "Book of Shadows" may have origins in eastern Sufism rather than Western European occult practice.*

It was not until the early 1990s that the origins of the Book of Shadows were really seriously questioned, and this was done again in a book: *Crafting the Art of Magic (Book 1)* by Aidan Kelly.† Janet and Stewart had, of course, questioned its origins in *The Witches' Way* (and in the combined edition, *A Witches' Bible: The Complete Witches' Handbook*) with the help of the "mother" of modern Witchcraft, Doreen Valiente. Kelly's eventual conclusions were correct: the Book of Shadows was a created

---

* "The Book of Shadows" in Sufi practice is a method of divination involving taking a measure of head, chest, and height. The measurements are then compared to notes within the book. As noted by Ron Hutton in *Triumph of the Moon* (page 273), there was a Sufi among Gardner's circle: Idries Shah, author of *The Way of the Sufi*. Wicca is mentioned in his introduction as one of the many spiritual traditions of the West influenced one way or another by Sufism.

† Many of Kelly's suggestions on origins have since been questioned, although his basic conclusion—that the Book of Shadows was a creation of Gardner and Valiente—is considered correct.

work put together over a period of time by Gerald Gardner and Doreen Valiente. To date, we have seen many copies of the Book of Shadows. We know that there are at least three distinct phases in its development, scrupulously catalogued and dated by Aidan Kelly. There are also five root copies, each with differences, related to Gardner's high priestesses, who all changed material after hiving off from him. There are also Alexandrian versions of a Book of Shadows, and other ritual books created by Alex Sanders that have no relationship to Gardnerian practice at all.

The Book of Shadows was never intended to be dogmatic. We strongly believe Gardner intended it to be something that Witches added to in an organic fashion. It was supposed to be more like a Witch's notebook reflecting their ongoing development rather than a bible or ancient grimoire of magical secrets. One story that came from an original Gardnerian initiate is that Gardner actually changed material around in one version to make his initiates think for themselves.[1] Unfortunately, this didn't work out the way he expected, so there is now a Gardnerian line where one of the rituals is still in the wrong place even though it disobeys magical lore.* This is one of the dangers of dogma taking hold and the reason why fixed traditions are facing the question of "adaption or extinction."

The Questioning of Tradition

It is important to understand what tradition is. A tradition is a set of workable ideas, philosophies, and practices that are passed down from one person to another over a period of time. The process of transmitting a tradition over several generations often has the result of inspiring reverence for the tradition's content. Sometimes the reason why the actual tradition is passed down is lost. This doesn't in any way necessarily mean that the tradition is obsolete or no longer valid. It may still work, particularly in occult practice. But a tradition with a lot of reverence placed on it by the users can be hard to change if the situation changes and the material no longer performs the original role for which it was created. The people might say, "It's traditional; we've always done it that way." The tradition becomes an end unto itself, and no longer performs its original purpose.

Progressive Witchcraft adapts the idea of tradition into something more tenable. This is where a coven—be it of Gardnerian, Alexandrian,

---

* It is our belief, and experience magically, that the consecration of wine should in fact take place immediately after the invocation of Deity and before the raising of energy.

or self-initiatory origin—has developed its own system, and then members hive off to develop their own covens. A good example of this is an American tradition called Blue Star. According to an article written by Cat Castells and Amy Douglass:

> Blue Star Wicca is a centuries old Pagan tradition founded in the mid-1970s. Originally established as a single coven in Pennsylvania, Blue Star evolved over the next decade or two into a collection of more than a dozen covens all across the U.S., all working in what is essentially the same framework and therefore recognizable as a tradition.[2]

Janet and Stewart first encountered Blue Star in 1991 when they met Tziporah and Kenny Klein. It was Tziporah and Kenny who went on to develop Blue Star into a viable system of training.[*] We have since met many of its members and can honestly say that we find their approach to Wicca one of the most refreshing we have come across. First of all, there are no claims of heredity. In fact, they are very proud of their modern origins and see this as no hindrance to being a viable system of Witchcraft. They also see evolution as an important factor, and actively encourage each hived-off coven to develop its own way of doing things rather than sticking to dogmatic tradition, while still maintaining the core beliefs unique to Blue Star; these core beliefs keep them a coherent and recognizable system. Most prominent of these is their code of conduct related to the Rede, and their system of training and education. They consider themselves to have one of the most strenuous training regimes of any Wiccan tradition, hardly surprising as Blue Star had its origins in the Pagan Way and the Alexandrian Traditions, which both pioneered the idea of fixed training systems within modern Witchcraft (see pages 30, 101–102). We have come across several other similar coven-based traditions out there, and have regular contact with many of them. We see this rather than the inflexible monoliths of the past as the future of tradition within modern Witchcraft.

Evolution, Cultural Selection, and Lineage
History shows that witchcraft is an adapting, evolving tradition. You can easily apply the ideas of Charles Darwin to its development, and witchcraft's religious and philosophical beliefs certainly do not disagree with

---

[*] Blue Star was originally formed in 1971 by Frank Duffner. At this time, Tziporah Klein (then Katz) joined the coven, married Frank, and met Kenny Klein—who was to become her second husband.

the ideas of Darwin. In fact, the infamous "Darwin fish," which mocks some Christians' refusal to accept evolution, is commonly found as a bumper sticker on the fenders of cars owned by modern Witches. Is this surprising? No, as at the core of Witchcraft is its reverence for nature and the belief that we are not separate from it; an idea the monotheistic religions have tried to discourage. What is happening in modern Witchcraft is cultural selection.* If something contributes no positive benefit within Witchcraft, it is rejected. If this rejection doesn't happen, then the tradition that maintains the noncontributory element becomes dogmatic and eventually disappears. The most obvious example of this is the differences in the development of Wicca in the United States and in the United Kingdom. The culture in the United States is much more open in its approach to religion, as the first amendment of the United States' Constitution protects the right to religious freedom. In some areas of the United States, you can easily have an open public Pagan festivals. In other parts, individuals and magical groups still have to remain highly secretive and alternative religions face daily prejudice. Because of this, Witches in these areas will have very different outlooks about what they are doing.

In California we have seen more openness toward Wiccan practice, which includes "outer courts," which are Circles in covens that welcome visitors and newcomers. This has, in turn, resulted in a more progressive attitude towards Wicca and a questioning of its structures and doctrines. This is not a bad thing in our eyes. But in other states the situation is very different. From conferring with Wiccans in the heavily evangelical southern states, we know that heavy vetting of those who come looking for Wicca, and strict abidance by rules of secrecy and tradition, has resulted in a very closed approach to Wicca. We believe neither approach is wrong—each is what is required in each specific environment for Witchcraft's survival. We have also witnessed situations where a coven with its origins in the Gardnerian Tradition has more in common with a local

---

* Darwin's idea of "nature red in tooth and claw" was rejected long ago, as it was found that cooperation and mutual altruism is equally capable of enabling not "survival" as such, but *reproductive success*. Anthropologist Marvin Harris has proposed this idea of "cultural selection," as it is called, in his book *Our Kind* (page 127). In this system, the criterion for success is, as Harris puts it, "well-being." In short, a new variation in the way individuals think and behave is propagated if it enables the individual, or group in which the individual exists, to obtain more of the good stuff in life: more food, better shelter, more sex, more leisure time, more fun, more intellectual or emotional stimulation, more power, more access to resources, and so on.

Alexandrian coven than with the coven it originally sprung from in a neighboring state (because of the aforementioned factors). Here we see cultural selection at work—nature (and thus, the Goddess) loves diversity, and it is this diversity that has allowed Witchcraft to survive.

One of the effects of this evolutionary growth has been the questioning of what some have seen as the cornerstone of Wiccan practice: *lineage*. The current interpretation of lineage has now become a burden, stunting the growth of some of the traditional lines due to its inflexibility. It has been misused as an excuse for elitism, and a rationale for being insular—which separates the Witch from the real world around him or her, including modern Paganism and Witchcraft. In the worse cases, it has become a method of control over coven initiates. In a time when information on Wicca is freely available, lineage has become an anachronism. The result is that a new type of Witch has appeared who rejects the concepts of lineage and tradition. Many have decided just to label themselves *Witches* rather than *Wiccans*, because of Wicca's associations with these twin dogmas.

We should point out that lineage does have its positive side: it gives many a sense of security in what they doing. They know that they can trace their teachers' origins and that their teachers have had at least some sort of spiritual instruction. It offers a sense of belonging and membership in something larger than one's self and immediate surroundings, and the need to be accepted and to belong is quite high in Maslow's hierarchy of needs (see pages 96–97). It is perhaps time for the concept of lineage to change its significance and function in Pagan culture rather than be simply dismissed. For this reason, we do feel that this rejection is unfortunate, but we also agree that it is perhaps time for Wicca to realize that spiritual training must take precedence over the idea of apostolic succession—which is actually alien to Pagan practice, although possibly originally rooted in it. Here we not only see evolution at work, but also a cycle: Wiccans are returning to many of the old pagan values and seeing their practices as a spiritual path rather than those of a secret society influenced by pseudo-Masonic ideas.

The Witch Versus Wiccan Debate

We, personally, do not actually believe there is any difference between the words *Witch* and *Wiccan*. The two words, as we have shown, come from the same root source (see pages 3–4). The differentiation of *Witch* from *Wiccan* originated in the 1960s when Sanders first faced rejection from the Gardnerians and went his own way. It came about as a result of the nonacceptance of those who were not seen as correctly initiated or as having correct lineage. The two main traditions refused to accept those from outside their traditions as Wiccan or even as "real Witches." For many years, this divided the Witchcraft movement into two camps, and has blurred the meaning of the words *Witch* and *Wiccan* purely for the sake of political expediency. This division has been perpetuated with the statement "All Wiccans are Witches, but not all Witches are Wiccans." Some of us who have been around for a while find this amusing, as we remember when the statement was "All Witches are Pagans, but not all Pagans are Witches!" We, with many others, realized the divisive nature of this situation early on. We have always refused to accept these artificially created divisions. As time has gone on, these divisions have broken down due to the necessity for communication within the Pagan community. This interaction has now resulted in the majority of the old traditions accepting that you can be self-initiated, or be from reconstructionist traditions, and still be a Witch. Some have even accepted that you can be classified as a Wiccan, resulting in the term *Initiatory Wicca* to define those of Gardnerian or Alexandrian origin.

Of course, what is really going on here is the continual cycle of need for the new generation of Witches to prove themselves to their perceived elders before being accepted. ("Second-degree syndrome" can also be a factor in this cycle. See page 57.) We have no doubt that, as the new generation of young Witches that are now appearing strive to assert their own way of doing things, new semantic divisions will occur until they are also finally accepted; just as the reconstructionists and self-initiates were in the past. For this reason, we continue to believe that "Wiccan" is the more correct way to define anyone who is following the modern spirituality of Wicca. It does, of course, very much depend on your individual view and whether you believe Gardner and Sanders really found any survivals of ancient witchcraft.

The Predominance of Training and Ethics over Doctrine
While Witchcraft remained underground within a culture that did not accept religious differences, it was necessary to have the ideas of lineage and fixed traditions with the resulting attitudes to initiation. These allowed Wicca to retain a coherent practice, while keeping it secret and out of public view, but with the opening of attitudes, these doctrines have now become redundant and only exist for "traditions sake." The two most important doctrines that have kept Wicca from degenerating and losing

cohesion as a spiritual path is its system of ethical principles—the Wiccan Rede—and its system of training. If these systems didn't exist within Wicca, someone would end up creating them—regardless of whether tradition or lineage continues as a prevalent factor.

The Wiccan Rede ("An it harm none, do what thou will") has origins with Gerald Gardner. Many have noticed its similarity to Aleister Crowley's "Do what thou wilt shall be the whole of the Law. Love is the Law, love under will." There is no doubt that there was communication between Gardner and Crowley (see footnotes page 13). The occult writer Francis King goes further and suggests that much of the original Book of Shadows was written by Crowley for Gardner, and a substantial financial sum was exchanged for his services:[3]

> He [Gardner] accordingly hired Crowley, at a generous fee, to write elaborate rituals for the new "Gardnerian" witch-cult and, at about the same time, either forged, or procured to be forged, the so-called *Book of Shadows* . . . but betrayed its modern origins in every line of its unsatisfactory pastiche of Elizabethan English.[4]

Here again, as with the Rede, we see elements of practice possibly absorbed into Wicca from another system. Although it is unproven, there is little doubt that there are strong elements of OTO ritual style in the original Book of Shadows. These origins are irrelevant, however. What is important is that it worked and gave Wicca a ritual and ethical base, something possessed by all other genuine spiritual paths. The Rede has become the central defining ethical tenet for nearly all Wiccans regardless of tradition. It not only reflects the golden rule found in other religions, but should also be seen as an ethical imperative that encourages the Witch to learn and train so that they do no harm. It has remained the main focus of modern Wicca's philosophy, and is always the first statement used when Wiccans face the ignorant and discriminatory accusation of being evil. We have even heard it being used by those who are quite adamant that they are Pagans, not Witches, as no other ethical principle fits the neo-Pagan movement so well. If the glove fits, why not wear it!

Secrecy has remained one of the main precepts of Wicca, and in the Gardnerian initiation ritual, it is very prevalent. In the first-degree rite, initiates are pushed into the Circle in a particular way, so they do not see their initiator. An argument leveled at Alexandrians by hard-line

Gardnerians is that some Witches are "not real Witches" because this was not part of their initiation rites.* Secrecy within Witchcraft was, of course, necessary in the 1950s when there was still serious prejudice. But even the founder, Gerald Gardner, continually broke the rules of secrecy to seek media exposure for the growing Craft of Wicca—as did Alex Sanders. Strange as it may seem, without this rule-breaking there probably wouldn't be a Pagan movement today, or the amount of interest in Wicca that there is.

Secrecy exists within Witchcraft for three reasons:

1. Protection of the individual members from suffering discrimination outside of Circle.
2. Prevention of information about coven meetings and the magical practices of the coven from becoming available to nonmembers.
3. Stopping the secrets of the Craft—the written material and practices of the coven—from being passed on to those outside of the coven, or even to those within the coven who are not prepared for them.

Although we see good reasons for the first two points, the last is now an anachronism. Within our coven, we still maintain secrecy from the outside world. To quote Doreen Valiente, "Witchcraft doesn't pay for broken windows," and even in a world with a more liberal attitude, there are still those in our society likely to cause problems for self-professed Witches. Regarding the second point: what goes on in our coven is the business of nobody but the members; and more importantly, an outsider's awareness of the rites you practice can dissipate the energy. It is the third reason for secrecy that we have the most problem with and which, on numerous occasions, we have been accused of breaking in the publication of our books.† Janet and Stewart found it interesting to be accused of breaking oaths by writing about rituals they had researched and created themselves. One reason for this was that some individuals didn't want to be seen as not knowing about this material, even though it was new. The very idea of a "tradition

---

* Monique and Scotty Wilson once informed Stewart that he was not a "real Witch" for this reason.

† Many people are unaware that all the material from the Sabbats that Janet and Stewart published in *Eight Sabbats for Witches* and *A Witches' Bible* was in fact not traditional, and was created by ourselves from sources of literature. The ritual framework and the Drawing Down the Moon ritual were Gardnerian not Alexandrian, and were published by permission of Doreen Valiente, their coauthor.

of secrets" has degenerated Wicca into a second-rate form of Freemasonry in many people's eyes. Hardly surprising, since the Co-Masonic Fellowship of Crotona is one of Wicca's sources.

Witchcraft, the Mystery Tradition

Some of Wicca's origins seem to be in the concept of a mystery tradition (see chapter 3). This means that the mysteries or secrets are *experiential* (for more on this see pages 42, 44–45, 109, 172). This is important if you are going to understand the true nature of Witchcraft. Many people have given away the secrets: it started with Gardner, proceeded with Sanders, and continues today. There is not one element of original Gardnerian or Alexandrian practice that has not been published somewhere—be it in a book or the Internet—but these secrets are meaningless as they are no more than words. You have to experience the mysteries to understand them; they cannot be conveyed in language; they are the very spiritual essence that is sought from the pursuit of ritual and magical practice, and they create communion with the divine. This is the important spiritual truth within Wicca. If someone explains to you what is going to happen to you when you go on a roller-coaster ride, describing initially to you how the roller coaster works, and then how it feels, does it detract anything from the actual experience? No, of course not, particularly because the person describing how it feels is describing something subjective, and your experience will be very different to theirs. The same applies to the mysteries. It is the idea of *experiencing* spirituality that is one of the main causes of interest in those seeking Witchcraft. In a world governed by logic and science, where every question is answerable with a mathematical equation, it is not surprising that we seek a return to magic. This need can sometimes develop into a romanticism about the past, a nostalgia, which sometimes has been channeled into the idea of hereditary witchcraft or the idea of witchcraft's continued survival through the Middle Ages and up to the present day. It's a nice image, but it's unlikely to be true in the way that some expect. Yes, there are hereditary survivals, but no dusty grimoires or secrets from the past that aren't already known.

If this romanticism is directed properly, then we see the links with our own ancestors through culture, such as in Celtic, Norse, Egyptian, or Anglo-Saxon symbolism. This is the reconstructionism that we mentioned (see pages 10, 17), which is highly creative and expressive in its form and has helped to guide Wicca back to its spiritual origins. At the end of the day, this is all that Gerald Gardner did when he and Doreen Valiente put

Wicca together as a viable system; taking material from the Fellowship of Crotona, from Aleister Crowley's OTO, and from several pieces of literature of the period, including the accounts of Isobel Gowdie's witchcraft trial.* The only difference is that he claimed it was hereditary and was of ancient origin, which he apparently considered necessary to gain acceptance in a critical occult world. This has led the writer Raven Grimassi to suggest that Wicca's origins are actually in Strega, as the only real hereditary witch material present was from Charles Godfrey Leland's *Aradia, or the Gospel of the Witches*. From the perspective of a practitioner of Strega, he is correct, although others may disagree. What is often overlooked is that surely any true British hereditary, traditional material would have been about Anglo-Saxon magical practice, as the New Forest is situated in the old English kingdom of Wessex. Perhaps, without realizing it, Ray Buckland stumbled on an important truth with the publication of *The Tree: The Complete Book of Saxon Witchcraft*.

We have always strongly believed in the free flow of information about Wicca. It is this very process that has kept Wicca a thriving spiritual path—along with the Rede, which we mentioned earlier. One of the triumphs of the modern neo-Pagan movement is its progressive attitude to new technology. It would have easy for Wicca to have become a religion of luddites, but it did not. Wicca has embraced the computer revolution; our Book of Shadows became a Disc of Shadows in 1995 and continues growing to this day. Since the 1980s, one of the "pre-Christian values" that Witchcraft has returned to is the absorption of that which works and aids the belief structure of the individual.

Within our own coven, we do not keep secrets from members of the coven, including information about the origins of the material we have in our Book of Shadows. There are a few exceptions. One is information from private conversations. Another is that, when it comes to initiation, the initiate is kept from knowing exactly what is going to happen during initiation to help build suspense. We strongly believe that people will understand what they're taught when they're ready. As we have previously mentioned, the mysteries have to be experienced. Initiations, rituals, and magical practices in the context of the mysteries are tools to assist in the spiritual experience of the Witch initiate.

---

* In four separate confessions made in 1662, Isobel Gowdie gave what amounted to a resume of popular beliefs about witchcraft in Scotland. A source of material for anyone researching witchcraft, such as Gardner.

Freemasonry and the Origins of the Degree System

One other doctrine that has come under scrutiny is the degree system. There is no doubt about the origins of this system, as it clearly has overtones of ritual magic and Freemasonry. It certainly isn't a system you would imagine being used in a hereditary witchcraft family of the Dark Ages. Again, Crowley's relationship with Gardner comes into the picture. One suggestion we have heard many times is that Gardner attempted to align his system of Wicca with that of the OTO—in which he had a charter granted to him by Crowley.[5] The first degree of Wicca can be seen as equivalent to the first three degrees of the OTO; the second degree, the next three, etc. The other possibility is that the degree system is purely Masonic in origin. After talking to practicing Freemasons, we consider this to be more plausible and think it shows the Co-Masonic influence. But if the former is true, you can certainly understand Gardner's reasoning behind this. It goes back to the need for acceptance. Perhaps he felt that by doing this he could gain universal acceptance amongst the fickle middle-to-upper-class occult community of Britain at the time, although he was probably a bit optimistic about how this alliance with "the mad, bad, and dangerous to know" Aleister Crowley would be taken.

The main criticism of the degree system is its hierarchical nature. We couldn't agree more, but it has not stopped individuals from adapting it. A good example is the system used by the incredibly nonhierarchical neo-Pagan Church of All Worlds.* Although not Wiccan, it has a system of "circles" through which its members pass as they head toward Scion or clergy status. The system was created because there are good psychological reasons for a system of levels (which are covered more fully in chapter 6).

Even we attempted in the 1990s to finally do away with the hierarchical degree system. We initially adopted an organic system based on the ideas of dedication, initiation, and eldership. We hoped this would result in a one-initiation system. It sounded good on paper and felt more like a method that could have been used by the village witch. The problem was that our initiates continued to refer to themselves as "first," "second," and "third." They were familiar with this system and felt secure with it.

In the end, we ended up with a system that has not one, but four initiations: dedication, first, second, and third. We have come across other adaptions: Alexandrians with five degree systems; Seax-Wicans using a

---

* The Church of All Worlds was founded in 1961 and based its theology on Robert A. Heinlein's science-fiction novel *Stranger in a Strange Land*.

three-degree system—even though Raymond Buckland's book only had one initiation. At the end of the day, a degree system should not be hierarchical, but a reflection of the competency and spiritual experience of the initiate. We feel it is up to individual covens and Witches to decide

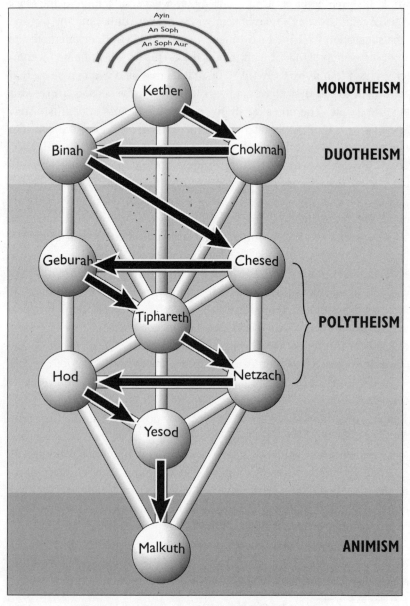

Figure 1 Polytheism, Duotheism, and the Lightning Flash

whether they should use this system. There is no reason why it cannot be adapted to suit specific needs. It is a useful system, a tool, and should not become dogmatic—and it certainly should not become a system of hierarchy with individuals achieving a higher status than any other member of the Craft. This is stated clearly, but seldom heeded, in Gardnerian law with the phrase: "All members of the Craft are equal." Somehow the Orwellian *Animal Farm* joke, "but some . . . animals [witches] are more equal than others," crept into the older traditions of Wicca. But we believe we have found one other reason for the existence and continued use of a degree system in modern Witchcraft, and that is its unquestionable link with the ancient mysteries.

Defining the Modern Witch

We now come to one of the most difficult questions to answer: what are the modern definitions of witch and witchcraft? This is a question that has continued to be debated ever since Gardner went public in the 1950s. Before the 1990s, the terms were pretty much interchangeable—before the new trend appeared that we mentioned earlier (see pages 29–30). This is, of course, the same rebellion against dogma that all the main figures of Wicca have gone through since Gardner's expulsion from his first coven. As we've seen, it isn't a path based necessarily on the form that it takes; for example, its lineage, tradition, or sacrosanct secrecy. What seems to define modern Witchcraft is its belief structure. The first obvious thing is the presence of Deity in some form; the principle forms in Wicca are the God and the Goddess. There are two approaches to them: the duotheistic "all gods one god; all goddesses one goddess" and the polytheistic belief that the divine has many faces manifest as the many gods and goddesses of the different cultures around the world.

Duotheism within Wicca actually has its origins in the work of Dion Fortune, and it was she who made the often-quoted statement previously mentioned. Dion Fortune, though, was not a Witch, but a follower of the heavily Cabalistic-influenced Western tradition of occultism.* In the ten sephiroth of the Cabalistic Tree of Life, duotheism is found in the sephira of Binah, the Goddess principle (sphere three, Mother, understanding, outer intellect) and the sephira of Chokma, the God principle (sphere two, Father, inner intellect, wisdom). These sephiroth, along with the first, Kether (Crown) make up the supernal triangle. Kether is the androgynous fusion

---

* Dion Fortune (1891–1946) was a widely published writer of her time (see Bibliography). She founded the Society of the Inner Light more on Christian gnostic and theosophical principles than pagan ones.

of both the previous sephiroth. What we have in duotheism is a heavily Judeo-Christianized idea of what the divine is (see figure 1).

From the perspective of Cabala and Western magical traditions, polytheism is the descent down this tree. These two principles split into a myriad of forms and personalities, gods and goddesses. Thus polytheism and duotheism are not exclusive of each other. In fact, one could argue that polytheism is the eventual goal of duotheism. The idea of polytheism in the modern Witchcraft community seems to be gaining ground on duotheistic ideas. It is hardly surprising then that modern Witchcraft has started to become more spiritual in its perspective, as it is successfully bringing the "lightning flash," the power of the divine, down into its practices and into the world in general. The eventual conclusion of this process would be the embracing of animism,* which is still found in contemporary shamanic practices today. Animism is a practice only really understandable if you live a lifestyle close to the earth, something that few modern Witches are capable of doing. But embracing polytheism is important for another reason. It comes with the idea of "many truths," the acceptance of the many different paths to Spirit within Witchcraft. The increasing acceptance of polytheism has resulted in the realization that it is spirituality that is important—not the form used to reach it. This embracing of polytheism is itself a result of the fact that monotheistic religion is no longer taught in schools the way it used to be. In the first years of the new millennium, the first generation of truly non-Christian moderns who have an innate understanding of the nature of modern Pagan spirituality is emerging.

Any definition of Witchcraft must therefore be related to the divine itself, and the role of anyone who brings Spirit to Earth. In Wicca, we can see this symbolized in the process known as Drawing Down the Moon, which is the most important sacrament in Wiccan practice (see pages 177–179). Witchcraft must therefore be a priesthood by its very nature, and the priesthoods of ancient paganism have always been mystery schools (see pages 45–46). All priesthoods must serve; it is their nature. To be a Witch, therefore, is to serve the divine—not in a slavish way, but in a joint partnership for the good of the Witches' community (see pages 170–172). Therefore, there should be no overblown ego when it comes to being a Witch. We see this partnership in the ancient forms of witchcraft and shamanic practice

---

*   Animism is the belief that everything in the material world is alive and sentient on a spiritual level—the divine Spirit made manifest universally.

that were mentioned in chapter 1. Magic can therefore be seen to be principally about healing.* To heal is the only truly ethical reason for performing magic, and the priest/priestess works to heal the world in some form. Magic therefore ceases to be about controlling natural forces, a principle of ceremonial ritual magic, but instead becomes about working in synergy with natural forces: flowing with the divine energy of the universe (see pages 132–133).

At the beginning of the new millennium, the stage that modern Wicca is now at can be likened to the self-awareness a child develops in their teens as they strive to understand their world. It has begun to question its parents and their values, and like an obstreperous teenager, has entered into a period of rebellion. It has rejected the old doctrines, lineage, tradition, and even the old rules related to initiation, regardless of the parents' protestations. By doing so, it has rejected the root causes of many of the problems that have caused arguments in Wicca in the past. It is quite simply that the older generation of Witches had continued to hold on to the Christian values of their time, without realizing it, only because they were so deeply ingrained. These included the monotheistic doctrine of "one God, one Truth, one Way." True polytheists believe that there are many truths, and therefore many ways to Spirit, Deity, or whatever name you wish to call it. By definition, this encourages acceptance of the paths of others, as well as acceptance of a diversity of practice within one's own path.

Where else do the seeds of the rebellion lie but in the Woodstock generation of the 1960s? It was a generation whose main catchphrase was "Question authority." When individuals set themselves up as self-professed "authorities" on Witchcraft, it was inevitable that they would be questioned. Feminist Wicca, the reconstructionist traditions and their authors, and even ourselves, have the origin of our Witchcraft in this generation. The idea that just because someone was old didn't necessarily mean they were right began to permeate the blossoming Witchcraft community. This rebellion was possibly connected to the very origins of ancient tribal witchcraft and the initial cause for its creation: survival. The return of this imperative is at the very roots of why a shamanic, magical approach has returned to the modern world.

So what has changed since witchcraft first began to disappear during the Middle Ages? We just have to look at the history of the twentieth century to understand why; the First World War, the Second World War,

---

* For more on this idea, see our previous work *The Healing Craft*.

the nuclear Cold War, and now potential environmental disasters, have threatened the world since the 1900s. For the first time in humanity's history, we are capable not only of making our own species extinct, but also of reducing the whole planet to a pile of rubble. It is a hardly surprising that two of the main doctrines of modern Wicca is reverence for nature and the pursuit of world peace. These values were incorporated into Witchcraft from that 1960s generation, which rebelled against the materialist values of the previous generation that caused this situation to arise. The role of Witchcraft is no longer just to help the tribe or clan to survive, but also now to help the survival of the whole of humanity and the world in which we live.

So now we're going to do something that few people would dare do, as it has always been so controversial. We are going to try and give our definition of a modern Witch or Wiccan. As magical workers in a community setting have always been referred to as priesthood, we therefore define Witchcraft as

> *An evolving, magical, nature-based priesthood with service to its community as its main role. A Witch is also, therefore, a craftsperson with well-developed magical skills and an emphasis on religious and spiritual practice.*

This definition is also, of course, a cross-cultural definition that could easily include Vodoun practices, Strega practices, and similar practices of other cultures.

Spirituality and Progressive Witchcraft

As we have seen again and again, Witchcraft is in a continual growth process subject to evolution. In some cases, aspects of it are becoming extinct as they cease to have any purpose. Wicca is, quite simply, dynamic—as all living spiritual paths are. It does not remain still; it is continually changing and going through cycles. Witches see this all the time in the natural cycle of the seasons, which is referred to as "the Wheel of the Year" (see chapter 9). Many Witches have now begun to realize that these very cycles appear in spirituality itself, obeying the occult law "As above, so below." These are principles also found in shamanism, an area neglected by many in modern Witchcraft in favor of Western ritual magic—thereby ignoring the fact that ancient witchcraft and shamanism are similar in essence. Witches with a progressive outlook have come to realize that Witchcraft is dynamic and cyclical to its very core. To try to hold back these forces, which are evolving Witchcraft into a new form of spirituality, would be like the story Gavin was told as a child about the Dark-Age Danish ruler, King Canute, who tried to hold back the sea at high tide. There will always be some who will try to hold back the sea of change for the sake of tradition, or rather for the sake of their positions of power and ego, but they will ultimately fail. This realization comes from the conclusions drawn through a process of understanding Wiccan history. We have decided to call the results of this process *progressive Witchcraft*. Our attempted summation is as follows:

Tenets of Progressive Witchcraft

1. *Progressive Witchcraft* is not a tradition, but a name describing the evolution of modern Witchcraft into a coherent magical and spiritual path for the next millennium. Those following this path may not necessarily even name themselves progressive Witches, and may classify themselves as belonging to one of the many traditions of Wicca that exist; it is their actions and beliefs that dictate their belonging to progressive Witchcraft.

2. Evolution is an important aspect of this path, particularly in the understanding that all that has gone before in Wicca has been part of its growth process, whether perceived as negative or positive. Because of this, progressive Witches believe that there are no "good" or "bad" experiences, only experiences that can be learned from.

3. Spirit is at the core of any religious belief structure. Those who are progressive Witches realize that spirituality must be at the center of Wiccan belief, training, and practice. The emphasis is therefore on connection with the divine by whatever names it is called. For those on a progressive Wiccan spiritual path, connection and union with the divine is the ultimate goal of being a Witch.

4. With connection to the divine comes the realization that we are servants of Spirit and not the masters. The terms *priestess* and *priest* are therefore put back into their original context as servants of the divine, and the implications put on them by two thousand years of hierarchical abuse of the words are thrown aside. Within progressive Witchcraft, a priest or priestess is someone who has union with Deity for the benefit of society, humanity, and the world around them. They also see their role as assisting others to make this connection, realizing that there is no monopoly on it, as there has been within the monotheistic religions. There is no room for *ego* within the words *priestess* and *priest*; they are a description of what someone does, not a hierarchical title to be bestowed.

5. Progressive Witches do not feel that initiation can only take place in a "properly prepared circle." Individuals may have initiatory epiphanies outside of Circle as the result of divine intervention. There is only "one true initiator" to quote an old Gardnerian Wiccan law and Dion Fortune. This is understood to mean that it is not a priest or priestess who initiates someone into Wicca, but the divine as God or Goddess or even the Higher Self. The doctrine of lineage is therefore seen to be irrelevant, and the term 'self-initiation' misleading, as Deity will always manifest at a true initiation if the person has reached the right level of spiritual growth; even if the person alone is physically present.

6. Although much can be learned from books and from word-of-mouth (in formal or informal teaching situations), progressive Witches know that Wicca is a mystery tradition and that experiential knowledge is the most important form for spiritual growth. They also know that the mysteries can never adequately be explained by word-of-mouth or written word, as it touches the individual's very soul. It is therefore impossible to give away the true secrets of the Craft.

7. All genuinely spiritual paths have a firm ethical and moral base; anthropologists often refer to this as "the golden rule." Wicca has the Wiccan Rede: An it harm none, do what thou will." This is more a philosophy of ethical living than a prohibitive law—as you can do harm by inaction as well as by action. The implication is that to obey this law you must strive to be the best that you can be by accumulating knowledge and experience as a priestess or priest, as this is necessary if you are going to do your best to avoid doing harm in any of your actions—be they magical or mundane.

8. Spirit is seen as immanent in nature. Although complex, Wiccans see an inherent polarity within existence; day/night, growth/decay, life and death, et cetera. In Taoism, this is referred to as the ideas of Yin and Yang; in Wicca, as God and Goddess. Although we refer to God and Goddess in a duotheistic fashion, we are naturally polytheistic, believing that the divine has many faces that manifest as individual deities, be they ancestral, of nature, or even deities who govern a specific human skill (e.g., Hephaestus, god of smithcraft).

9. Those who follow the path of progressive Witchcraft seek for that which is best for all—both from nature and from themselves. "Good" and "evil" are recognized as human concepts, alien to nature and arising from imbalance. They therefore seek to balance themselves, and by doing so, the world around them. For this reason, progressive

Witches are intrinsically healers in all aspects of their work. They see magic, ritual practice, and the use of psychic skills as nothing more than tools to achieve this goal of balance and harmony.

The next chapter covers in more depth the subjects of initiation and the spiritual experience of initiation (mentioned in tenet five), because it is such a large and important subject in the evolution of Witchcraft. We will expand the subject of training in chapter 6.

NOTES

1. The originator of this story, Fred Lamond, has since published this with more detail in an article entitled "Gerald Gardner's Teachings" in the U.K.-based *Witchcraft and Wicca Magazine* (Beltane to Lammas, 2003).

2 Cat Castells and Amy Douglass, *The Witches' Voice*, 26 May 2001, http://www.witchvox.com/va/dt_va.html?a=usvt&c=trads&id=13922/.

3 First published in *Ritual Magic in England: 1887 to the Present Day* (1970), 179–180.

4 Francis King, *Ritual Magic in England*.

5 Again, found in Francis King's *Ritual Magic in England*, pages 179–180.

3

At the Heart of Witchcraft:
Spirituality and the Mysteries

And thou who thinkest to seek for me, know thy seeking and
yearning shall avail thee not, unless thou know this mystery:
that if that which thou seekest thou findest not within thee,
thou wilt never find it without thee.
—DOREEN VALIENTE, THE CHARGE OF THE GODDESS

This chapter is about the spiritual experience of Witchcraft. Spirituality is a word we have so often found lacking when people talk about Paganism and Witchcraft. In this chapter, we try to explain the origins, both ancient and modern, of the mysteries within modern Wiccan practice. We also try to explain what the mysteries are. Because experience of the mysteries is subjective, the best way we have come across to try to explain them in words is with adjectives and descriptive nouns. This explains why storytelling—the role of the bard and their Northern equivalents, the Skalds—was so important in ancient cultures. To quote Brendan Myers, a research associate of philosophy at the National University of Ireland, Galway:

> If you think about the mysteries you will find that while it is certainly the case that everyone's experiences of the mysteries are their own, nevertheless the mysteries are their own entities, "out there" to be experienced by every seeker who finds them. The mysteries themselves may be indefinable in words but the experience of the mysteries is describable. Also since the mysteries are eternal,

immutable, and immaterial and one (i.e., each mystery is a unity in itself, not the sum of its parts), therefore they are the same for everyone. Thus, people's spiritual experiences can be compared with each other, and one person's vision of an otherworldly landscape or figure can usually be confirmed by another person's vision.[1]

It is for this reason that some of the material in this book is anecdotal. We will, of course, give more objective information regarding the rites and rituals we went through to attain these experiences, and some of the psychology behind them, but these (as we have clearly stated) are *not the mysteries*. We hope that this chapter guides the reader in how to have his or her own experiences as an integral part of the spirituality of Witchcraft.

At the heart of the spiritual experience within modern Witchcraft is the idea that Wicca is a mystery religion. Although this is true of modern Wicca, there is little evidence of it before Gardner and the 1950s. The mystery practices of modern Wicca seem to have been drawn from the Mediterranean—more specifically, from the Greek and Egyptian cultures and their established priesthoods—rather than from any form of Northern or Western European village or tribal magical practice. Such village or tribal mystery practices would have surely been more shamanic in nature. Rosicrucianism and Co-Freemasonry follow mystery cycles from these Mediterranean cultures combined with heavy Christian gnostic* influences. Gardner, of course, was originally a member of the Rosicrucian theatre and a member of the Fellowship of Crotona, and therefore was heavily influenced by Co-Masonry. This is important, as it is R. E. Witt who points out in his work *Isis in the Graeco-Roman World* that Freemasonry was the natural successor of these mysteries, and of course Co-Freemasonry took an even more esoteric and gnostic path:

> The affiliation of Freemasonry with the rites of Isis and Osiris was recognized years ago by the percipient genius of Mozart in *The Magic Flute*. When Tamino and Papageno are led within the temple for their initiation into the mysteries of Isis they must be thought of from two standpoints. They typify modern Freemasonry. They also follow in the steps of their ancient brethren, the Cabiri, and Isis who went in search of the slain Osiris, or met the same god, no longer a corpse but resurrected as the god Ptah, The

---

* *Gnosis* is not strictly a Christian term. According to the *Oxford English Dictionary*, it means "knowledge of spiritual mysteries" and can just as readily be applied to the Wiccan mysteries.

Lord of Life, opening and closing the day, creating 'with his heart and tongue', superintending architects and masons at the building of temples and pyramids, ordaining that the house should be established firmly, and holding the *djed* column as his emblem of stability.[2]

It is very likely that Gardner incorporated into Wicca the form that the mysteries took within the Fellowship of Crotona and the Rosicrucian theatre, which he was familiar with. This was also probably his reason for incorporating the Masonic-style three-degree system, which acted as the vehicle for these mysteries. Like R. E. Witt, he saw Co-Freemasonry and the Rosicrucians as the successor to the ancient mysteries, and for Gardner, these mysteries were at the core of what he considered Witchcraft to be. He may have been right. From examining the myths of cultures closer to hand—those of the Celts and the Norse—we have seen parallels with those of the Greeks, Romans, and Egyptians. It is probably not that the mysteries did not exist within these closer cultures, but that the evidence for their existence was trampled underfoot by Christian-influenced thinking. The question is not whether Gardner was right, but *whether the mysteries still belong at the heart of modern Witchcraft.* We believe that they do, and that they have an important place within Wicca as a vehicle for the spiritual experience. The developments of the mystery schools within Greek and Egyptian culture are no more than the evolution of a shaman's journey into the underworld and his or her experiences there, and it is in shamanism that Witchcraft ultimately has its origins. We think the only major difference is the form of practice used to experience the mysteries—but the mysteries remain the same. Consciously or unconsciously, by reintroducing the mysteries into Witchcraft from Co-Freemasonry, Gardner returned them to their origins and fulfilled a cycle.

The First Thing that Magic Changes is the Self

One of the first things we are taught as Witches is that "the first thing that magic does is change the self," and we feel this should still be taught first. An understanding of psychology is essential to the understanding of the processes in magical practice, and to correct interpretation of the mysteries and the spiritual experience. The theories of the psychologist Carl Jung have been the mainstay of such interpretation though, because he analyzed both myth and the occult experience. The psychological theories of importance to the Witch are related to ego, id, Shadow, and to the anima/animus complex. You may ask what the theories of a scientist have to do with the mysteries. Jung's theories are important and relevant for a good reason—his outlook was gnostic, as were the origins of his psychological theories.[3]

Jung's concept of the ego was adopted directly from Freud. Freud believed the human personality consisted of two components: the *ego* and the *id*. These terms are Latin and mean, respectively, "I" and "it." In everyday life, we normally refer to ourselves in the context of the semi-conscious ego, hence we refer to ourselves as "I." If we become controlled by our instinctual impulses—such as hunger, thirst, sexual arousal, or aggression—we fall under the control of our id. When this happens, we may very likely refer to these forces as "it." For example, when talking about being envious they may say, "It's that green-eyed monster in me!" In a normally adjusted individual, the function of the ego is to serve (and to a certain degree, to control) the instinctual id. Hence we are prevented from taking off all our clothes in a public place in hot weather by our ego, which will fear ridicule. This is a good example of the ego-defense mechanisms that develop in an adult; but in a child, the ego has not yet developed, so a child may very likely do such things without fear. Not stripping publicly in hot weather is an example of the control function; an example of the serving function is that when we are hungry, the id only knows the hunger and the demand to be satisfied, but the ego knows how to open the can of food!

When the ego finds itself trying to cope with over-demand from the id—which is only interested in satisfying itself—the ego copes by using several defense strategies. It may push the unwanted impulses, thoughts, and ideas into the unconscious. This is called *repression*. The ego is also responsible for projecting these impulses and ideas onto others, so that sometimes what we most hate in others is what we are trying repress within ourselves. It may also displace the unwanted impulse, for example, by taking out anger for the way we are being treated on someone who is not connected with the cause of this anger. We may try to intellectual-ize and rationalize these impulses by developing elaborate excuses for our behavior when we succumb to the demands of the id. Other ways of coping with the demands of the id are as follows: to regress to a childlike state where the ego is less developed; to deny consciously the cause of an impulse, whether it be fact, feeling, or memory; and sublimation, the channeling of unacceptable impulses into acceptable everyday behavior. Many sports perform this function by channeling unwanted aggression. While the ego is still only partly conscious, these methods of ego-defense always remain unconscious.

Jung differed from Freud, for he believed that we develop a *persona* at the outer edge of our functioning egos. This is an outward mask, and a compromise between what the ego aspires to be and the limitations and social functions imposed upon it. If there is no compromise between the ego's aspirations and the social limitations, then the persona becomes a rigid stereotyped mask. In a balanced state, it is supple and pliable; being able to adjust to life's everyday situations.

The Shadow is the antithesis of the persona. Just as the persona lies in front of the ego, the Shadow hides behind it. It is the "unacceptable" face of the ego, the part that has been rejected. This pattern has appeared in mythology and literature for centuries. In Norse mythology, Odin's Shadow is Loki; in Egyptian mythology, Osiris's Shadow is Set. Biblically, Satan can be seen as Yahweh's Shadow; in modern writing, the concept is typified by the characters of Dr. Jekyll and Mr. Hyde. Because of the ego's rejection, the Shadow is often found portrayed as evil in nature, as can be seen from the examples given previously. This is an oversimplification, however, because when the ego sublimates some of its aspects, it may sometimes "throw the baby out with the bath water," so to speak. For example, if aggressive aspects are sublimated, individuals may also lose their ability to be assertive and make decisions. Sometimes exploration of our Shadows (an essential aspect of many forms of occultism) can restore these lost aspects and complete the wholeness of the individual's psyche.

The *anima* is the buried feminine element in a man, and the *animus* is the buried male element in a woman. The neo-Jungians believe it can be found in the area they call the "Bright Shadow." This is best symbolized in the fairy tale of Sleeping Beauty,* which features the beautifully draped room where Sleeping Beauty (the anima) sleeps, surrounded by the dark ominous castle (the Shadow). It is here that positive, repressed aspects of the individual can also be found. Apart from fairy tales, they are often found—like the Shadow—in art, literature, and (of most importance to the Witch) in mythology. In Welsh poetic tradition, the *Arwen* is the female soul-spirit of the poet and artist, and in Irish tales, the *Leannán Sidhe* fulfills the same function. The Arthurian Nimue is the anima representation of this within Merlin. Many male Pagans relate to the Goddess principle via their anima, as female Pagans do to the God principle via their animus. When we first fall in love, or have "crushes," we tend to fall for this soul image (regardless of sexual orientation), unconscious of the fact that

---

* Many of the Grimm brother's fairy tales are in fact a retelling of mystery stories originating in pagan mythology.

we are falling in love with ourselves. The results, if we remain unaware of what is really happening, can be disastrous, as with Lancelot and Guinevere within medieval Arthurian mythology. (The original Guinevere was a very different woman, but that is another matter.) If recognized and harnessed, the soul-spirit can act as an inspiration and a guide.

An example of this can be found in the Welsh bardic tradition where the anima appears as the Arwen—the female spirit of inspiration that eventually comes to claim the bard's soul while he is still young. Perhaps within this myth there is a veiled warning—that the exploration of the anima can go too far, eventually destroying important parts of the individual's persona. A similar theme can be discerned in Norse myth, with the Valkyries coming to claim the souls of the warriors, and within the Celtic myth of the Morrigan, the crow goddess who claims Cuchulain.

Even the myths revolving around various pagan deities show the pattern of the anima/animus concept's role in the formation of the human psyche. In the Greek myth of Theseus and the Minotaur, we see all the above aspects come together. King Minos represents the ego, who tries to deceive Zeus and deprive him of the offering of the white bull that, interestingly, is given to Zeus by Poseidon, the god of the sea (water and the sea are traditionally associated with the unconscious mind). As punishment, Zeus makes Queen Pasiphäe, the wife of Minos, fall in love with a bull and conceive the Minotaur with it. The Minotaur is placed in the labyrinth because he is so hideous and dangerous; the Minotaur represents the id and the labyrinth represents the Shadow area of the mind. Seven boys and seven girls are brought regularly from the Greek mainland to Crete as punishment for the death of Minos' son Androgeos at the hands of Aegeus, the son of King of Attica. The youths are thrown into the labyrinth to be devoured by the Minotaur; this represents the ego suppressing and forcing down into the Shadow not only unwanted impulses, but also those of a positive nature. It is Theseus who challenges this process and seeks the mysteries. From a psychological perspective, Theseus represents the personality on a journey of discovery. He travels from Athens with the others and is thrown into the labyrinth to await his fate. While there, Ariadne (the daughter of Minos) sees him through the bars of his cell and they fall in love. She is clearly the anima, which is one of the first aspects anyone venturing on the journey of discovery must find. She tells him how to beat the Minotaur by finding him before he wakes and killing him; this represents the unconscious mind controlling the id. She helps him by giving him a ball of golden thread that he must unreel to find his way back out of the Labyrinth. This act is important, as it clearly shows the dangers of embracing the Shadow without first seeking the anima/animus complex. Not to do so could result in becoming lost in the labyrinth of your own mind. Theseus does, of course, triumph—defeating the Minotaur just as it wakes.

We see a similar myth enacted in the second-degree rituals of both the Gardnerian and Alexandrian Traditions of Wicca. This is the Legend of the Descent of the Goddess, which is probably based on the myth of Demeter and Kore and the Sumerian myth of Inanna. Unlike the myth of Theseus, there is an agricultural aspect related to the Wheel of the Year in the Legend of the Descent of the Goddess,˙ (for more on this see pages 156–162) as well as a psychological one. This is important, as the fertility rites of the community that related to birth, death, and rebirth also echoed the deeper mysteries of the soul. The occult law of "As above, so below" seems to come into play again in the mysteries, and this is also found in the Egyptian mysteries related to Isis and Osiris.[4]

Legend of the Descent of the Goddess

Now our Lady the Goddess had never loved, but she would solve all the Mysteries, even the mystery of Death; and so she journeyed to the Underworld.

The Guardians of the Portals challenged her: "Strip off thy garments, lay aside thy jewels; for naught mayest thou bring with thee into this our land."

So she laid down her garments and her jewels, and was bound, as are all who enter the Realms of Death, the Mighty One.

Such was her beauty, that Death himself knelt and kissed her feet, saying:

"Blessed be thy feet, that have brought thee in these ways. Abide with me; but let me place my cold hand on thy heart."

She replied: "I love thee not. Why dost thou cause all things that I love and take delight in to fade and die?"

"Lady," replied Death, "'tis age and fate, against which I am helpless. Age causes all things to wither; but when men die at the end of time, I give them rest and peace, and strength so that

---

* The cycle of the Wheel of the Year in Wicca consists of the eight festivals, or the Celtic fire festivals of Imbolg, Beltane, Lughnasadh, and Samhain plus the solar festivals of spring equinox (Ostara), summer solstice (Litha), autumn equinox (Mabon), and winter solstice (Yule).

they may return. But thou! Thou art lovely. Return not; abide with me!"

But she answered: "I love thee not."

Then said Death: "An thou receivest not my hand on thy heart, thou must receive Death's scourge."

"It is fate—better so," she said. And she knelt, and Death scourged her tenderly. And she cried, "I feel the pangs of love."

And Death said, "Blessed Be!" and gave her the Fivefold Kiss, saying:

"Thus only mayest thou attain to joy and knowledge." And he taught her all the Mysteries, and they loved and were one, and he taught her all the Magics.

For there are three great events in the life of man: Love, Death, and Resurrection in the new body; and Magic controls them all. For to fulfil love you must return again at the same time and place as the loved one, and you must remember and love them again. But to be reborn you must die and be ready for a new body; and to die you must be born; and without love you may not be born; and this is all the Magics.[5]

This myth teaches reincarnation, particularly for those who have learned to love. The process of life, death, and rebirth—which the observant will see in nature—is an important part of neo-Pagan belief. But the experience of passing through this process as a mystery also gives those experiencing it the feeling that they have passed through death itself. This is one of the effects of passing into and facing your own Shadow—the death of the old personality as you come to understand your own ego.

The second degree is the most important rite, because it is the time when the initiate actually encounters the mysteries and faces the greatest challenge—the embracing of the personal anima/animus while descending into the personal Shadow. The first degree can be seen as no more than a preparatory initiation leading to this process, while the third degree is the initiation marking a witch who is capable of taking an initiate through the process. These levels are no different from the system of degrees found in the traditional Isis/Osiris mysteries mentioned earlier in this chapter. In these mysteries, Isis governs the first degree and Osiris the second.[6] It can be no chance then the first-degree sigil in Wicca—the inverted triangle—is a Goddess symbol, while the second-degree symbol—the inverted pentagram—is a symbol of the resurrected Horned God of nature.

The Shamanic Revival and the Mysteries

In the 1980s, shamanic practices began to appear in the general Pagan communities of both Britain and the United States. The major influences for this were the fiction of Carlos Castaneda, the academic works of anthropologist Mircea Eliade, the writings of mythologist Joseph Campbell, and (more importantly) those of Michael Harner, an American anthropologist who had traveled extensively in South America. Harner's interest was such that he began to do seminars and workshops on the practices of the Conibo and Jivarí Indians, whose shamanic practices he had been involved with. Harner eventually published *The Way of the Shaman* in 1980, which was the first practical Western guide to shamanic practice. For modern shamanism, the influence of Michael Harner can be considered the equivalent of Gerald Gardner's influence on Wicca.

In some of the magical communities of the eighties, Cabalistic ritual magic was being rejected in favor of more ancestor-based magical systems. To a certain degree, the mysteries within the more dogmatic traditions of Wicca had been lost in meaningless complicated ritual, and many initially attracted to Wicca rejected ritual dogma in favor of the spiritual trance experience of shamanism. Numerous Witches began to look at native forms of shamanism for this reason, including Gavin. Here we see an example of the new Witchcraft movement coming of age as Witches reject dogma they find to be outdated and of no use. If you have an understanding of shamanic practice, then you realize that the reintroduction of shamanism has not caused the mysteries to disappear, but shamanism has, in fact, brought back an earlier form of mystery tradition, one more relevant to a generation that no longer needed the mysteries shrouded in the same level of symbolism.

The first of these mysteries is the reconciliation of the personality with the id/the power animal (we would like to point out that the totem animal is very different from the power animal, and is associated with the ego, see page 47). It is believed that the power animal comes to you in tribal/native shamanic practice. It is the spirit of the id itself, which connects you with the animal side of your nature. One belief of ours is that animals, like humans, have their own collective unconscious, or astral plane. The result is that the animal, be it bird or mammal, connects to you across a bridge from their astral plane to yours. The prominence of animals in the mysteries of Greece and Egypt points to the animal as an important symbol for the id. We consider their equivalent of the power animal to have been the *psychopompos* (conductor of souls). Anubis is a perfect example; in Hellenistic Egypt, it was Hermes Trismegistus—a conflation of Hermes and the ibis-headed Thoth. At a later date, these two were in fact combined within the mysteries of the Cabiri in the figure of Hermanubis.[7] In tribal/native shamanism and the Greek and Egyptian mysteries, the role of the psychopompos and the power animal is the same: to escort and protect the seeker of the mysteries (for more see pages 123–124).

Hermanubis

The second stage in shamanic practice is the retrieval of the soul, which in some cultures is believed to manifest as the anima/animus complex. This is hidden in the *Bright Shadow*, an area where positive aspects are repressed due to cultural or social pressure. The anima/animus must be retrieved with the protection of the power animal—the Underworld Guide. This is the hunt for the soul, or *soul retrieval*. In the traditional Greek and Egyptian mysteries, this may be seen as the connection to the Goddess herself for the male seeker and the God for the female. Again, the same process is at work.

Finally, there is the third challenge, the facing of death. In shamanism, the practitioner must go in to the chthonic Shadow Realm, the Ancestral Realm of death itself, and return. To do this, they must be challenged by the guardian who guards the gate of death—the Guardian of the Mysteries. This closely follows the previously mentioned Legend of the Descent of the Goddess, indicating a relationship to the mysteries of Greece and Egypt.

Versions of the mysteries can be found in the Northern cultures of Europe. Myths related to the descent into the underworld can be found in both Celtic and Norse tales. Northern myth is particularly full of psychological analogy; Odin's hanging on the world tree, Yggdrasil, can be seen as the shaman's decent to find the mysteries. After being close to death, he looks down into the Well of Urd or Wyrd (fate) at the base of the great tree and sees the runes; the word *rune* itself means "secret" or "mystery." He then takes on the role of the psychopompos, escorted by his two wolves and two ravens, to guide others through the same process. It is no mistake that his name was given to Wednesday, Woden's day, as this day is also equated with Mercury, the Roman equivalent of Hermes.

Spiritual Initiation Versus Ritual Initiation

As every Wiccan knows, initiation takes place in Circle. Or does it? We have come to question this idea. It was toying with the concept of "walk-ing the tightrope" that triggered Gavin's initiation. To walk the tight-rope is to balance the right-brain and left-brain functions, which both Janet and Stewart had previously written about in several of their works. Gavin realized that it was in fact a dynamic process: we swing between these influences. Although neurologists and psychologists today debate whether these sides of the brain actually are separate in function, this was the prevalent theory at the time, and the magical process is relevant regardless. The general theory is that the functions are divided into two hemispheres: the left brain is primarily concerned with logical thinking and speech, and the right brain with instincts, intuition, and feelings—the two halves complementing each other. In our society, emphasis is put on logic and the scientific process: the left brain, while for our ancestors, more emphasis may have been on belief and emotional relationships: the right brain. To connect with deities you must have an emotional relation-ship with them, must know them to be real personalities, and understand their nature (for more on this see chapters 4 and 10). But you must also realize the psychology through which we experience them, and recognize them as numinous archetypes within the purview of left-brain function. This is like balancing on a tightrope as you shift your weight, trying to reconcile both concepts being true at the same time. If you don't, one of two things can happen: you cannot connect with the deity, thus forcing the ego to control your spiritual practices, or you develop an unbalanced obsession with the deity, which is what fundamentalism in the monothe-istic religions is. This does, of course, relate to the concepts of polytheism and monotheism (see pages 37–38).

We feel the connection to Deity on a personal level should be the goal that the Witch is working to achieve after the first-degree initiation (see page 172). This process also results in the discovery of the individual's *anima/animus*—their contrasexual self that is normally hidden, an idea put forward in Jungian psychology. The anima is analogous to the Muse in Greek myth or the Arwen of the Welsh bardic tradition. Both are said to inspire creativity and art. It is the division into female/male role models that represses the anima/animus. In the male, those aspects that are considered feminine are repressed by the ego and pushed into the Shadow. Men are therefore expected to be unemotional, detached, et cetera. For example, the idea of men kissing each other is considered a minor taboo, although it is acceptable for women. In some shamanic traditions, particularly Norse/Anglo-Saxon, the anima/animus can be considered your very soul. In the priesthood of Frey and Freya, both men and women were expected to embrace the contrasexual aspects within themselves in the practice of Seith: men had to embrace Freya, while women had to embrace Frey. Hence, the gods and the individual's anima/animus became the same. Seith is, of course, a shamanic tradition, which was considered by the Norse to be witchcraft, making this process even more relevant to the modern Witch. The same practice occurs even today within Tantrism or Shaktism.

There is balance in all things, and we would like to point out that there is a dark side to this process. This is found in Irish myth as the Leannán Sidhe, the fairy woman who inspires young men in art and music, and then destroys them at the height of their fame. Herein lies a warning of the dangers of allowing our anima or animus to dominate our lives, an act which can be seen to be ultimately self-destructive for the personality.

Gavin's first experience with his Arwen was not quite what he expected. His first meeting with her was during a past-life regression with a Buddhist counselor, and he assumed that she was one of his past lives. For some time after, she began to appear in his life in different forms. The most shocking were the several occasions when his face shape-shifted into hers. This was, to say the least, somewhat disconcerting for those he was with at the time! Several witnesses were able to describe her, and confirmed that it was the supposed face of the past life. In fact, Janet, being a psychic and an artist, has drawn her several times. Initially, this left Gavin with a conundrum: was he manifesting a past life, or was he manifesting his contrasexual self? One of the conclusions we've come to is that it could be possible for both to be true, and that the personality from the previous life can take on this form in the next. It was this past-life experience that began to make him look at his ancestry from a magical viewpoint.

It has been our experience that the magic practitioner who has done this is more in touch with their psychic abilities, their emotions, and their true nature. This does, of course, make the old argument against homosexuality in Wicca redundant, as it has been our experience that most (but not all) homosexuals who join the Craft are already in balance with these aspects and are quite capable of assuming either sexual polarity related to energy. The argument against this has, of course, come from those in the past that have held on to rigidly exclusive male/female role models (as well as the ethical models of Christianity) and have not come into internal balance themselves via this process. Many of the older members of Witch-craft—including Patricia Crowther, Starhawk, the late Doreen Valiente, Victor Anderson, Leo Martello, and Janet's late husband, Stewart—have all spoken out against such discrimination.

Gavin's experience of initiation was very different to the one you see in books written about Wicca. He believes his "true" initiation took place outside of Circle when he went through a difficult phase of his life. Lead-ing up to this, he had been exploring a particular magical aspect of his own ancestry and had found himself being pulled toward one specific goddess. He actually had done his best to try to avoid this form of magical working—Anglo-Saxon and Norse runes—because of their associations with the magical practices of Nazi Germany. Regardless, their attraction wouldn't go away, and he describes finding himself pulled toward using them. When he first became involved with Wicca, he had tried to be fash-ionable by taking on the practices of Celtic magic, and particularly Arthu-rian symbolism, even though he was originally initiated into Seax-Wica. Much of this was related to the associations of his name with one specific character. For a while he had worked that archetype, and discovered that every archetype has a negative as well as a positive aspect. It led him into lots of trouble, resulting in several confrontational situations. It seemed strange to him that he should now embrace its historical polar opposite!

Gavin finally gave into the pull of the Northern magical practices and this specific goddess, as she was now beginning to invade his dreams. He went about preparing for a dedication ritual to her and finally on one night gave himself to her as her priest. It was then he learned an important lesson: be careful what you ask for, as you may get it! His life turned upside down for the next year while she gave him the lessons he'd needed to learn. Gavin often describes this time as being an epiphany, a series of awakenings and understandings of the nature of Wicca and spirituality itself. One of the things he did was face his own inner demons while taking responsibility for his actions. He actually went about apolo-gizing to those that he perceived as doing him wrong on the belief that he was ultimately responsible for the hurt they had caused him. In Cabalistic terms this is recognized as the *Tipharethic* experience, when the initiate passes through the sphere of his essential nature. He became acutely aware of his own failings and the faults in his personality and entered a "dark night of the soul." The initiatory question of "Art thou willing to suffer to learn?" took on a whole new meaning for him during this time. For Gavin, this was his true initiation, one that occurred in everyday life, not in the pomp and ceremony of a magic Circle. It was this experience that he considers made him a priest of Freya, not lineage or tradition, but one-on-one contact with a face of the divine Goddess.

What actually happened to Gavin is the experience the initiate should go through at the second degree within Wicca. It is during this that ego, id, and Shadow are recognized by the individual within their personality. You become aware of your faults and failings. By acceptance of their existence, you are hopefully able to change them, or at best learn to live with them. If this process doesn't happen, several things can occur— particularly within a coven setting.

We have coined a term for something we have seen regularly happen within Wicca, and for that matter, within everyday life: *second-degree syndrome.* Over the years, we have noticed a trend within covens: Witches rebel against the leaders of their covens and leave on acrimonious terms. Our theory is that it is not so much the student's fault, as the teacher's, or the method of teaching employed—particularly when there is no understanding of the processes involved. It is a by-product of dogmatism. If the high priest/priestess of the coven claims to be all-knowledgeable and infallible, then the inflated ego of the high priest/priestess becomes recognizable to the initiate, along with his own ego, after this initiation. If the student initiate does not go through the process properly, recognizing their own ego, then they will become an imitation of the teacher and will very likely enter into competition with the leaders of the coven. Whatever happens, the initiate will leave the coven, either rebelling early on and going their own way or, in the latter case, competing with the teacher by leaving and carrying the process on, replicating it like a virus. In such groups, the attainment of status overrules achievements of spiritual discovery. This is one of the reasons we no longer use the terms *high priest* and *high priestess* to describe ourselves: we feel the terms encourage ego inflation. We still use the terms *priest* and *priestess,* but we use them as a job description rather than a statement of status. It is not that we feel that everyone should drop these titles, just that they are no longer right for us. We feel that it is up to the individual to decide whether to use them, but they should be aware of the dangers to their ego such titles can carry.

One problem for Wicca is that such spiritual experiences are so subjective that it is hard to judge their validity. A high priest or priestess can only really take any such experiences voiced to them on face value.

This is a problem when you have an inflexible system based on dogmatic ritual rather than a spiritual process. How does a coven cope with a new member joining a coven and claiming to have already been through such an experience, but who doesn't necessarily have a good deal of knowledge about Wicca? We think training systems within Wicca should be based on both practical and academic techniques for the attainment of spiritual knowledge, while still having a flexible framework for initiation. Ritual initiations only have value if they stimulate a spiritual change—a true initiation—or if they recognize that an individual has already been through such an experience.

Gavin does point out one thing that is of importance: he became aware that there is very little difference between real spiritual initiation in Witchcraft and the experience an evangelical Christian goes through when they are "born again." They are, in fact, the same experience: that of the death and rebirth of the individual's persona as a part of a spiritual experience. The only difference is that most Wiccans are trained or encouraged to be aware of the processes involved. Although most Wiccans are not necessarily encouraged to look beyond Western Paganism at the experiences of those following other faiths such as Buddhism, Hinduism, or Shintoism, we have come to realize that this level of spirituality goes beyond the normal ancestral and cultural boundaries. There are, in fact, big gaps in much of the training in Wicca relating to spirituality and how to deal and comprehend spiritual mystery, which can now only be addressed by looking at contemporary pagan and post-pagan cultures in the East. For a long time, Wicca has been very insular in its approach to culture, looking at only the current Cabalistic-influenced Western magical tradition to base its practices on, or attempting to reconstruct past practices from over fifteen hundred years ago. Eastern culture has been generally ignored on the grounds that you "mustn't mix traditions" (another dogma from Western magic). There were, of course, those who broke the rules; Aleister Crowley was one of them. This dogma ignores the fact that Hinduism incorporates elements of Assyro-Babylonian and Persian religion. Eastern culture may show us how European pagan mystery practices might have developed if they were still around today; they put spirituality (the experience) above ritual and practice (the form) in importance. We see Wicca slowly moving in this direction, where experience and belief becomes more important than form—particularly when it comes to working with the gods and goddesses that are a central part of the belief structure. Wicca is now becoming more deity-centered and less magic-centered.

NOTES

1 Personal communication between ourselves and Brendan Myers. Myers is inspired by the works of eminent philosopher Paul Ricoeur.

2 R. E. Witt, *Isis in the Graeco-Roman World*, chap. 12, p. 157.

3 Jung was heavily influenced by his study of Gnosticism, particularly the Gnostic Gospels. They became a cornerstone for his psychological theories, particularly those related to Valentinus, according to Elaine Pagels in *The Gnostic Gospels*.

4 The same myth is, in fact, found in many cultures, including that of the Assyro-Babylonians in the myths of Tammuz and Ishtar.

5 Janet and Stewart Farrar, *A Witches' Bible: The Complete Witches' Handbook* (Phoenix Publishing, 1996, 2002).

6 From R. E. Witt's *Isis in the Graeco-Roman World*. He recounts Lucius's journey through the Isiac Mysteries. It is interesting to note that he takes also takes his third and is accepted into the priesthood.

7 According to R. E Witt (pages 153–154 of *Isis in the Graeco-Roman World*), the Cabiri were "originally demi-gods, sons of Hephaestus, who could themselves share in the chthonic rites of Demeter and Kore." Herodotus wrote about the rites of the Cabiri being a combination of both Egyptian and Greek mysteries and the originators of the word *mysterion*, from where our word *mystery* derives.

4

The Gods and Goddesses: Deity-Centered Witchcraft

God[dess] must become an activity in our consciousness.
—JOEL S. GOLDSMITH, *THE INFINITE WAY*

Janet lovingly calls our home the "house of a hundred deities." The reason is obvious if you have ever visited us. Statues and pictures of deities can be found in every room of the house. One room is given over completely to Far Eastern and Buddhist statuary. In the passage way are Native American representations. The kitchen has plates from Crete representing the Greek myths. But the majority of representations are in the living room. These range from traditional bronze and brass Hindu deities—including Shiva, Krishna, and (of course) foremost of the Indian gods, Ganesha†—to the common white plaster figures of the Greek gods and goddesses: Zeus, Athena, Artemis, and Ceres. Modern neo-Pagan representations also appear: a beautiful statue of Odin holding his spear Gungnir, escorted by his two wolves, and two ravens; Gaea clutching the

---

* Joel S. Goldsmith lived from 1892 to 1964. He was a great mystical teacher, author, and healer. In 1947 he gained national recognition with the publication of his book *The Infinite Way*. This book came about as a result of Joel's many years of study and meditation, his healing work, and the spiritual revelations that came to him during the course of his lifetime. He went on to write numerous books on mysticism and mystical living.

† Ganesha or Ganesh is the first god to be worshipped in the Hindu pantheon by decree of Shiva, as an act of recompense for the loss of his human form and its replacement with that of an elephant. He is the most worshipped god-form in the world.

world, decorated with the beasts of land, sea, and air; and a haughty Morrigan with her shield, her head up high with an air of disdain about her. We have lost count of the number that we have. They grow every time we enter an occult shop or go on a new odyssey abroad.

There is an old occult law that "you don't mix traditions"; maybe that should be that you don't mix gods! For although they all get along, there is the occasional spat between them. We discovered very quickly that some of the Japanese deities don't get on with the Celtic, but it is just a difference of temperament more than anything. The standoffish Greek gods prefer to be higher than anyone else in the room; hence, they are on a shelf above the library door. The Indian deities, by contrast, are always chatty and willing to please. This has a habit of winding up the Greek gods no end, much to Odin's and our amusement. We have been plagued with stray cats in recent years due to the increasing number of Bast statues on her shrine in one corner of the room. Additionally, we have a statue of the Hindu Mother Goddess Durga with her lion on the mantelpiece. This is just ask-ing for an ever-increasing cat food bill. Being priest and priestess of a cat goddess, we are obliged to find room and board for every one of them.

In the corner of the living room is Freya, the most important deity to both of us. She is represented by a statue crafted by Paul Borda, which Gavin took a part in designing. Freya sits permanently on a shrine in the

Shrine to Bast

corner of the room, surrounded by the amber and trinkets that she loves, such as a drinking horn, a rune circlet, and numerous precious stones. She is our principal deity; she guides our lives and our practice of Witchcraft. She is also in our genes, as an ancestral deity of the Anglo-Saxons and the Norse. Some may think it odd that she sits in a house nestled in the wilds of Ireland, but both of us are English with strong magical connections to our roots. Over the years, Freya has guided what direction we should be taking. She is a loving, consoling, flirty guide, who sometimes likes us to be outrageous to get the message across! We've had our ups and downs with her, just as you do with any friend, but she's never let us down. She is a goddess of love, but more importantly, as the older pre-Indo-European, pre-Ásatrú goddess,* she is the principal deity of magic and shamanism for her peoples. (We work with her for ourselves rather than for anyone else.)

It would be insulting of us to ignore the spirits and deities of the land we live in. When working magically outside, we first find ourselves having to appease the spirits—the fairy folk.† Not to do this is to ask for trouble, for they will delight in upsetting your working, such as by tipping things off the altar, etc. We also respect the deities of the land of Ireland. They surround us, for the Irish gods and goddesses are in the landscape itself: in the rivers, the hills, and the mountains. Close to us is the River Boyne—the goddess Boann—and Slieve na Callaighe (the "Hill of the Witch"), named after a Crone goddess of Wisdom. Most important of them all locally, is the Hill of Ward, the residence of the goddess Tlachta, the Irish goddess of witchcraft and Samhain. When we work, we pay respect to them all. Not to do so would not only be bad magical practice, but it would also be downright rude.

Of course, this was not the way either of us were taught to relate to the gods. Janet and Stewart were originally taught there were only two true deities of Witchcraft: Aradia and Karnayna. Aradia is Italian/Etruscan in origin, and Karnayna—often thought by Stewart to be Alex Sanders' mispronunciation of Cernunnos—was, in fact, an egotistical joke: it was the name given to Alexander the Great by the Carthaginians on his

---

*   Ásatrú is the practice related to Odinism as "All-father." Freya and her brother, Frey, belong to an older group of gods and goddesses called the Vanir, who are agricultural and magical in nature.

†   The fairy (or faery) are a folk memory of the Tuatha De Danann, the older gods of Ireland who are similar to the aforementioned Vanir, in fact there are strong similarities, and evidence that in many cases they are the same gods and goddesses with different cultural overlays.

reaching godhood.[1] After moving to Ireland, Janet and Stewart changed their God name to Cernunnos, a more generic term of Gallic/Latin origin meaning simply "Horned God." The dogma of only two true names for the God and Goddess continues today among some hard-liners of Alexandrian and Gardnerian Wicca. On moving to Ireland, Janet and Stewart were faced with the realization that they were surrounded by a country full of its own mythology. Aradia began to take a back seat in their practices, as the old Irish gods demanded recognition.

Gavin's experience was different. Right from the beginning he was encouraged to choose two deities at his initiation into Seax-Wica, although this was not strictly a practice of this tradition. Gavin had had little contact with the spiritual aspects of Witchcraft at that time, so his choice was guided by ego more than anything else. Later on, he received similar teachings from Janet and Stewart related to Aradia, from an orthodox Wiccan coven. Like Janet and Stewart, he was also taught the dogma that Aradia was the only true Goddess of Wicca.

Deity and Religion

The basic deity-teachings within Wicca centered on a triple goddess and a dual god, although the origins of these teachings are far from ancient. The concept originated in Robert Graves' work *The White Goddess*,[*] which draws the theme of Maiden-Mother-Crone from the historical Roman goddess Diana Triformis,[†] and the theme of the dual god from the Oak King and Holly King of English folklore. *The White Goddess* was standard reading for anyone coming into a coven at that time. There was little theological instruction such as would be found in other contemporary religions. Students of Witchcraft were pretty much left to develop their own belief structures and ideas about the nature of the divine, particularly when it came to connecting with a deity. Of course, when there is a vacuum in such circumstances, something has to fill it. By the late 1970s, Cabala was filling that gap. Cabala, being of Judeo-Christian monotheistic origin, was not a very good example of what our pagan ancestors believed about their deities. But it was easy for the Witches of that period to

---

* Grave's *The White Goddess* was compulsory reading material for most Witches, although very few ever managed to read it from cover to cover due to Grave's style of writing.

† Diana Triformis was a triple goddess consisting of Prosperpina, Diana, and Hecate respectively. In his book *Moonchild*, Aleister Crowley views Hekate as a Crone Goddess (page 188). Many neo-Pagans still work with her in this aspect due to this, even though historically she is portrayed as a much younger goddess.

accept, as its teachings did not contradict the religious norms and values they had been taught in a predominantly Christian culture.

Gerald Gardner and Doreen Valiente—the original founders of Wicca—referred to it as "the Old Religion," but it is neither particularly old, nor strictly a religion. The religious beliefs of Wicca have always been based in paganism. There are of course, those who would argue with this statement, particularly those of a Judeo-Christian Cabalistic bent, but we have presented the evidence for Wicca's pagan origins clearly in the first chapter of this work. It was called 'the Old Religion' because Gardner and Valiente believed at the time (the 1950s) that it was the only survival of ancient paganism. Arguably, there was also Druidism, but Druidism at that time was heavily Christian and also influenced by freemasonry. Thus it was possible for a previous Archbishop of Canterbury, Dr. Owen Williams, to be ordained a Druid. * As we have shown, witchcraft isn't a religion as such, but the survival of the priesthood of the pagan religions of old.

It is important to understand what the word *religion* actually means and where it comes from. The etymology of the word is from the Latin *lige,* which means "to join." Such words as *ligature*, an item that binds or ties, have their origins in this root word. Religion therefore can mean to rejoin, or reconnect to the divine. According to Merriam-Webster's online dictionary, in modern usage *religion* has come to mean several things:

1. The service and worship of God or the supernatural.
2. Devotion to a religious faith.
3. A personal set or institutionalized system of religious beliefs, attitudes, and practices.
4. A cause, principle, or belief held to with faith and ardor.

Only the first meaning seems to link directly to the original etymology of the word *religion*. This is important, as when Witches talk about "the Old Religion," they are most definitely talking about it in this respect,

---

*   This took place on Monday 5, August 2002, at the National Eisteddfod in Wales. According to the Welsh Gorsedd, this was acceptable as "The Welsh Gorsedd of Bards, into which the Archbishop was initiated, is not now, and never has been, a Pagan institution. It was founded in 1792 by Iolo Morganwg, a stonemason, failed farmer and shipping magnate, revolutionary, sometime jailbird, laudanum addict, collector of medieval manuscripts, forger of same, poet and antiquarian. He was also a minister of the Christian Unitarian church and composer of a number of hymns still popular in Wales today."

as witchcraft has always been nondoctrinal.* For Wiccans, the religious aspects of their practices are about reconnecting with the divine by interacting with one of its many faces—faces that manifest within the myriad of gods and goddesses that exist for the Witch.

The word *pagan,* from the Latin word *paganus,* meaning "country dweller," describes a series of ancient beliefs related to the natural environment. For a modern Pagan, and therefore the Witch, the divine is perceived as immanent in nature. This means the divine is believed to be present in the animate: the plants, the trees, the wildlife; and in the inanimate: in the wind, in the rivers and the rocks; and (most importantly) Deity is believed to be within us. Animistic beliefs still thrive today in the practices of the Sami-Lappish tribes of Finland, the Native American tribes, and the Aboriginal peoples of Australia. We believe animism represents the original beliefs of humanity before the coming of organized religion.

We are not separate from the divine, or from the dynamic, ongoing process of creation. The saying "Thou Art God/Goddess"[2] is often used by neo-Pagans. This is not to say that we are all deities in our own right (we find this to be a very egotistical concept). It simply means the divine is in us, just as it is in every aspect and part of creation. Everything we see around us is sacred and should therefore be treated as such. It is not surprising to find that Witches can be found actively involved in protest and direct action to protect the environment.

These concepts are very different from the teachings of monotheistic religions that base their belief structures on the idea of faith in a single invisible entity, one that has created us as separate from itself and has created the world for our personal use. A Witch does not require the concept of "faith" (although they may have faith in an individual deity with whom they have connected). They just have to smell a flower, listen to the call of a bird, or watch the waves roll onto a beach to see the divine and realize that they are an active part of what monotheism calls *God.* Although faith is not required, belief in the spiritual concept of immanence is. This is also more commonly referred to as pantheism. This is an important concept when it comes to magical work, particularly when it comes to working with the four elements and other areas of magical practice.

---

* There is no evidence to suggest that witchcraft as a practice has ever had a doctrine, as opposed to Wicca or derivatives of witchcraft with origins in ritual magic practice. Likewise, there is no evidence that it hasn't!

An example of this is when a Witch calls a "quarter" to protect the Circle that they are casting. In this act, they call the spirit or "Lord" of the element. Here we see the concept of divine immanence applied practically in a magical rite, as the Witch calls the divine manifest through the four elements.

Witchcraft and Our Relationship with Deity

So where does Deity, and the individual personalities that are the gods and goddesses, come in? Is Deity part of Witchcraft? Yes. From the historical evidence, there is plenty to prove that gods, and more importantly goddesses, were central to historical witchcraft practices. Even the bard himself, William Shakespeare, refers to "pale-faced Hekate" when speaking of the "three weird sisters," the soothsaying witches who meet Macbeth on the road. He does not have the witches commanded by a Christian Satan, but by a classical pagan goddess—in what can be seen as an act of Drawing Down the Moon (see pages 177–183).

One of the biggest problems that modern Witches have had to face is the fact that there are few written records of what the actual philosophical beliefs of our ancestors were concerning Divinity. We can surmise some ideas from the writings of the ancient Greeks, but the Christian monks who wrote down the mythologies of ancient peoples have influenced the histories of the Celts and the Norse. This can be seen in the major Norse-Icelandic work, *The Prose Edda*, where Snorri Sturluson tried to align Odin with the Christian God by identifying him as "the All-Father." We have no real idea of how Odin was seen by his peoples or what their belief supposed him to be. Modern Witches have had to draw on works that have a presupposition of the monotheistic and patriarchal Christian idea of God,* thereby resulting in a concept of the divine with strong Christian philosophical overtones. We can see this in the concept of duotheism, that "all gods are one god, and all goddesses are one goddess," which became a major doctrine of Wiccan thinking (see page 37).

Over the years, many Witches began to question the ideas about what a god is. They began to look away from Cabala, seeking what the true belief structure of paganism really was, or for that matter, really is. We've

---

* The doctrine of monotheism found in the Middle East is believed to have derived from Akhanaten heresy of Egypt of the eighteenth Dynasty (1567–1320). The heresy was crushed by the priesthood of Amun-Ra, but not before it had gained root in the foreign workers within the Northern Kingdom. Judaism and Islam are believed to have derived their doctrinal origins from these Semitic peoples who continued in their cult of the only god, the Aten.

encountered many, including ourselves, who have started looking into contemporary non-monotheistic religions. Polytheistic belief systems, untainted by monotheistic thought, can be found in Africa, India, and the Far East. During the 1990s, we began to look to these religions for understanding regarding the nature of the divine. We are sure we are not the only ones. In Shinto, Hinduism, and the practices of the African diaspora religions (Vodoun, Santeria, et cetera), we can see ancient worship of Deity, both preserved and evolved, just as we might have seen it in Europe if pagan practices had developed unhindered. The biggest problem many modern Witches have when examining these contemporary religions is that the cultural symbolism is so alien to them. As evidence, it may be seen that many Western Pagans have great problems understanding the Vodoun deities (loas) or those of Santeria (orishas), as they fit neither into their concept of a spirit or that of a god. Yet the Vodoun concept of Deity is probably closer to our ancestor's idea of the way gods and goddesses worked than what was originally taught within Wicca. The major obstacle in the development of Wiccan spirituality has been the monotheistic idea of God, which most of us were brought up with in Western culture.

In Vodoun, the relationship between the follower and the Deity is a very personal one. Trance and ecstatic vision are an important part of the practice, just as it would have been in ancient witchcraft. There are important similarities between the practice of being possessed, or *ridden*, by a loa and the central Wiccan rite of Drawing Down the Moon—where the priestess becomes the vessel through which a goddess communicates. The major difference is the nature of the ritual. The fact is, Witchcraft has become less spontaneous and more *Apollonian* in its approach (logical and systemized); whereas, Vodoun is more shamanic, ecstatic, and *Dionysian*[3] (spontaneous and emotionally orientated). During a Vodoun ceremony, anyone who is present may be ridden by a loa, thereby becoming a vessel for that deity. Connection with the divine in Vodoun is therefore an integral part of the religion, enabling the practitioners to talk directly with their deities during the rite. It is the ultimate example of immanent divinity. The Vodoun or Santeria belief in god-spirits is probably little different from ancient witchcraft beliefs; certainly ancient witchcraft would have been more spontaneous and Dionysian in its approach. More importantly, like modern Witchcraft, Vodoun is an initiatory mystery tradition, but unlike Wicca, the initiations are related to specific loa. A Vodoun priest (houngan) or priestess (mambo) is therefore a servant of a specific deity, but is expected to be capable of bringing through any loa.

Vodoun also uses a system of offerings for each loa, similar to the Western magical system of correspondences. Specific offerings are ritually made to the loa by their followers on particular days of the week. There are also specific taboos. Followers may not eat certain foods, for example, or have certain things in their homes that may offend the loa. Similar practices exist in Santeria, the kin-path of Vodoun, which evolved in Spanish America. In Santeria, followers may place a clay or cement head with cowrie shells for features next to a door to represent Elegguá (Legba). They will regularly "feed him" with toys, candy, and even cigars, to bring good fortune to their home. As Elegguá is the Guardian of the Crossroads and the gate-guardian to the otherworld, he is always the first to be recognized or worshipped in any ritual. In this respect, he has strong similarities with the Hindu Ganesha.

Most people would be quite shocked to know that the most worshipped male deity-form in the world is none other than the elephant-headed Hindu god Ganesha; the most worshipped overall form being the Eastern bodhisattva Kwan Yin (a goddess by any name). In Hinduism, Ganesha is "the foremost of the gods." He is the first to receive offerings, in order to ensure that the way is open for the devotees to send their messages to the gods of their choice. Hinduism has been developing since pre-Christian times, and it gives us an idea of how Paganism might have developed in Europe had Christianity not put in an appearance. Within the religions of the Indian subcontinent, there are many similarities with Western and Northern European paganism, partly due to the strong link through the ancient migration of the Indo-European peoples. As in Wicca, there are multi-formed goddesses, such as the Durga, who also incorporates Kali, Lakshmi, and Sarasvati. There are two principle male deities: Shiva and Vishnu.* There is also a plethora of less well-known local and tribal deities, with many being incorporated into the main gods and goddesses of the religion. There are also fairy folk: *devas* and spirits of nature; so the divine is seen to be immanent in nature, just as in neo-Paganism. In many Hindu festivals, called *pujas*, we see similarities with traditional pagan festivals of Europe. Diwali, the Festival of Lights, is one good example.

---

* Along with Brahma, Vishnu and Shiva also create a triple god (creator, preserver, and destroyer respectively), although paradoxically, they are also seen as aspects of Brahma. Which of these male gods takes precedence depends upon the locality of the Hindu temple and the area of India it originates from. It should also be remembered that Krishna is an incarnation of Vishnu.

Many of its practices mimic both the festival of Yule and Imbolg, which are both traditionally festivals of light.*

Primary to Hinduism is the idea of the unknowable divine—Brahma. Brahma is often portrayed as a wheel, as found on the Indian national flag. Brahma is not directly worshipped, but is approached through the other gods and goddesses of the religion, a concept not alien to modern Pagan thought, but only now developing. We would recommend any Witch to at least once in their life go to a Hindu temple to experience the nature of this concept. It has to be experienced, as it cannot be put into words and written about. When we have entered Hindu temples, we have always been warmly welcomed. The first thing that strikes you is the shrines and the statues to each individual god or goddess or sometimes to groups of gods and goddesses. Hinduism is idolatrous. It is believed that Deity is present within the statues themselves. We have actually felt this when entering these temples. The power of the Deity shines from them. The statues of the gods are regularly washed and dressed as part of the rites, while being talked to as if they are alive: because to the priesthood, they are. An established priesthood does exist within Hinduism, but it is not centralized, like that of Christianity. These small priesthoods often operate from a temple devoted to one specific deity, but other major deities of the religion are also present. Could this be what the old priesthoods of Europe (and therefore Witchcraft) might have developed into? We believe so.

In Vodoun and Hinduism, we see the idea of immanence and the idea of absolute belief in the deities being worshipped. They are not seen as any form of psychological principle, as has occurred in recent years within Wicca, but as real personalities in their own right. In both these traditions, the belief in Deity is at the center of their practice, be it magical or religious. We are only now seeing the return to true belief in the old gods of Europe within the modern Witchcraft community. So what is a god or a goddess? Carl Gustav Jung, the great psychologist, refers to them as "archetypes." But this is an intellectual approach, which needs to be balanced with spiritual experience.

---

* Diwali is the major festival of truth and light. It is celebrated on Amavasya—the fifteenth day of the dark fortnight of the Hindu month of Ashwin (October/November) every year.

Archetypes, the Goddess, and the Pagan Philosophy of Creation
Archetypes are elements of the collective unconscious, what occultists
call the "astral plane." It is part to the psyche, which is universal to all
periods and cultures; hence, mother goddesses appear in every culture
in the world. We inherit it from the human experience as a whole, not
through the filter of our parents or the culture we are brought up in.
Right from the beginning of the modern Witchcraft revival, there was
the idea of the Goddess taking precedence over the God in Wiccan
thinking. One of the primary reasons for this was the rejection of the
patriarchal values of monotheistic religion. Intrinsic to this was the idea
of creation. Philosophically, the Goddess as the center of the universe
is incompatible with the mechanistic creation of the universe by a male
god who creates or molds the cosmos as a craftsman. In the Goddess-
centered belief structure, that idea is replaced with the more natural
idea of the universe being given birth to by the divine itself. That act
is not dependent on the egocentric symbolism of human craftsmanship.
More importantly, the natural world replaces man as the central focus
of the theology. This takes away the emphasis on science and a mechanistic explanation of the cosmos. It makes us consider the possibility
that our planet, as well as the universe, is actually alive, and it supports
the idea of immanence. In many cultures, this divine Mother figure
has become symbolized as the cow, such as Hathor of the Egyptians,
Audumla of the Norse creation myth, and Boann of the Irish Celts. In
contemporary Hinduism, cows are sacred for this same reason. They
are considered "The Mothers of the Universe."[4]

The symbols by which we become aware of the archetypes may be
culturally or individually conditioned to a certain extent, but the archetypes themselves are not. They "continue eternal and always after the
same manner."[5] As Jung says of the term *archetype:*

> This term is not meant to denote an inherited idea, but rather an
> inherited mode of psychic functioning, corresponding to the inborn
> *way* according to which the chick emerges from the egg; the bird
> builds its nest; a certain kind of wasp stings the ganglion of a cater-
> pillar; and eels find their way to the Bermudas. In other words, it is
> a "pattern of behavior." This aspect of the archetype is the biologi-
> cal one—it is the concern of scientific psychology. But the picture
> changes at once when looked at from the inside, that is, from the
> realm of the subjective psyche. Here the archetype presents itself
> as numinous, that is, it appears as an experience of fundamental

importance. Whenever it is clothes itself with adequate symbols, which is not always the case, it takes hold of the individual in a startling way, creating a condition of "being deeply moved" the consequences of which may be immeasurable. It is for this reason that the archetype is so important for the psychology of religion.[6]

We believe Jung's concepts are intellectually correct and show a deep understanding of the subjective psyche. But from a spiritual and occult perspective, something else is also happening. Quite simply put, we cannot experience the Ultimate Divine. We would be like ants trying to understand a computer. The divine is unfathomable and beyond our comprehension. This idea is common in ancient religions. Even in Judaism, it was believed that you could not look upon the face of God and live. Hinduism expresses this idea of the Ultimate Divine as Brahma. Many religions have attempted to focus worship directly at the unknowable divine, but most fail. Judaism, Christianity, and Islam have all attempted to encourage worship of this faceless divine only to have human nature put a face on it. A good example of this is in Christianity, where the Jewish god was personified as Jesus. By the time of the Renaissance, Jesus had developed the visual personification of God along the same lines as the classical Greek Zeus, as can be seen in the Sistine Chapel. Islam regards images of Allah as blasphemous, which has resulted in his personification through the use of Arabic script and cult-like devotion to his prophets. Each time this personification happens, it produces a deity—as we understand it to be in Witchcraft and the occult sciences.

This is also one of the reasons why the faceless concept of duotheism, which existed in early Wiccan practice, will ultimately fail to fulfill the needs of the new generation of Witches. It is human nature to anthropomorphize the world around us. When we paint and draw as children, we put smiley faces on flowers, the sun, and the moon. As we grow up, we give inanimate objects names and personalities—cars and boats for example. This is the *inherited mode of psychic functioning* at its most basic level. What Jung doesn't cover is the result of this personification, the creation of supercharged thought-forms that we call gods and goddesses, which have developed personalities as real as our own.

One big problem for modern Pagans is that the old gods and goddesses have been asleep. Devoid of worship and recognition for so long, they have become psychically dormant. In other religions this is not the case. Both in Hinduism and Vodoun, their deities are wide-awake and kicking, so to speak. We have found almost direct results from working with the

Hindu god Ganesha because he is so extensively worshipped around the world, and we know of practitioners of Santeria and Vodoun who talk about similar experiences. This is because there is an unbroken level of devotion to them that has kept them charged psychically over the years. It is not surprising that many Pagans are drawn to these religions. We see it is as the role of modern Witches and Pagans to "wake the gods" just as Tim Robbins' character "Erik" did in the film *Erik the Viking.*

The Gods and Goddesses are Alive!

The unknowable divine is the source of power for the numerous gods and goddesses that exist around the world. But it is humanity and its culture that gives them their personality and attributes. Stewart Farrar often quoted the well-known Greek philosopher Xenophon,[†] saying, "If I was a horse, my god would be a horse"—a statement reflecting this same idea. They have developed personalities like us, no different than our own. We mold the divine power like clay through worship and belief over periods of time, just as it takes each of us twenty years or more to fully develop our personalities. They differ in that they have no bodies, and their spirits remain directly connected to the ultimate, unknowable divine. Gods and goddesses also have personas, but theirs may have taken much longer to develop than ours, and their connection with the ultimate, unknowable divine is more direct.

From our personal experiences, we can say without doubt that the gods and goddesses of the ancient world are real. Like human personalities, they can have strange nuances and flaws. For this reason, the faces of divine should always be accepted and respected as individuals. You must believe in them as persons in their own right if you are going to connect and work with them. It is not recommended that you work with them as Jungian concepts alone, as it simply won't work. It is necessary to personally experience them if you are going to connect and work with them.

The principle deities of Witchcraft have always been goddesses. Witchcraft has always been a feminine art, regardless of which sex practiced it. In European culture—Northern Germanic, Western Celtic, and Southern Graeco-Roman—our ancestors had deity-forms that related to specific

---

* Produced by Handmade Films in 1989. In the story, Tim Robbins as "Eric" (a sensitive Norseman) goes in search of the "Horn Resounding" to wake the gods and end the bloody world of Ragnarok. The Gods turn out to be children, and clearly not in control of the fate of man.

† An Athenian, the son of Gryllus, Xenophon was born about 431 BC. In his early life, he was a pupil of Socrates.

crafts. There were also therefore specific goddesses related to "the dark arts" (the occult crafts of dealing with spirits for the purposes of healing or oracular work). Nearly all of these goddesses have an association with the moon and water, and the cat is also a common symbolism related to them. One of the reasons for this is that they all stem from the same archetype, and in some cases have the same historical roots.

It is impossible to remove the idea of the Mother from any goddess archetype; she is simply too strong a force. Even the Christians had to bow to the pressure of this archetype in the human psyche and incorporate Mary as a major part of the Roman Catholic Church's theology. Mary was a reflection of Isis/Artemis, whose symbolism she incorporated (see page 226). We are all born from mothers, so it is the first archetype within our subconscious minds to surface after birth. It is therefore not surprising that this archetype quickly bridged the gap between the psychological and the spiritual in human consciousness and culture.

The Triple Goddess is the most common deity-form taught within Wicca. Always lunar, she represents the three stages of the moon. The waxing, full, and waning moon echo the three stages of womanhood: maiden, mother, and crone. The moon has always been associated with magic and witchcraft, because of its psychological and psychic effect on the individual, and because of its associations with the woman's menstrual cycle, which was considered by the ancients to have magical properties. But the concept of the Triple Goddess in this form may be quite modern. When we look at more ancient forms, such as those found in among the Greek and Norse, we find triple goddesses that all are bracketed into the same age groups—for example, the three maidens of the muses, or the three mothers, or the three crone witches surrounding a bubbling cauldron as found in *Macbeth*. We believe the modern Wiccan concept of the Triple Goddess is probably a synthesis of three-times-three goddesses. The concept has nine specific archetypes,[7] not necessarily associated with Witchcraft or the magical arts themselves. This synthesis from nine to three can be attributed to Robert Grave's work *The White Goddess,* a major source of inspiration for the early founders of Wiccan theology.

The male god of Witchcraft has always been problematic from a theological viewpoint. Basically, he is the Horned God of nature, commonly known within the orthodox Wiccan traditions as Herne or Cernunnos. He is divided though into two aspects: the god of fertility and life; and the god of death, the underworld, and resurrection. He is an essential part of modern Witchcraft belief as he plays an important part in the mysteries of Wicca. He is the god of life, and the guardian of the gateway to death. Unlike most of the goddesses, there is little history about him or his archetype. The name *Cernunnos* was found on a stone in Notre Dame. It was a Latinized Gaelic inscription simply meaning "horned one." That is the actual historical limit of our knowledge of Cernunnos. Herne, whom he has come to be strongly associated with, is a different matter. He is of Anglo-Saxon origin, with a central myth related to the Tudor period and a woodsman of Great Windsor Forest named John Herne. This histori-cally recorded figure was convicted of poaching the king's deer and was hung on the great oak in the forest. Many of the attributes associated with him were adopted from myths of other gods. He is said to haunt the for-est and lead the Wild Hunt, also associated both with the Northern Odin and the Welsh Gwynn ap Nudd—both underworld deities. The percep-tion of Herne in modern Paganism also has to do with a British television series from the 1980s called *Robin of Sherwood*.* Here we see both aspects of the Horned God coming together. Like the Triple Goddess, the modern Wiccan movement has filled in the historical scaffolding with archetypal understanding. Does this invalidate him or the Triple Goddess? We would say no, as what has occurred is the natural understanding of these deities by those who have connected with them on a psychic and spiritual level. At the end of the day, we believe you can learn more about the gods and goddesses from meeting and connecting with them than you ever can from reading about them in a book, and we believe this is what has oc-curred on a collective level with modern Witchcraft.

Our experience of meeting deities has been an interesting one. In many cases, we have found that they have updated their appearance. Janet once had a vivid dream that she was at the "Club at the end of the Universe." There was a host of many different gods and goddesses there, but they were not dressed traditionally. Frey, the Norse of god of abun-dance, peace, and prosperity, was in an Armani suit with a wad of credit cards in his wallet. He was chatting up Aphrodite who was standing at the bar in a "small black number" with high heels and bright red lipstick. Anubis was the bouncer at the door. No jackal-headed mask, but a black suit and tie and a Doberman by his side. Then there was poor old Yah-

---

* A highly successful series from Harlech TV. It prominently brought mysticism and magic into the Robin Hood legend. Herne was portrayed by John Alberini as a real man who played the part of a shaman-figure for the local village, Wickham. At different times, the series explored Cabala, Luciferian Satanism, Witchcraft (positively), and Anglo-Saxon, Norse, and Celtic myth.

weh in the corner; everyone was ignoring him. He wasn't having a good time, as he was standing there propping up the bar, dressed in a white nightshirt. Why shouldn't the gods and goddesses change their appearance, particularly as many of them are traditionally shape-shifters?

Gavin had such an experience with one shape-shifter after some magical work. He had been working with runes at the time. He had finished learning the Anglo-Saxon futhork (a thirty-three-rune system) and was creating his rune staff. He had done it traditionally through a process known as *blatting* where you paint the runes down the staff while doing the appropriate invocation. He was not doing this at home, but at a friend's house where he had to leave the staff as it was too big to carry on his motorcycle. A few days later, his friends telephoned him and sounded very upset. A figure had started to appear on the landing at the top of the stairs. They described him as wearing a long leather coat and having a wide-brimmed hat pulled down over his face, which they could not see. As they were also Witches, they realized some sort of manifestation was occurring and that it was related to Gavin's staff. They wrapped the staff up, put a magical binding around it, and put it in the basement for Gavin to collect later.

So what had happened? Gavin had used a traditional invocation for the god Woden (Odin) without realizing it, and Woden had come looking for the owner of the staff. But he had appeared in modern dress appropriate for his personality and magical nature. Woden is traditionally a shape-shifter in northern European myth. There is an important point here. Be aware that many magical invocations and charms are specifically aimed at manifesting Deity, so you must research them fully before using them.

NOTES

1   The name can, in fact, be found with reference to Alexander in the Koran, the holy book of Islam.

2   A term most commonly used by the U.S.-based Church of All Worlds.

3   The terms *Apollonian* and *Dionsysian* derive from the philosopher Frederich Nietzsche and his work *The Birth of Tragedy*.

4   This statement comes from Bhishma, in the *Mahabharata*, Anusasana Parva, Sections LXXXIII, LXXVII, LXXVI. In Vedic script, there are seven mothers: the birth mother, the nurse, the wife of the father (if she is not the birth mother), the wife of the king, the wife of the spiritual master, the earth, and the cow.

5   C. G. Jung, *The Collected Works of C. G. Jung*, vol. 9, part 1, "Archetypes of the Collective Unconscious" (London: Routledge and Kegan Paul, 1968).

6   Ibid.

7   Cherry Gilchrist in *The Circle of Nine*, pages 4–13, points to this idea's importance in mythology and its continued relevance today.

5

The Progressive Coven: The Witch's "Family"

Call it a clan, call it a network, call it a tribe, call it a family.
Whatever you call it, whoever you are, you need one.
—JANE HOWARD, *FAMILIES*

The origins of the word *coven* do not seem to go any further back than the Middle Ages. It is doubtful that any form of village priesthood would ever have used it. Etymologically, its origins are in the word *covenant*, which has its origins in the Middle English *covin* and Anglo-French (Norman) *covine*. In all cases, the word is related to a person or group making an agreement. Of course, the traditional perception of the witches' coven comes from this period, so a coven would have been perceived as consisting of a group of witches who had made an agreement or oath together. Gerald Gardner adopted this concept of the coven into Wicca, of course, when he introduced the oath taken at initiation. In our view, these origins do not negate the importance of the coven in creating a group of Witches who are of like mind and mutually supportive in their practices. Traditionally, this is said to have been thirteen witches or less. Any larger and the intimacy required for magical working would be lost. Doreen Valiente in *An ABC of Witchcraft, Past & Present* states that there were also covens of eight

---

* Jane Temple Howard (1935–1996) was born in Springfield, Illinois, USA. Journalist and author, Howard's first book, *Please Touch: A Guided Tour of the Human Potential Movement*, was published in 1970. *A Different Woman* appeared in 1973, *Families* in 1978, and the biography *Margaret Mead A Life* in 1990.

more-experienced witches who came together for purely magical work.[1] Nearly the majority of all covens nowadays are training covens, so we feel that the meaning of the word *coven* that relates to oath-taking remains the most workable definition that you can come across. It is still appropriate to the way modern covens work, particularly those that fall under the category of progressive Witchcraft.

The coven as the primary social unit for Witches is important for another reason. In the last few decades of the twentieth century, the extended family had almost completely broken down and been replaced with what sociologists refer to as the *nuclear family*. Before then, families consisted of several generations living together, including grandparents and even aunts and uncles—not only in close contact but also in many cases in the same home together. The elders shared their wisdom and knowledge with the younger generation who grew up around them.

From the 1970s onward, the nuclear family became the norm, consisting of just parents and children living under the same roof. The wisdom of the older generation ceased to be passed down.[2] You may think this has little to do with Witchcraft and the coven, but many who come into Witchcraft are in fact looking for an extended family. The coven provides this, as the average coven consists of a mix of age groups.* Those interested in Wicca are often drawn to the closeness and intimacy within the coven, as well as the knowledge that it can provide on a mundane as well as a magical level. For some, the coven becomes a surrogate family. The parental figures are the high priestess and high priest, and the older brothers and sisters are the senior members of the coven. Some might query whether this is a valid way to view the coven, but it should be remembered that any original hereditary coven prior to this time was most likely an extended family in the true sense of the word. The coven has now really become a family affair. Members bring their children along to the more-open festivals, and coven members become adopted "aunts" and "uncles" to the children of the other Witches. We have attended several such coven meetings in Europe and in the United States. This style of coven was unheard of during the time of Gerald Gardner and Alex Sanders.

---

* During our time as coven leaders, our age range of members has been from 18 to 74.

Coven Structure

There are many different ways of running a coven, all of which can be successful. Janet and Stewart were taught in the more formalized Alexandrian Tradition in which there was a fixed method handed down during training. In this tradition, as well as the Gardnerian, it is a benign dictatorship in which the high priestess of the coven rules jointly with the high priest, although she traditionally always gets the last word. She is expected to follow the "Craft Laws" in her rulership. In the Alexandrian Tradition, there are 161 of these[3] (some have been added or removed by various covens); in the Gardnerian Tradition, there are approximately fifty laws.

In Seax-Wica, in contrast, Raymond Buckland created a democratic system. The high priest and priestess are elected yearly by the coven. This was the system that Gavin was first introduced to. As Seax-Wica covens still survive using the same system, which is proof enough that this can work. Buckland's reasons for introducing this system are given below, from a letter he wrote to us on the subject:

> One of the problems that led to the ego-trips in Gardnerian was the degree system. It had always worked fine in the past, due to the very slow growth, with accompanying careful selection of leaders. But with the then new desire to expand and embrace everyone, it inevitably led to poor quality leaders (not all of them, obviously. There were and still are some excellent ones.) Anyway, to counteract this possibility I gave Seax-Wica a more democratic form; no degrees, leaders chosen by the group, to lead for a year and a day.[4]

Ray Buckland's points are quite valid. The degree system is not at the center of Seax-Wica practice, so there is no reason why such a coven cannot run without it. The same applies to the idea of a coven run by a high priestess and priest. A democratic leadership is just as effective if not more in newly formed groups of self-initiates, which the Seax-Wica system appeals to.

Over the years, we have come across other ways of structuring a coven. There are no right ways or wrong ways, just different ways suitable for different situations. Many covens that are newly formed may experiment with several ways till they are happy with one. This is to be expected, particularly in a coven that is progressive in nature. We have done this ourselves: we have amended the way we work over the years, so that our method of working is now very different from the way it was when we formed our first working magical group. Our experiences show that most good covens develop a family atmosphere, regardless of how they work, and tend to develop their own unique ways of doing things over time.

We here give an outline of the most common systems we have come across. Many of these systems may incorporate ideas from each other. We also try to show the basic underlying principles of each:

High Priestess Oriented

This is the system used in traditional Gardnerian and Alexandrian covens. It is based on the idea that the high priestess acts as the voice for Deity in Circle and therefore "the Goddess" directs the coven's activities through her. This does, of course, require a trance component to ritual within the magical practices of the coven. The high priestess must be able to successfully channel the divine wishes of the Goddess rather than her own ego. She must also possess excellent leadership skills. This system only really works when there are differences in the levels of training and experience amongst the members, with the most experienced individuals being the high priestess and priest. By nature, these are ideal training covens.

Elected Priesthood

The leaders of the coven are elected on a regular basis—monthly, annually, or whenever the coven decides. Seax-Wica works on a yearly basis, and this seems to be the most effective time span. This system works best when a group of Witches are forming a new coven as equals, whether they have all had experience. It is common to find such covens formed by those who have been Witches many years who want to come together in a group for magical work rather than for training. This is also the system we recommend to those with little experience who are getting together with others to form a coven for the first time and wish to train together on an equal basis.

Democratic Coven

All members of the coven have equal say on decisions made within the coven, either by vote or consensus of opinion, where compromises are made to accommodate everyone's view. In practice, we have found that it normally takes someone to act as a chairperson to make it work. You may get combinations of this kind of coven with the other ways of working, such as a high priestess-oriented coven where she refers decisions to those over second degree. It suits covens that are likely to be short-term—for example, one doing purely magical work within a given time frame.

Rotational Priesthood

When the coven is formed, the existing members take turns filling the roles of high priestess and high priest over allotted periods of time—for example, from Circle to Circle, or from month to month, or even from year to year. If the period of time is short, decisions affecting the whole coven will need to be on a democratic basis.

Constitutional Priesthood

The high priest and high priestess rule with the consent of the coven. This is confirmed on a yearly basis, sometimes by symbolic ritual. This is very similar to the high priestess-oriented coven. The major difference is that the priestess and priest refer decisions back to the whole coven on matters such as acceptance of new members on a regular basis. They both retain the right of veto on decisions if they feel it threatens the cohesion or security of the coven, but such vetoes are only used if it is really necessary, as the members of the coven might not reconfirm their position if the veto has been used unwisely. In our view, this coven structure has the best elements of all of the above. We feel it is a truly progressive way of working, which retains flexibility while allowing the leaders of the coven to express their leadership skills.

This is, in fact, our current way of working. The most important reason for using this system has to do with the group mind and the effect new members can have on it (see pages 85–90). The sword, as a magical tool, has taken on a new significance for us, as it now represents the sovereignty of the group (as opposed to being the coven leadership's symbol of power), and belongs to the whole coven. We now have a ritual related to this concept that involves the whole coven handing the sword to us for a year and a day. This system is written into our coven's rules, which override the old Craft Laws that were received from our Alexandrian heritage. The coven rules form the basis for the coven and the level of power given to the priesthood.

Laws and Rules

The original Gardnerian laws were apparently drafted by Gerald Gardner after Doreen Valiente and other members of their existing coven at the time presented him with "The Provisional Rules of the Craft."[5] This came about because Gardner had a habit of breaking his own oath of secrecy every time the press appeared on the doorstep! It was apparent to the coven members that a written set of rules was necessary to keep old Gerald under control. The history aside, it is our experience that any group of people working together for a period of time will need some set of rules. This is reflected in the rules you find in the workplace and even the unwritten rules you find in the family home. Rules within Witchcraft should be no different; they need to be practical and appropriate to now.

Over the years, we have found the Laws of the Craft as they were handed down to us are unworkable anachronisms. To give his laws weight, he attempted to make them look old, but he failed to make them very practical. Janet's late husband and coauthor, Stewart Farrar, was particularly critical of Gardner's laws, as the language in them wasn't even consistent with Old English, the pronunciation of which Stewart was an expert. Most working covens of Gardnerian or Alexandrian origin that we have talked to have created their own coven rules to supplement the Craft Laws they first received.

The first thing that any set of rules has to do is lay down how the coven system works. They must describe the degree system, or system of levels (if there is one), and the individual rules of behavior for the individual members—such as the level of secrecy, preparation required for Circle, et cetera. Here is an example of a set of rules that is loosely based on what we use today. Please note that we have included reference to the level system that we have incorporated into this book in the following chapter (see pages 97–102). This set of rules can easily be amended to suit any coven and the structures they choose to incorporate:

Coven Rules

1. All members of the coven are governed by these rules regardless of initiatory status.

2. These rules may be changed only by a majority decision of the coven.

3. The Coven Priest and Priestess rule by consent of the coven. A yearly ritual will be performed to confirm that sovereignty is granted to them by the will of the coven.

4. The level system within the coven is that of the four elements. Dedication: Path of Earth, first initiation: Path of Water, second initiation: Path of Fire, third initiation: Path of Air. The decision to initiate a member to a specific level is based on completion of work over a year and at the discretion of the Coven Priest and Priestess.

5. The basic ritual frame is the system of ritual that is laid down in the coven's Book of Shadows.

6. All members of the coven are oath bound to maintain the anonymity of the other members of the coven.

7. All members of the coven are oath bound not to reveal the secrets entrusted to them in Circle, and not to reveal the activities of the coven.

8. All members of the coven are to attend Circles "properly prepared" This means to be ready with appropriate robes and working tools as needed. They are also expected to maintain a high standard of personal cleanliness before Circle.

9. Potential members must be introduced to the other members of the coven. A unanimous decision must be made if they are to be asked to join, and even after this they must attend three Circles before the Coven Priest and Priestess confirm this decision.

10. It is intended that the coven will hold twenty-one or more meetings in a year. These will consist of the eight Sabbats (festivals) and thirteen Esbats (full moons). There may also be supplementary training Esbats, workshops, and seminars. All members are expected to try to attend. If they are unable, they must inform the coven.

11. Coven business is carried out after the Blessing of the Cakes and Ale at the end of the ritual. Every member has the right to speak freely about anything related to the coven and its running. It is also a time when disputes should be settled, if present between coven members, adjudicated by the Coven Priest/Priestess or someone appointed by the other members.

12. All problems within the coven should be brought to the attention of the Coven Priest/Priestess or brought up at coven business. It should not be discussed inappropriately with other coven members outside of Circle.

13. A member may leave at any time, but they must give notice of their leaving and their reasons why in a letter to be read out at coven business. This allows appropriate action to be taken to remove any psychic link they have with the coven.

Roles within the Coven

Coven Priestess and Priest

Traditionally known as the high priestess and high priest. It is the Coven Priestess who is considered to the head of the coven in Gardnerian and Alexandrian Witchcraft, as she is the representative of the Goddess. Likewise, the Coven Priest is considered the representative of the God. In most covens we know, including our own, they tend to be an equal partnership. In the past it was necessary to have the high priestess as the principle leader because society was so male-oriented. This ensured that she received an equal say and that there was a true balance of male and female energy within the coven. The Priestess and Priest are the leaders of the coven—directing ritual and training and enforcing the rules and the laws the coven runs by. In ritual, the Priestess takes on another role: that of directing any psychic energy raised by the coven. In this respect, she is not unlike the conductor of an orchestra, allowing the coven (the orchestra), to concentrate on the raising of energy (the music).

Leadership skills are essential in this role. The best Coven Priestesses and Priests consider themselves guides of the coven. They tend not to *rule* so much as assist the coven in the direction its members want it to go. Like all good leaders, they listen carefully to what the coven members want before making any decisions. Humility and a good sense of humor are essential.

An effective Coven Priestess or priest looks for and encourages the inherent skills in each member of the coven. They give out unconditional love to the members equally, and they act as mediators if problems occur between members. They are not judgmental regarding the personal or private lives of the individual members, and do not interfere in them, although they are willing to give unbiased advice if it is requested.

Like all good leaders, they should stand by what they believe in, particularly when it comes to the ethical principles that they follow. But it must be remembered, like all humans, they can make mistakes. They are likely well aware that they are not infallible; they are aware of the dangers of ego inflation. They know when they have made a mistake, and will admit openly when they have been wrong.

They do not necessarily have to have a lot of knowledge, but they must have the willingness to learn and have a good dose of common sense.

Assistants to the Priestess and Priest

The female assistant to the Coven Priestess is traditionally known as the "maiden." Her role is to assist the Priestess during ritual. Her counterpart is the Assistant Coven Priest, whose purpose is self-explanatory. Together, they act as support to the Priestess and Priest: they hold the Circles when the Priest and Priestess are not present, and they assist in training. Traditionally, there is also a figure known as the Man in Black, or coven "summoner." We have even heard the name "Black Rod" used. He is responsible for calling the coven together, hence the traditional name of summoner. Sometimes his role is combined with that of the Assistant Coven Priest. He may also move between covens, acting as a messenger between different groups, so he needs to be someone that people trust. He can be likened to being the coven's "diplomat."

Another role is the scribe. His or her job is to take and keep notes on the ritual workings performed by the group. This can also include updating the Book of Shadows in both its handwritten and computerized forms. In today's modern world, the scribe has to have computer skills to do this, as the days of keeping purely handwritten notes for the coven are now pretty much over.

In covens with a system of degrees, these roles are given normally (but not necessarily) to those who have reached second degree (our Path of Fire). In a new coven, it may be necessary for first-degree initiates to take on these roles. Second degree is normally a preparation for members to hive off and run their own covens in the future.

Types of Meetings

Festival Circles: These are the traditional Witches' Sabbats held eight times a year—on the four Celtic fire festivals and the four solar festivals (i.e., equinoxes and solstices). These tend to be celebrations rather than working Circles. The Wheel of the Year is a standard teaching in Wicca, particularly regarding what is referred to as the *power tides*—the ebb and flow of fertility energy during the year (see pages 164–166). Any magical work carried out during a Sabbat will be related to this flow, particularly on the naturally occurring solar festivals.

Moon Circles: These are the traditional Esbats held on (or close to) every full moon, although they may also be held on the new moon or during the waning moon. The moon is considered to have a psychic effect on the individual in occult teaching, and its phases therefore have particular influences magically.

Training Circles: Most covens have additional meetings or Esbats for the purposes of training. They may be less formal that the other Circles, with members in everyday clothing and possibly even no Circle cast if there is going to be a purely teaching session. Most covens try to keep these meetings during the phases of the moon from waxing to full, and try to avoid dark of moon.

The Coven Mind and Its Creation

Understanding that a coven is more than just a group of people worshipping together is vitally important if it is going to run successfully. Spiritual experiences, psychic skills, and the use of magic within the coven develops a group mind; it becomes an entity in its own right, developing its own personality and ways of expressing itself. The words "perfect love and perfect trust" (the passwords used at traditional Wiccan initiation) are an expression of the bonding of the individual into the coven. These words have become an important ideal within modern Witchcraft: that coven members have unconditional love for one another, resulting from the formation of the coven mind. An understanding of some aspects of psychology, including Carl Gustav Jung's theories regarding the collective unconscious and Max Wertheimer's Gestalt theory, are therefore essential.

According to Jung, we are all psychologically connected on a level known as the collective unconscious. In occult practice, this is believed to directly interface with the different levels of reality that make up spiritual and magical cosmology—for example, the elemental, underworld, and Astral Realms (for more on this, see pages 118–122). We are unaware of the collective unconscious in our everyday waking consciousness, although we may enter it to a certain degree during dreams or rapid eye movement (REM) sleep (for more on this, see page 182). Those adept at visualization and trance techniques can also achieve this, hence their importance of these techniques in magical practice. Every time a Circle or a magical item is consecrated, an astral double (a magical reflection—for more on this, see page 147) is created in the collective unconscious. A coven therefore works principally within this area of consciousness when it performs any form of magic.

Many animals work on the collective unconscious level all the time, hence herd behavior and the collective instincts that some animals seem to manifest. In humans, it sometimes manifests as psychic experiences in which someone is aware of something traumatic happening to a loved one, or a feeling that something isn't right in the world when something disastrous has just happened, but such genuine experiences are uncommon.

Here is how Max Wertheimer explained his Gestalt theory:

> The fundamental "formula" of Gestalt theory might be expressed in this way. There are wholes, the behavior of which is not determined by that of their individual elements, but where the part-processes are themselves determined by the intrinsic nature of the whole.[6]

This can be summed up quite simply as "the whole is more than the sum of its parts." Gestalt theorists use this process in education as well as in therapies for cognitive disorders. It is also applied to groups that develop their own identities within society.

When these two theories are applied to a group like a coven, it comes to light that any group working closely together on a collective unconscious, or astral level, will develop its own personality separate from those of the individual members; it creates a permanent astral imprint similar to the consecration of a magical item. This, of course, can have both positive and negative effects, which anyone running a coven should be aware of.

First of all, anyone joining a coven that has been running a long time, needs to be allowed to enter the coven mind slowly. If they enter it too fast, it can be like a body rejecting a transplanted organ. This is one of the many reasons why we have incorporated a dedication ritual (Earth initiation) into our practice: it allows the newly accepted Witch to enter the gestalt mind of the coven slowly (see page 98).

As most coven leaders know, the moment you form a coven successfully, you set up a flashing beacon on the astral level (so to speak) that will attract those who are suited to the coven. This is one of the reasons why there is no reason to actively recruit. Proselytizing will very likely create members who do not naturally adjust to the coven mind.

One of the biggest dangers of group mind is its manipulation by those who run cults. Leaders of such religious groups manipulate the gestalt created by the group of people they are trying to control so that they act, in essence, as the group's nervous system. If this occurs within a coven, it will be noticeable that the leader not only becomes the dominant personality, but will also attempt to control its members. They may even try to prevent members from leaving or try to interfere in their everyday lives. If the leader is successful, the members of such a group lose their personal autonomy outside of the coven. This sort of situation can be avoided by ensuring that everyone has equal rights within the coven's system of rules and laws, with adequate checks and balances. This is why we have incorporated the idea of a constitutional Coven Priestess and Priest within our current coven rules, and encourage individuals to follow their own spiritual paths. This is what separates Wicca from the many religious cults that are out there: free expression, creativity, and the *encouragement* of individual identity within the group mind.

The positive aspects more than compensate for the awareness needed to counter the negative ones. The first noticeable effect is from a magical perspective: the coven raises more energy than "the sum of its parts." Members of a coven with a healthy group mind find that they are strongly linked, like a family, and have caring and loving feelings toward each other. Strong psychic connections naturally exist, and we have experienced psychic experiences between members; for example, when a member is suddenly aware that another member of the coven is in trouble. Magic in such an environment becomes natural, and it is not unknown for spontaneous flowing rituals to occur without preplanning, and without any specific individual directing the group. The coven does, literally, take on a mind of its own and begin to run itself.

There are several ways we have learned to encourage the development of a coven mind, and most of these revolve around creating a specific identity. We have listed these below:

1. **A Name that Identifies the Coven's Personality:** Just as a name comes to represent you to other people, a coven name does the same thing. We have come across several different types of names for coven: ones related to deities, totemic ones using the names of animals or mythical beasts, ones related to myth, and ones related to places such as sacred sites. Sometimes names can be a combination of all of these. Our current coven's name incorporates a goddess, a sacred site, and a myth, and for this reason is quite powerful. Whatever name is chosen, it should reflect the aspirations, personality, and feel that the members want for the coven.

2. **Coven Deities:** When Gavin joined his first coven, there was nothing but arguments over the names for the deities of the coven. Everyone wanted his or her own deities, so in the end they just used Lord and Lady as titles and let the gods decide who was going to turn up! Within the more rigid traditions, coven deities are fixed—such as Aradia and Cernunnos in the Gardnerian Tradition, or the use of hidden or secret names. More progressive covens are likely to have a more

flexible approach. We certainly see no point in having an Etruscan goddess, such as Aradia, for a coven in central Ireland. Whatever is decided, the deities chosen should be the coven's deities, not those of the individual members. They should, like the name, reflect the innate nature of the group: if it is oriented toward healing, it should be a healing deity; if a coven is oriented toward environmental work, it should be a deity of nature, et cetera.

3. **Symbols that are Specific to the Coven:** Symbols are powerful things, and there is nothing more effective in uniting a group of people than the use of a flag or emblem that represents the group identity. Symbols have always been used in Wicca in this way. They can be found on the handles of athames, on the pentacle, and on the wand. There is no reason why a coven cannot have its own separate symbols to represent itself, without excluding the traditional symbols. We know members of one tradition that actually have a tattoo put on their wrist after initiation, as a memory of the "witches' mark" of the Middle Ages. Some may consider this extreme, but the members of the tradition are certainly not alone in this level of committed practice.

4. **Magical Items Given at Initiations:** The first item we give to our initiates at dedication is a plaited cord of three colors. (It has actually replaced the measure during the taking of the coven oath.) The colors were chosen carefully, as they are connected to the deity and name of our coven. Every time a member of our coven puts on their cord, they are reaffirming the coven's collective mind; every time they take them off, they are disconnecting from it on a lower level. We must point out that these are not the traditional cords given at first degree; they do not make someone a Witch, but a coven member. Within the mainstream forms of Wicca, it was traditional to give a chalice and the magical cords at first-degree initiation. We still do this, as well as giving other items related to the system of levels, or degrees, that we work with. (These are unique to our current coven.) There are other items that may be given. For example, jewelry or combinations of jewelry that identify the coven members in a subtle way. Some covens also have embroidered patches made up for robes and cloaks.

5. **Robes and Cloaks:** It is not uncommon for some covens to insist on specific colors for their initiates. A few covens go so far as to have both robes and cloaks made especially for them. White and black are the commonest colors used, then greens, browns, and other natural

colors. The use of robes in a single color actually performs the same role as going *skyclad* (nude); robes merge the initiate into the group identity by removing clothes, which are expressions of individual identity. Our preference is for our coven members to choose robes for themselves, so they maintain their own individuality rather than being uniformed.

6. **Creation of Coven Rituals:** The use of unique rituals that belong only to a specific coven is incredibly powerful for creating a coven mind, particularly if the rituals are created by the whole coven rather than passed down from a previous one. This allows the magical creativity of the coven to flow rather than be stifled in dogma. By doing so, the coven also creates its own nondogmatic Book of Shadows (BOS). In our current BOS, we have no scripted written rituals as such, but only directions on how to perform them.

7. **Use of Energy Work:** Using energy, or *prana* (to use the Hindu term), is essential for the creation of a coven mind. Yet we have found few covens that consciously work with energy. Moving energy around the Circle in visualizations helps to build the gestalt on an astral level, just as ritual does. Understanding the chakra system and the levels of the aura is therefore essential learning for anyone involved in running a coven, as well as for the individual members of the coven (see pages 133–137, 203). We now use chakras as the basis for our magical teaching.

8. **Secrecy and the Measure:** We have put these together, as they both represent the old method of creating a coven mind (we have already discussed the pros and cons related to secrecy in chapter 2, see pages 31–33). One of the advantages to a newly formed coven of keeping its existence secret for a period of time after formation is that it helps to birth the coven mind—normally a year is adequate. Secrecy prevents energy being dissipated psychically, by people talking about its existence. The measure was traditionally taken at initiation in the Gardnerian and Alexandrian Traditions of Wicca. It was originally a method for maintaining the secrecy of the coven's existence, and preventing the coven oath from being broken. At initiation, the Witch was measured with a piece of string from feet to crown, and the string was cut to that length. It was then measured around the forehead, the heart, and the hips, and marked off with a knot each time. A threat was then made that if the secrets were revealed the initiate would be "damned to hell of the Christians," and the measure would be thrown

into a bog or marsh so that the perpetrator themselves would rot. To this day, many covens still keep the measure, but we quickly changed this; as an act of love and trust, we ritually returned it to our initiates. Today, we have done away with the measure completely, feeling it is an anachronism. In fact, we have discovered evidence that indicates the practice's origins may be in a Middle Eastern system of divination rather than European witchcraft (see footnote page 25). We have replaced it with the coven cord and dedication ritual, which involves the taking of the oath.

A specific problem may occur when a member leaves: it can leave a gaping hole in the group mind, which needs to be filled to prevent problems. This gap is by nature a vacuum, which could easily fill with paranoia, mistrust, and even hate toward the person—particularly if they left on bad terms. Ideally, a leaving ritual should be performed with the person present, but this may not be possible if there is acrimony involved. The members of the coven should be encouraged to express their feelings about the situation. Afterwards they should aim toward a resolution and wish well to the person leaving on their new path. This reveals another reason why we have coven cords given at dedication: these should be returned when the member leaves, to break the psychic bond between the coven and the person leaving.

Grounding Your Coven

This is an aspect of covencraft that we have rarely found published in books. Grounding the coven is the process of linking the coven to the area it works in. It is no different to the grounding process an individual goes through when they work magically (see page 151). This is more complex with a coven, though, as we are talking about a gestalt entity, and the grounding process is ongoing. Grounding is necessary as it prevents the coven from becoming spiritually and psychically unbalanced. The rule "As above, so below" applies as much to a coven as it does to an individual. An ungrounded coven is likely to be overly concerned with psychic matters while ignoring everyday concerns.

In Ireland, grounding a coven is a very simple thing to do, as there are plenty of ancient sites for a coven to link to. Our current coven is linked to a series of megalithic tombs not far from our home, as well as a set of holy wells of ancient origin. This is common practice among the few covens there are in Ireland, and this is also common practice if you live in England or Europe, as there are plenty of such sites. Of course, this may not be so easy if you live elsewhere, particularly in parts of the United States, or if you are "townbound" so to speak. We do know of covens in the United States that link to local sites, sometimes of Native American origin, and they do so with great reverence and respect.* But there is no reason why you can't create your own sacred site. To a Witch, the whole earth is sacred, not just a series of sites that emanate power.

Sacred sites actually come about as a result of long periods of continual worship at them, so any outdoor site where rituals take place over a period of time becomes powerful, owing to the magical residue and astral imprint that is left there. After a while, such places are even detectable by dowsing; the only difference between them and the ancient megalithic sites is that they are just a bit more modern. This is particularly useful to know if you live in a town. We have heard of such a site developing within Central Park, New York City.

There are several methods to link a coven to a specific physical place. The first obvious one is regular ritual at the site. This is fine in secluded places, but it is not always possible in the middle of town. The next way is to leave a physical link. We have done this in Ireland by leaving ribbons tied to nearby trees; this is a common folk practice in Ireland. A physical link is very effective. We know some people who buy two identical crystals, burying one at one site and keeping the other at their altar. But you should be aware that by doing this you are likely to pick up on any activity at the place, so you should be quite knowledgeable about what activities go on there.

---

* We'd like to point out the incredible importance of gaining permission from the local magical tradition when using such sites, as well as the importance of using rites appropriate to that tradition.

NOTES

1 Reference to this can be found in Doreen Valiente's *ABC of Witchcraft*, pages 69–73.
2 From *Sociology: Themes and Perspectives*, pages 344–346 and 400–401. This is basic sociological theory, which also recognizes that alternatives (e.g., the coven) will form to replace the extended family.
3 These can be found in their most complete form in June John's *King of the Witches* (1969), pages 130–140. They were published again two years later in Lady Sheba's *Book of Shadows*.
4 Ray Buckland, private correspondence, 28 November 2002.
5 These rules can be found in *Crafting the Art of Magic* by Aidan Kelly on pages 103–105. According to Kelly, this story originates from Fred Lamond who claimed it was Doreen Valiente's high priest who drew up the rules.
6 Lecture for the Kant Society, Berlin, 7 December 1924.

6

Making the Witch:
Training within Witchcraft

You can tell whether a man is clever by his answers. You tell whether a man is wise by his questions.
—MAHFOUZ NAGUIB*

We can imagine the traditional form of training that a British village witch of the Middle Ages would have received if Christianity had not arrived. This would probably have been what we shall call generational training. A child would have been taught the family trade from an early age. Their mother would have taken them into the fields to collect herbs, and then they would have assisted her in making healing potions and balms. For community rituals, all the family would have assisted, and the younger members of the family would have prepared the ritual space: decorating it, setting up the altar as they had been taught, et cetera. They would have then watched their parents at work, later asking questions and receiving answers. Most training would have been one on one—the origin of the sorcerer's apprentice image so loved by fantasy movies. There would have been no large group of people sitting down, learning by rote, researching or reading. This would have been unlikely, as there were no books, and no one (for that matter) could read. These methods of training are a modern creation. Generational training was slow but it worked, quite simply because the length of training was from birth to death. By the time a child reached their teen-

---

* Born in 1911, Mahfouz is the grand old man of Arabic fiction, enjoying the affection and reverence of both critics and a vast readership.

age years, their breadth of knowledge would have been quite astounding, particularly if there were no other forms of education available. Most modern Witches start learning from the age when a hypothetical village witch from the past would have already been working with their parents in ritual for at least five years.

There is, in fact, an ethical imperative at work to take training seriously within Wicca. Not training or gaining knowledge breaks the Wiccan Rede itself, the very core ethic of Wicca. Similar ethics can be found in the medical professions, where there is an obligation for doctors and nurses continually educate themselves in the latest healing techniques. You may wonder what this has to do with Wicca, but it should be remembered that the ancestors of modern Witchcraft are the village healers and shamans of the past.

In Gardnerian/Alexandrian Wicca, training was not aimed at solitary Witches or self-initiates. You had to join a coven or formal group of some sort to receive instruction. When both Janet and Gavin first came into Wicca, you were not expected to learn anything prior to initiation. In fact, you couldn't be taught anything by the coven until you were actually initiated, due to the oath that none of the "secrets of the craft" could be passed on until the person receiving them was "properly prepared," in other words, initiated in Circle. The result was that there were many initiated first-degree Witches who knew next to nothing. There were few relevant books around, so it wasn't unusual for the initiate to have read only one book prior to being brought into the Craft.

This was, to say the least, a rather unsatisfactory situation that continued in some covens right up until the 1980s. There was, in fact, no system of training within Witchcraft up until then. It was a conversation with Doreen Valiente that made us realize this. Gavin asked her what she thought about covens assigning essays for their student initiates. She was visibly shocked by the idea and said, "In my day it was on-the-job training!" What she meant was that once you were initiated, you were left to learn by watching the coven at work. There was no formal system of teaching sessions, and any one-on-one training would have been an informal affair. The only thing the new initiate was expected to do was faithfully copy out the Book of Shadows, spelling mistakes and all! Initiates were left to teach themselves. They were generally guided in what to read and left to watch what happened in ritual. In the 1970s this began to change within some covens.

During this time, Alex Sanders heavily influenced the incorporation of ceremonial ritual magic and Cabalistic teachings into Wicca in the United Kingdom. There had been influences prior to this, but not to the same degree of intensity. He changed Wicca's orientation from Low Church folk magic to High Church ceremonial magic. A single book seemed to be the major influence on him to cause this change: W. E. Butler's *The Magician: His Training and Work*. Part two of this work looks at the information that was conveyed to the postulant during training. Janet's late husband, Stewart, was quick to notice this influence in the notes he and Janet took from Alex while training with him. He went about researching and listing Alex's sources in a work Stewart labeled as "Wicca Transcriptions." Stewart noticed that Alex also scavenged information from several other works—passing them off as his own teachings—including Franz Bardon's *Initiation into Hermetics*. (But to be fair, much of Alex's teachings derived from his own philosophy and beliefs.) Alex created several books of out this information, including a second and third "Book of the Law," and several updated versions of the Book of Shadows. All remain unpublished and are only are passed on to recognized initiates of the Alexandrian Tradition. Alex changed the information in them over time, continuing to tinker with the content up until his death. It is for this reason that there are several different versions of each book in circulation.

Of course, what Alex was doing was turning the traditional coven structure into a magical lodge. He did so by putting the emphasis on ritual magic as the main magical practice within Wicca. His way of teaching was to sit his pupils down and to dictate to them, as a schoolmaster does to a group of twelve-year-olds. He even went so far on some occasions as making student Witches write out lines because they misbehaved! His usual method of teaching consisted of demonstrations instead of practical workshops or one-on-one instruction. Janet recounts one demonstration that consisted of Alex running around in a loincloth with a feathered headdress while summoning an Aztec spirit. At the climax of this bizarre ritual, Alex put a hot poker in his mouth.[1] After Janet and Stewart left to form their own coven, Alex's system of training continued to develop. Meanwhile, things were progressing somewhat quicker in the United States than in the United Kingdom.

In the United States, the Pagan Way group had formed and was beginning to put forward a viable system of training accessible to all. According to Ed Fitch, the Pagan Way ". . . came out of a general round-robin correspondence in 1969–70 which involved Joe Wilson, Tony Kelly, John

Score, and several others in the U.K., plus John Hansen, Fred & Martha Adler, and myself in the U.S. There was also some consulting with the late Susan Roberts, who had just written *Witches, USA*."[2]

Ed Fitch is a practicing Gardnerian high priest, although he has also written books on Ásatrú, and was partly responsible for the creation of the group rituals and teaching structure of the Pagan Way materials. These were later published anonymously as *A Book of Pagan Rituals* by Herman Slater, then by Llewellyn Publications, and still later by Samuel Weiser. The original idea was that the Pagan Way materials should be public domain because it was felt that such material needed to be freely available to the public. The original cooperative of writers, including Ed Fitch, never actually made a penny from it.

Fitch later went on to publish the book Magical Rites from the Crystal Well in 1984. This was, in fact, a compilation of material published in the Pagan Way magazine, *The Crystal Well*, that Fitch had been involved in publishing with John Hansen.[*] This material confirms that there was a system at work, although the introduction claims there was no consistent method. The second section of the first chapter, "Forming a Pagan Training Group," goes through eight ways to form a magical training group, and suggests ESP exercises, research and reading assignments, and meditative exercises.

Level Systems and Training

A Witch's training goes through several specific phases, from accumulation of knowledge and skills up to their final implementation in a practical environment. In our current way of training, we try to break these phases up by the elements and the system of degrees. We have found that a system of levels is necessary, as a training coven will over a period of time have individuals with different levels of knowledge and skills. This can be a problem, as you may find yourself repeating the learning process with the same students time and again when new members join. Of course, repetition itself is part of the learning process, but a student who has been through the same seminar for the third time running is likely to get bored, and their time would be better spent learning something else. A system of levels, degrees, or otherwise, helps to split the coven into useful levels of ability and avoids this problem, as you can have separate training sessions with each level.

---

[*] The magazine *The Crystal Well* was originally published as *The Waxing Moon*. They were give out free of charge through two mailboxes, one in North Dakota and one in Philadelphia. Donations were asked for just to cover mailing costs.

Figure 2 Maslow's Triangle

Some have rejected the degree system on the grounds that it is too hierarchical (see pages 35–37). We believe that degrees are not supposed to be a reflection of status, but of the individual's ability. We ourselves rejected it for a short period for this reason, but found it necessary to reinstate it. This made us examine the reasons why people found security in it, particularly in a training environment. We discovered that levels of attainment exist in all successful educational systems. In his *Hierarchy of Needs,* the eminent psychologist Abraham Maslow sums up the reason for this in his "positive theory of human motivations." This was a theory Gavin had been taught while training as a nurse, and although he had always been a critic of the degree system in Wicca, he realized the necessity for a system of levels.

---

* In 1954, Abraham Maslow formulated a positive theory of motivation derived from clinical experience, which by integrating earlier theories arrives at a dynamic-holistic theory. Although taught to health-care professionals, this theory easily applies to all situations to explain motivational imperatives.

Maslow's theory is often portrayed as a triangular diagram divided horizontally into five levels (see figure 3). He described a hierarchy of needs as follows (from the bottom of the diagram to the top):

- **Physiological:** air, food, water, warmth, and rest
- **Safety:** security, stability, protection, and order
- **Love and Belonging:** affection and friendship
- **Esteem:** recognition, dignity, worth
- **Self-Actualization:** the development and fulfillment of potential

The final two are important here, as they motivate individuals to achieve. Maslow believed that if people did not have goals, they would create them to assist in their motivation. This answered our question of why it was so hard to reject the degree system. In its purest form it is no more than a system of attainable levels for the student to work toward. They may actually mean nothing (as we shall show), but as most occultists know, it is the quest that gives meaning to the Grail, and not the other way around. The quest is therefore more important than the actual Grail itself, which is ultimately a symbol.[3] It is for this reason that initiations become triggers for spiritual change in the seeker in Wiccan and other occult practices. It is also important to point out that the serious quest for spiritual experience can only really take place at self-actualization. In other words, when the seeker has achieved the first four needs to some extent and has become grounded in the process. Here we see the importance of the coven in this process, particularly in giving the seeker the love, sense of belonging, and esteem mentioned by Maslow.

The Elemental System

We have related our current system to the four classical elements: Earth, Water, Fire and Air. These are the four basic correspondences that most Witches learn early on in their training. Gavin belonged to a clan that did similar work, and we are sure there are others who have done likewise, as it is such an obvious way of doing things from an occult perspective. These are often referred to as the "Platonic" elements, from the philosopher Plato, but it was his contemporary, Empedocles, who theorized that they were the building blocks of creation.* The currently accepted

---

* Empedocles was a citizen of Agrigentum in Sicily, around 444/3 BC. He unreservedly accepts the doctrine of Parmenides that *what is* is uncreated and indestructible, and he only escapes from the further conclusions of the Eleatic by introducing the theory of elements or *roots*. Of these he assumed four: Fire, Air, Earth, and Water—and in some respects, this was a return to primitive views that the Milesians (Celts) had already left behind them.

symbol of Witchcraft is the pentagram worn around the necks of so many Witches. The pentagram is representative of Spirit in control of the four elements. It is also safe to say that most Witches, being polytheistic and believing in many truths, also believe that Spirit is attained by the fusion of the four elements together to create Ether. This Idea is often symbolized by the Celtic cross.

It is within the elements that the Witch can find a key to understanding the mystery tradition within Wiccan practice. We have organized this by the use of the degree system into a series of goals to aim toward. The four passage rites are related directly to the elements:

- **Dedication:** the initiation and commencement of the **Path of Earth**

- **The First Degree:** the initiation and commencement of the **Path of Water**

- **The Second Degree:** the initiation and commencement of the **Path of Fire**

- **The Third Degree:** the initiation and commencement of the **Path of Air**

Our use of an extra initiation—the dedication—came about for several reasons. First of all, there was an inherent problem in the old system of secrecy. When Janet and Stewart came into the Craft, they were not allowed to learn anything before they were initiated because of the oath of secrecy that Witches took at the time. This was very unsatisfactory, as it meant that you had many initiated Witches with very little knowledge. Many left covens because they hadn't known what they were getting involved in, nor really understand the nature of the coven until after they had been initiated into it. This was not necessarily a fault with either side, but a problem due to the lack of a waiting period when the coven members and the potential new initiate could get to know each other. We therefore introduced a dedication ritual to try to remedy this situation. Again, this is not new, and has become common amongst many covens for reasons similar to ours. Another reason for a dedication is that there is now a wealth of information available for the student Witch—something that was not true in the past. Most solitary Witches or pre-initiates who approach a coven for initiation already know so much about Wicca that it is necessary to have some sort of buffer to discover what knowledge an individual has before serious training can commence. This buffer also allows the initiate to get a real sense of belonging to a working group. After dedication, the potential initiate also tends to show their real personality, which helps the members decide if the individual is suitable for joining a coven that has already formed a group mind.

Path of Earth: This commences after dedication. The element of Earth is the element of stability and foundation. It is the first element that needs to be addressed by anyone commencing training as a Witch. It lays the foundation of values that they will need as a Witch and a Priest/Priestess. Training during this stage is therefore initially centered on basic knowledge: the Rede—the ethical code of modern Witchcraft; the history of witchcraft, both ancient and modern; the structure of Wicca and what a coven actually is; the nature of Deity; the Wheel of the Year; basic magical principles and laws, et cetera. Practical knowledge is also important and relates to the techniques that the initiate needs for the learning process after their second initiation (for example, visualization and meditative techniques).

Path of Water: This path commences after first-degree initiation. This element relates to emotion, connection, and flow. The path starts with the customary first-degree initiation found in both the Gardnerian and Alexandrian Traditions. This is where the real training starts, as far as we are concerned, because Water is the first element of the mystery of connection with Spirit. It is during this time that the initiate is encouraged to find their personal god or goddess. Water is also the element of connection with the Arwen, or anima/animus to use the Jungian psychological term. This is an experiential process not an intellectual one. We actually encourage our students to build a shrine and altar if they believe they have found the deity who they can relate to. At this stage the initiate also starts to learn the more practical side of Witchcraft: Circle casting, working with energy, and commencement of psychic and astral training.

Path of Fire: This path commences after second-degree initiation. We were taught that the old second-degree ritual was about facing our fears and understanding where they came from. Fire is about the use of will to do this, as the will is governed by the element of Fire. During this time, the Witch faces his or her own "inner demons." The initiate learns, in terms of Jungian psychology, to recognize and to come to terms with their own primal nature, the id, the Shadow, and the ego. This can be a difficult process, for it is as much about personal growth as spiritual. The traditional symbol of the second degree was the reversed pentagram; it represents the Horned God of nature, the god who not only rules our own natural instincts but is also the psychopompos—the Guide to the Mysteries.

Path of Air: This path commences after third-degree initiation. The element of Air relates to wisdom and knowledge. Traditionally, the third degree in Wicca is marked with the symbol of the pentagram surmounted by the triangle with point upright. This is, of course, the symbol of Fire, and is used to mark the completion of that path. There is no training for Air. The reason is that by the time any Witch reaches this stage, they should be (to use Maslow's wording) self-actualizing; they should be able to guide themselves or seek guidance from the higher forces. It does not mean that the Witch has finished learning, even though she has finished training. Life is a learning process: even after death, this continues as you go through life after life. This is why the idea of reincarnation is an important part of Wiccan thought. Janet always makes the statement, "If I say I know everything, kick me! I'm still learning, and the more I learn, the more I realize how little that I know."

One thing you will notice is that the elements seem to exist within one another within the individual paths. For example, knowledge is governed by Air, but can be found in the Path of Earth. This is intentional, as all the elements exist within one another. You will see this pattern again and again in any magical working you do. This is reflected in the use of the pentagram rituals of ceremonial magic where on appropriate occasions the ceremonial magician will invoke one element through all the others at each quarter in order to bring that pure element into the Circle.

This system is the way we work. There are other systems of levels that are just as valid. We are not the first to come to this conclusion. As early as the late 1960s a coven in New York was putting its initiates through the three-degree system twice, creating a six-level system. Alex Sanders in the early 1980s had instituted two more degrees, initiating Witches up to fifth degree. There is no reason why Witches should dogmatically follow the old three-degree system. Systems of levels could be related to the chakras in a seven-degree system, or to the four elements and spirit creating a five-degree system, et cetera. It is most important that any system of levels has a magical basis rooted in commonsense principles to make it viable; this includes the passage through the mysteries as an intrinsic part of its ethos.

In both Gardnerian and Alexandrian Traditions, there was a general rule of "a year and a day" between initiations, although there was originally no timescale prior to first degree. Janet was initiated by Alex Sanders within weeks of meeting him. Most sensible coven leaders have now implemented some sort of rule regarding this, just as we ourselves have.

The timescale for initiations was based on the premise that first degree made you a Witch, second degree made you capable of running rituals and a coven under supervision, and third degree made you a high priest/ priestess in your own right, capable of running a coven, initiating new Witches, et cetera. The normal practice was for third degrees to hive off after receiving this initiation. In theory, you were initiated into the third degree within three years. Anyone looking for a coven is going to find different rules regarding this. Some may still use the old timescale, others may have a flexible system, others no timescale at all.

There are, of course, several problems with implementing fixed time periods within training. People tend to learn at different rates, as well as the fact that you are trying to judge an individual's spiritual change. We have the rule that we should know someone personally for at least a year before dedicating him or her. Because of this, we were once accused of "only initiating friends." We consider this a compliment rather than a criticism. It must mean that we initiate in "perfect love and perfect trust," which must surely define the existence of a friendship.

In the elemental system we use, before dedication (Path of Earth) we must have personally known someone for a year, and in that time, they must have shown a certain amount of knowledge about Wicca. If someone comes to us knowing nothing, we send him or her away to do some reading. In the past, there was little reading material available so it was not unusual for people to be initiated with very little knowledge of what they were getting into. Today, this is not the case. We feel anyone seriously interested in becoming a Witch would have already read through several books before coming to us. First degree (Path of Water) is given after a "year and a day," or more, if the individual hasn't covered the necessary knowledge for that path. The same applies to the next two initiations. We try to base our decision on when to initiate someone on his or her personal spiritual growth, as well as his or her intellectual learning and practical ability. All the elements must be appropriately in balance for that person.

One problem for anyone running a coven is what to do when someone originally initiated by another coven asks to join yours. We are quite happy to accept anyone previously initiated by another coven, as long as they have left the previous group and they understand that they may have to start again from the beginning. This may seem quite harsh, but within Wicca itself there are no fixed levels of training or rules on initiation. Each coven, to all intents and purposes, sets its own guidelines. The

traditions within Wicca pass down rules regarding training, but you cannot guarantee these will be followed by covens that have descended from
them. There are some organizations that have tried to solve this problem, such as the Covenant of the Goddess* and the Aquarian Tabernacle
Church.† They have strict guidelines for their associate covens, which
need to be implemented if they are to remain members of their organizations, but generally these are related more to ethics rather than training.

Training Methods

Here we have tried to list the different types of training methods that can
be used by covens and other magical training groups, as well as solitaries. Most of these are tried and tested techniques used not just within the
occult community but also in educational establishments. Anyone who
comes to us for training must show that they are committed to learning. We do not wish to waste our time assisting someone if they are not
self-motivated. We feel it is important to honor the individuality in our
students, particularly with regard to their individual gifts. We feel it is
important for Witches to be "masters of one" rather than jacks-of-all-
trades—that is, to have a thorough grounding in Wicca, but specialize in
a particular occult area, be it spiritual healing or counseling and divination, et cetera.

We strongly believe that we all teach ourselves, so we tend to act
more as mentors in the way we train people—being supportive and giving individual tuition when necessary. It is important to remember that
not all methods of learning will suit every person. This is reflected in the
methods we have listed below:

1. **The Book of Shadows**

   "Now copy out the Book of Shadows," was the first thing said to a
   Witch after they were initiated into a coven. It is also the earliest form
   of training known in Wicca. It was traditional to write it out "in your
   own hand" but times have changed, and the initiate is just as likely
   to receive it on a CD, DVD, data stick, or even have it as an Internet
   download. The Witch will still, of course, have to copy it out in their

---

*   Covenant of the Goddess was formed in 1975 by thirteen covens and a number of
     solitaries in Berkley California. By 1980 it had members in at least fifteen states.
     (Abridged from Rosemary Ellen Guiley's *Encyclopedia of Witches and Witchcraft*.)
†   Founded in 1979 by Peter Pathfinder Davies. The ATC was formed as a coven
     dedicated to providing religious services to the larger Wiccan community. Today
     it has congregations in the U.S., Canada, Ireland (where we live), Australia, and
     South Africa. (Abridged from Raymond Buckland's *The Witch Book*.)

own hand. In our collection, we have over a dozen different books and their variations. Once kept highly secret, they are now regularly published in books. Some are traditional, some are freshly created. The Book of Shadows should not be regarded as the equivalent of the Christian Bible, but should be seen as an expanding magical diary being handed down from generation to generation, each adding their own material. We still make our students copy them out, but we also get them to compare the different ones we have. They are encouraged to add their own material as they learn as part of the process.

2. **Reading Assignments**

This is the standard basic method that has been used going back to Gerald Gardner's first coven, although it wasn't as formalized as it is today. There is nothing wrong with learning from books as long as you realize the basic rules. One is that they aren't always correct in what they're saying. Another is that you can't learn everything from a book. We once came across someone who actually believed they had the right to be initiated third degree because they had read our book *A Witches' Bible*. Books are objective ideas written by subjective people, and this should always be remembered. We actively encourage our students to question what they read, particularly as there are now so many books with few original ideas or that go to first sources for material. Reading assignments free up valuable time that can be used by the Wiccan teacher to show practical techniques. It also continues the learning process outside of the coven environment.

3. **Research**

We feel this is one of the most useful tools at hand for the education of a would-be Witch. This can include books, magazines, and the Internet. It has several advantages over just a reading assignment: it encourages students to use their own initiative, to think for themselves, and to develop their own ideas. Another result is that research sometimes unearths information we do not know ourselves. For this reason we get the student to feed what they have learned back to the whole group so the other members learn from it as well.

4. **Assigning Essays**

This is closely linked to the idea of research, but the person produces a paper on a given subject. One advantage is that the resultant essay can be used as part of the individual's Book of Shadows. The disad-

vantage is that the information in the essay is not really shared with
the rest of the coven. We have used essays in the past to assess those
who have asked to be trained with us prior to (or even during) the
Path of Earth.

5. **Group Demonstrations**
This is pretty much self-explanatory. Almost all the Circles we have
done with our covens have included demonstrations. It is, as Doreen
Valiente described it, "on-the-job training." We also give more specific
demonstrations on how techniques work—for example, talking the
coven through the Pentagram Ritual, Circle casting, and creation of
thought-forms, et cetera. In group demonstrations, though, there is no
participatory involvement for the student, unlike one-on-one training,
so it is more suited to those who have just joined a training coven.

6. **Group Practical Training**
This is similar to group demonstrations but with involvement of the
coven. We use this with magical techniques such as pentagram rituals,
meditation, and chakra techniques, et cetera, where it's possible for
our students to copy our actions while we talk through what is happening with energy, visualization, et cetera. We prefer group practical
training to group demonstrations, as the student gets a feel for what
they are doing. We therefore use this wherever possible.

7. **One-on-One Practical Training**
This is the most effective method when it comes to learning magical
technique. The drawback is, of course, that it takes time. We tend to
use it when we are training someone to perform rituals. Each meeting
we will choose the couple or individual who will do the next Esbat or
Sabbat. We then talk them through the technique. This actually helps
to build the student's confidence so they do not feel so self-conscious.
This method is also essential when you move on to experiential techniques, particularly in the second-degree phase of the person's path.

8. **Seminars and Talks**
Sit-down talks are useful for relaying information on more academic
subjects such as the history of witchcraft, the origins of the Wheel of
the Year, et cetera. But we never use it on its own, we tend to follow
it up with something practical to reinforce the information that has
been relayed. The reason for this is most people's attention span is
approximately twenty minutes. After this, their mind starts to wander,
so we tend to keep any talks short.

Coven Training

9. **Games and Quizzes**

We have learned over the years that the more enjoyable an experience is, the more will be learned from it, particularly if there is some sort of competition involved. We have found the use of games is a really a benefit in psychic exercises, where people try to guess what the other person has drawn or guess what tarot card they are concentrating on. Quizzes, on the other hand, are useful for assessing the progression of any student, while making them aware of what subjects they need to concentrate more on.

10. **The Internet**

Cyber covens are already a reality. They exist, to use a magical term, "in a place which is not a place," amongst the bytes and electrons of the World Wide Web. The Internet is an incredible teaching tool. Apart from the obvious ease of communication for teaching purposes and the unlimited research potential, it can also be used to set up "floating" coven websites, where training material and the Book of Shadows can be stored and easily accessed by the student. Such a site can be password-protected for coven members only and can also include a message board where subjects can be regularly discussed.

Magical Systems used in Training

The magical systems that are taught in Wicca are generally taught after first-degree initiation. We tend to use the analogy of the car when it comes to the importance of learning magical systems. Most Witches who practice magic know how to drive the car. They know what the controls (the magical tools) are for; and they know how to use them to drive the car (perform ritual). They also know the highway code (the laws of magic, et cetera—see Appendix A). The main problem we have found is that very few know how the car works, which, we'd like to point out, is very different from knowing how to drive. Here we are talking about ritual mechanics. This is why it is important to have an understandable magical system related to your work as a Witch. It is also important if you are going to create your own rituals and magical practices successfully and safely.

The four systems we list below are the ones we have found most often in Wicca. There are others, of course, which we have not mentioned. Here we give a brief outline:

Ceremonial High Magic and Cabala

When Janet and Stewart came into the Craft, the magical system used by Alex Sanders was Cabalistic ceremonial high magic. This is, of course, Air-based as opposed to Earth-based, which Witchcraft is supposed to be.[4] It is also of Judeo-Christian origin rather than being truly pagan; therefore, it carries with it many Judeo-Christian philosophies and values. Witchcraft's evolutionary process has included the slow removal of these influences. This is not to say that an understanding of Cabala or ceremonial high magic is not important in a Witch's training. There is much that can be gained from them. But its importance has been overemphasized within Wicca over the years. We now use it just for the purpose of explaining philosophical principles (as we have done in this book), and rely more on the following three systems:

Shamanism

Gavin started in a self-initiatory Seax-Wica group where there was only a basic structure with no central magical system. This led him into the natural direction of studying rune-craft and then into Norse/Anglo-Saxon shamanism. He discovered within this a natural system of magic, which seemed to have more to do with Witchcraft than Cabala, as it was Earth- rather than Air-based. With Janet and Stewart, he examined the similarities with the remnants of the Celtic system that they were working with in Ireland (which is less complete than the Norse/Anglo-Saxon) and created a root cosmology. We still teach this system. Shamanism is also much more experiential than Cabala and seems to explain the mystery tradition within Wicca more fully, as Jungian psychology fits perfectly into the shamanic cosmology of worlds (see "Spiritual Cosmology," chapter 7). One could even argue that we have returned to the probable origins of witchcraft by doing this, as a simplified version of this would more than likely have been the system used by the original village priesthood many centuries ago.

The Chakra System

This is a system of spiritual anatomy and physiology (see "Sorcery: The Magical Art of Witchcraft," chapter 8). One of the first books specifically about Witchcraft to put forward the idea of using chakras was Starhawk's *Dreaming the Dark*. Their use in Western occult practice, though, goes back to the end of the nineteenth century when they were incorporated into Theosophy. The Theosophists were heavily influenced by material emerging from the British occupation of India—particularly the translations of the Vedas. The chakra system became an accepted model of the energy centers of the human body among both Theosophists and occultists (see pages 133–136). The most common argument against using them is that they are not a part of the Western tradition and that by using them you are mixing systems. Our argument is that there is plenty of evidence to support the idea that a proto-energy-system was known in Western culture, and we have talked more about this in one of our previous works, *The Healing Craft*.[5] The chakras explain many of the techniques that Witches use in their ritual and magical practice from the perspective of energy, including Drawing Down the Moon (see pages 180–181), but more importantly for an Earth-based spirituality, they reflect the important occult law "As above, so below."

Jungian Psychology

You might ask what psychology has to do with Witchcraft, as modern science seems to be at odds with the idea of magic. But this is not the case from a polytheistic point of view. Jung's teachings are far from out of place. Jung developed and elaborated upon the teachings of his mentor, Sigmund Freud, by examining archetypes. He even published a treatise on the god Wotan[6] (Odin) while examining what was happening in religious and occult practices. His teachings remain standard reading for anyone involved in magical practice, and are highly relevant when it comes to understanding the processes involved in the mysteries (see chapter 3).

For example, in shamanism, the descent into the underworld is the descent into the Jungian idea of Shadow, the dark repressed parts of our nature. This is the same process that is triggered after the second-degree initiation in Wicca (our Path of Fire). Jung also gives good explanations of how the astral levels work—that is, the levels beyond our reality—as well as explaining the importance of symbolism in magical work.

Knowledge-Based Ritual

In the past, ritual was taught by having students memorize the ritual frame: Circle casting, calling the quarters, et cetera. They were encouraged to read it directly from the coven's Book of Shadows or learn it word for word before ritual. Both of us have fond memories of stammering over words while trying to conduct rituals from scrunched-up pieces of paper or ungainly folders. Most Witches before the 1980s tried to conduct rituals "from their heads" rather than "from their hearts." This resulted in the repetition of the same ritual over and over again. There were, of course, advantages to this system of learning ritual. The students would quickly learn the words for casting the Circle, as well as those for calling the quarters, or face embarrassment in front of other coven members. But in many cases, students didn't necessarily know the significance of the symbolism they were using, or even know the true significance of what they were invoking. The same, of course, applied to the rituals for the eight Sabbat festivals of the year. Here we see the development of a dogma—ritual for ritual's sake—as students continued to practice what they had been taught. The system did not encourage spontaneous ritual.

The influence of shamanism in the 1980s began to change things. Members of the neo-Pagan community began to do rituals straight from the heart that "felt right at the time"! Unfortunately, there was very little thought put into such rituals beforehand, and those conducting the ritual often had little knowledge of how ritual or raised energy works. Sometimes there were dire consequences, as when the energy of the Circle got out of control and members found themselves becoming emotionally distraught.

In both sorts of ritual, the cause of the problem is lack of knowledge. We still teach students to learn the ritual frame, but only initially as a discipline. Once they have learned the basic Gardnerian/Alexandrian method of Circle casting, we start to encourage them to merge "head and heart" in ritual. We do this by encouraging our students to learn the background knowledge of any rite they are going to perform. For example, if they were going to conduct a festival they would learn the origins of it, as well as the symbolism and its purpose. With this knowledge, they should be able to do a successful ritual "from the heart" that flows naturally. Such a ritual would be spontaneous. The only writing we have is a listing of proceedings: Cast Circle, Call Quarters, Invoke Deity, et cetera. When you do ritual in this fashion, it ceases to be dogmatic and becomes an art form in its own right. You start to feel the energy of the ritual at work in the magical act you are performing. As we mentioned previously, it is not enough for a Witch to drive the car. The Witch must also to know how the engine works. We feel this method of ritual is more in keeping with the progressive tradition that Witchcraft is becoming. The only exceptions to this are those that maintain a bit of continuity and "tradition." We still use the same words we always have for some parts of ritual, such as the consecration of Cakes and Wine, and certain initiatory oaths.

The Importance of Life Experience

For a Witch to really understand the mysteries of life, death, and rebirth, they must experience them. Our ancestors were faced with the realities of life and death every day as they struggled to survive in a potentially hostile world. It is from these experiences that they saw what we call the "mysteries" impacting on every aspect of their lives. At a young age, everyone had experienced death firsthand in the death of a tribal member due to to an animal attack, disease, or injury. It was even in the preparation of food. Through hunting, killing, and skinning an animal, our ancestors came to understand the cycles of life and death within nature. Nowadays, most of us live in a world where we are separated from nature within towns and cities where we rarely get to stare death in the face. Our meat is conveniently prepacked and sealed, so we do not have to deal with the spiritual implications of where it originated.

Witchcraft is a holistic spirituality teaching the balance of both the physical and the spiritual. It is therefore not enough for a student Witch just to learn from books, in ritual, or in meditative exercise; they must seek out the experience of life itself if they are to fully understand the mysteries of life, death, and rebirth. This is one of the reasons why a Witch must be over a certain age to join the Craft, but even at eighteen (the accepted minimum) we are only just beginning to gain life experience. Life itself is also training for a Witch, and any student of Witchcraft needs to realize this. The collection of degrees and titles that exist in Wicca are meaningless unless there is also the accumulated wisdom that can only be gained over time. The student Witch must therefore seek out the experiences of life if they are to truly understand the mysteries of Witchcraft. This is the most important training a Witch can have.

NOTES

1 This same rite was show in the documentary film *The Occult Experience* by Nevil Drury.
2 From correspondence with authors, September 2003. Tom Delong (Gwydion Pendderwen) may have been another possible contributor.
3 A general reference to the Arthurian myths and the quest for the Holy Grail, by those in the Western tradition of magic. In the quest, Perceval discovers that his experiences are more important than the Grail in saving Arthur and restoring Logres, the wasteland.
4 Both of us independently were taught this. Doreen Valiente also considered Witchcraft to be an Earth-based magical system. This was discussed personally between her and Janet.
5 *The Healing Craft,* chap. 6, pp. 91–100.
6 Can be found in *Carl Gustav Jung: The Collected Works* (Routledge, 1959).

7

Spiritual Cosmology: Walking Between the Worlds

The world of our present consciousness is only one out of many worlds of consciousness that exist . . . those other worlds must contain experiences which have a meaning for our life also.
—WILLIAM JAMES[1]

Wicca has never truly had its own cosmology. In Gardnerian and Alexandrian practice, Cabala and its Tree of Life were used as the major magical philosophy from the end of the 1960s onward. The Tree of Life with its ten sephiroth mimics many of the earlier spiritual cosmologies of the peoples of Europe, but it does not give a true map of the many other worlds that exist. A true spiritual cosmology is a graphic interpretation of the magical levels of reality. Such a map must include physical, psychological, energetic, and spiritual approaches, create a holistic view of the cosmos, and abide by the old magical law "As above, so below." In practice, this means that you should be able to stand in a Witch's Circle and see the worlds around you on all levels. Cabala, often described as a philosophical and magical filing cabinet, simply does not do this. You cannot use it to explain the levels of the other worlds or realms, or how to access them. It is odd that Wicca, with its claim of European origins, ignored existing European cosmological systems, but this can be accounted for by the fact that it adopted a Judeo-Christian ritual magic approach to the cosmos rather than a truly pagan one. Its creators used what was available at the time; Cabala was in the most accessible literature of the period.

As time has gone on, Witches have begun to question the practices they were originally taught. Cabalistic ritual magic was one of these, and it has slowly been abandoned. As a result, Wicca has had no useful cosmology to speak of. Not surprisingly, many Witches have been drawn to Celtic and Northern European (Norse, Anglo-Saxon, et cetera) magical worldviews. Both Celtic and Norse have integrated spiritual cosmologies of shamanic origin, which allow travel between different levels of reality. What becomes obvious when studying both Celtic and Northern European magic is that there are strong similarities between them, which has led us to believe that there was once a common European system before the cultural divisions of later times.*

In some early hunter-gatherer cultures, the first cosmologies to appear were probably based around three worlds: an upper world, the abode of the gods; a middle world, the home of man; and a chthonic underworld, home of the ancestors. To early man, these worlds were around him; he saw them in everyday activities. The cave became the gateway to the underworld, and the mountain—often hazardous to climb—became the abode of the gods. This basic cosmological belief structure can still be found in many shamanic cultures today (the Greeks used it too). Spiritual cosmologies therefore reflect the physical nature of the universe as well as the internal psychology of man.

These three worlds are reflected in Jungian psychology as aspects of the individual psyche. The upper world becomes the *personal unconscious* (Freud's *subconscious*); the middle world becomes normal everyday *consciousness*, and the underworld becomes the *collective unconscious* (for more on this, see pages 85–86). In ancient Greek mythology, these three worlds are referred to as Olympus, Earth, and Hades. The underworld, in all myth, is a place of darkness and fear. It is what Jung called the "Shadow," and is the first level accessed when travelling between worlds. Hence, ancient man associated it with caves due to his fear of darkness and the possibility that a ferocious animal lived in it. This fear of the Shadow Realm is the same as a modern child's fear of the dark or of a monster under the bed. Christianity perverted this concept into hell, a place of retribution and terror.

In the modern Brythonic Celtic and Druidic traditions, which visualize the three worlds as concentric circles, one extra realm joins the three

---

* One view is that the divisions between Celtic and Germanic peoples were in fact as much a creation by the Roman Empire for political reasons as anything else. For a long while, the Germanic peoples were simply known as "the Northern Gauls." Nationalism during the 1800s only increased this view of racial divisions.

worlds. In the center is Annwn, the underworld. In his poem "Preiddu Annwn," Taliesin talks about having to cross the sea to reach Annwn. A water-crossing to reach the Realm of the Dead is common in many myths. In Ireland, this is reflected in megalithic sites such as Brú na Bóinne (New Grange) in County Meath, where it is necessary to cross the River Boyne (a goddess herself, by the way) to get to the burial chamber.* Water can therefore be seen to represent the unconscious mind. The next realm from the center is Abred, the middle world of struggle and evolution, and the world in which we live. The upper world of Celtic/Druidic cosmology differs for it is split into two distinct realms: Gwynfyd, the realm of purity and attainment, and Ceugant, which in the bardic tradition is the abode of God. This division is similar to the one that occurs in the Northern traditions: their upper realm is Asaheimr (the equivalent of Gwynfyd) with the addition of Odin's throne, Hlindskjalf,† (this being analogous to Ceugant). In Jungian psychology this is referred to as the *superconscious*, the unknowable divine itself.

To the other three realms were added a further four elemental realms, Earth (or in Norse/Icelandic, Ice), Air, Fire, and Water. Again, all these are present in humanity's surroundings as the building blocks of physical reality and the four states of matter (solid, gas, energy or plasma, and liquid). They quickly became associated with the four cardinal points owing to the environment people lived in. In Northern Europe, the south is associated with Fire because of the position of the sun at midday. Water was associated with the west in Europe because of the Atlantic Ocean. Similarly, the east is associated with Air because of the eastern winds, and the north with Earth because the facing sun nourishes its fertility. Of course, in the far North, this does not apply; hence, in Norse/Icelandic practice, Earth becomes Ice.

In British Gardnerian Wicca, the act of casting a Circle mimics the movement of the sun, which is why many Witches start in the east where the sun rises, and then continue in a clockwise direction. This, of course, does not apply in the Southern Hemisphere (Australia and New Zealand)

---

* There has always been much debate over the symbols on the entrance stone at Newgrange, which traditionally had to be climbed to enter the chamber. During a visit by Isaac Bonewits in 2001, both he and Gavin noticed that the markings on the stones bear a strong resemblance to the eddies of the River Boyne. The stone may, in fact, be a representation of the river.

† In the Eddas, only Odin can sit on this throne, being "the All-Father." The only exception to this has been Frey, who surreptitiously mounted the throne (from *For Scirnis*, Elder Edda).

where, after rising in the east, the sun then follows an anticlockwise direction. This also affects the seasons, putting them 180 degrees out on the calendar. Hence, spring equinox in the Northern Hemisphere becomes autumn equinox in the South, and summer solstice becomes winter solstice, etc. Witches in the Southern Hemisphere have therefore had to adjust their practices accordingly, showing the necessity for flexibility and a lack of dogma in practice.

In Irish Celtic culture, these four elemental realms were referred to as the cities of Falias (north), Gorias (east), Finias (south) and Murias (west). The underworld was referred to as Tir Bo Thuinn (the Land Under the Water), and the Realm of the Gods (and, of course, the heroic figures of Irish myth) became commonly known as Tir Nan Og (the Land of Youth).*

The best example of these magical realms combined together is the Norse Yggdrassil, or the world tree. The most complete description can be found in the Icelandic *Poetic Edda*. In the first chapter, the "Voluspa" (the "Song of the Seeress"), a practitioner of Seidr, descends the tree in trance and describes the worlds that exist on its branches.† The tree is an ancient motif for the *axis mundi* (central axis) of the world and is sym-bolically important in numerous cultures.‡ In Ireland, it was believed that a great oak stood in the center of the island at Uisneach, County West-meath, one of the five great *Bilé* trees that brought luck to the provinces.§ In Assyro-Babylonian culture, there is the moon tree, and in Anglo-Saxon religious practice, a stone pillar was placed in the center of the temple to represent *Irminsul,* the axis of the world. Even in the Middle Ages, the

---

* Irish mythology was a fusion of many different regional mythologies, which became fused at the time of Christianity. There are many different names for the same realm to be found in Irish mythology because of this.

† This one description, from one Icelandic prophecy, has come to shape the whole Ásatrú view on cosmology. There is no doubt that it is an accurate portrayal of the Northern European Tree of Life, but it is nonetheless just one of possibly many interpretations. What has made it powerful is the fact that it is based on psychic rather than intellectual experience.

‡ In many cultures it is believed that man was originally born from the trees. In Norse, the first man and woman were Ask and Embla (Ash and Elm). It is interesting to note that even Australian aboriginals have a similar myth.

§ These five were the Bíle Uisnig at Uisneach; the Craobh Daithi at Farbill, County Westmeath; the Bíle Tartan, an ash tree, located near Ardbraccan, County Meath; the Eo Mughna, a yew tree; and the Eo Rossa, Old Leighlin, County Carlow, also a yew tree.

custom of placing *perrons* (stone pillars) in the center of a town or village was common practice. These represented the center of village life, and in the later Christian period, were replaced with the village or town cross.

The Norse world tree, Yggdrassil, includes the seven worlds we have already mentioned, plus a further two, making nine. These two additional realms probably belonged to the pre-Indo-European culture.* The central axis consists of the uppermost realms—

Perron, Rathkenny, County Meath, Ireland

Asgardhr, the abode of the gods and consciousness; Ljossalfheimr, the realms of the Light Elves and the intellect; Midgardhr, the abode of man; Svartalfheimr, the realm of the dwarves and emotion; and finally Helheimr, the underworld, the abode of the goddess Hel and the unconscious. These five worlds make up the Axis of Consciousness, connected by the axis mundi. Midgardhr has the four elemental realms revolving around it, making up the physical realms. These are Niflheimr—Ice and matter; Jotunheimr—Air and motion; Vanaheimr—Water and balance; and Muspellheimr—Fire and energy. This system of worlds continues to be taught within Ásatrú (modern Norse magical practice).

From examining Celtic, Norse, and other sources, it has become apparent to us that there is a common root source for the cosmologies we have mentioned. Over the last few years, we have tried to reconstruct

---

*   These two realms are Svartalfheimr and Ljossalfheimr; the Realm of the Dark Elves and the Realm of the Light Elves respectively.

this, with quite successful results. We believe the root source follows much the same pattern as Yggdrassil and its associated worlds. This is hardly surprising, as it is a reflection of magical reality. When you stand in the Witches' magic Circle, you stand within the first seven realms—you center yourself in the universe around you. This spiritual act of centering allows you to understand the universe and its levels of reality. It is the first act any magical practitioner does when creating sacred space.

Figure 3 The Lady's Star

Seven is an important number in magic. There are seven chakras, seven planetary correspondences, and seven days of the week. Although there can be said to be nine realms, only seven are fully accessible to the magical practitioner. In Anglo-Saxon magical practice, the most important magical symbol was the seven-pointed star—often called the "fairy," or more correctly, the "elven" star (see figure 3). It can still be found in stained-glass windows in churches in the south of England where it is called "the Lady's Star." It clearly has associations with the Madonna as *Theotokos*—and thereby the Goddess.

When standing in the magic Circle, you stand in the first realm; it is from here that you experience the others. The four elemental realms of Earth, Air, Fire, and Water are on a horizontal axis, with the two central realms above and below you on the vertical. The world tree therefore represents a common magical symbol. The benefits of this system are apparent, as no other system we have found offers the same level of integration into practical magical and spiritual work—but there is something more important about it. From our experiences, we have discovered it maps psychological processes, the levels of reality, and the physical realities of magic. This is particularly important when exploring the mysteries, as it grants the seeker a systematic guide by which he or she experiences the mysteries directly (given time and practice).

We have found a great deal of similarity among the experiences of people who use this schema. Without prompting, they often describe seeing the same symbolism and the same guardians while meditating. This has led us to use it as our primary spiritual cosmology when we teach our students how to "walk between the worlds" along the spiral paths that connect the realms. Our experiences have shown that there is a spiritual truth in this system.

One might think that after the advent of the Age of Reason and the Renaissance (when it was discovered that the earth circled the sun) that man would have gone past the point of centering himself in the universe as he did in pagan times. The facts actually show the reverse: man continues to create monuments in every major city to mark the center of his world. London has Nelson's Column, Paris has the Eiffel Tower, and Washington, DC has the Washington Memorial. While writing this book, a metal pole called the Millennium Spike was erected in the center of Dublin. The spiritual yearning for a physical center for our lives remains, even in modern society, and is reflected in these contemporary monuments. They are the modern Irminsuls and Yggdrassils. Our need for a center reflects the spiritual truth that we are all, ultimately, at the center of our own universes.*

---

* Albert Einstein validated this need with his theory of relativity—in that that our position and our movement within the universe is really relative to our perception of it.

A WICCAN COSMOLOGY

The Axis of Consciousness

The Realm of Experience: This is the central realm on the axis of the tree and corresponds with the *id*, the element of our psyche that strives for the most basic needs: food, shelter, sex, et cetera. The id forces us into the world and causes us to experience it. It is satiated or repressed by the effect of the other five realms that intersect with it, such as the Realm of Water that makes us feel emotion. This intersection of realms is symbolized by the crossroads, a traditional meeting place of Witches and

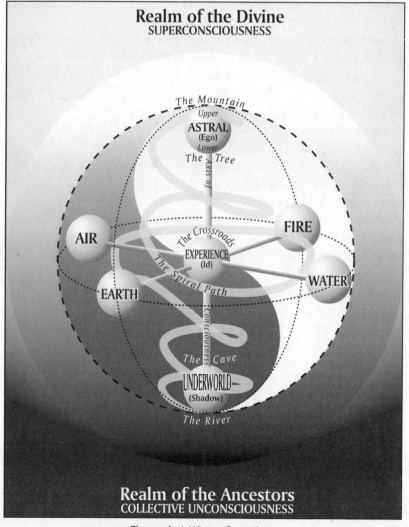

Figure 4 A Wiccan Cosmology

sacred to the goddess Hecate, and where she was traditionally invoked by Drawing Down the Moon.[2] In Celtic/Druidic mythology, this realm is Abred, and in Norse mythology it can be equated with Midgardhr, or Middle Earth.

The Astral Realm: This is above the central Realm of Experience. In both Freudian and Jungian terms, it is the abode of the ego, and thus anything we perceive here is clothed by our ego. Unfortunately, this makes our understanding of this realm subjective rather than objective, so to fully realize the experiences here, it is necessary to descend into the underworld (Jung's Shadow Realm) and to pass through the elemental realms. The Astral Realm is where one finds the world tree with which to travel between the worlds. The Astral Realm intersects with the world above it, the Realm of the Divine, where many of the entities and symbols found on the astral plane originate. It is in the Astral Realm that one meets both one's guide and guardian, and where the shamanic totem animal can be found. In Celtic/Druidic mythology, it is world of Gwynfyd; in the Norse, it is Ljossalfheim (the Realm of the Light Elves).

The Underworld: This corresponds with Jung's "personal unconscious" where the Shadow dwells. It is here that the ego sends the impulses it wants to repress. The Shadow can be likened to the Norse Svartalfheimr, the Realm of Dwarf and Dark Fairy, and the world of the Dark Elves. Deep within this realm are all the fears and negative aspects of the self that are rejected by the personality. Not surprisingly, many of the images are frightening. To understand what you see here, you must face yourself. Before exploring this realm, it is also necessary to find a guide— the psychopompos or power animal. In this realm, the seeker meets the Dark Goddess of Wisdom (the Goddess of Witchcraft) who travels up from the Ancestral Realm. It is she who holds the mirror up so you can see your true image. In this way, you can find your "soul," or anima/animus, which also abides here. The anima and animus exist in an area the neo-Jungians call "the Bright Shadow," which is often symbolized as a pleasant peaceful area hidden among the dark images of the Shadow.* The underworld can be accessed several ways, and each method allows access to different areas and grants specific kinds of knowledge. One way is to descend the roots of the world tree, found in the Astral Realm, or

---

* In the Sleeping Beauty myth, the underworld (the Shadow) is the castle and wasteland, and the Bright Shadow is the finely draped room that Sleeping Beauty (the anima) sleeps in, waiting to be rescued. She is of course, guarded by the dragon, the Guardian of the Mysteries.

one can descend the left-hand Spiral Path into the traditional entrance to the Shadow, which is the cave. There are, of course, other traditional entrance symbols, such as the well—an entrance taken through the Realm of Water. Whatever way is chosen, dark areas are always barred by the Guardian of the Mysteries unless the person is ready to proceed.

The Elemental Realms

The Realm of Earth: This realm (on the material level of reality) gives us our experiences of solid matter, form, and substance. Intersecting with the Realm of Experience, it gives the sensation of touch. It is therefore the element that governs manifestation. But it also intersects with the lower area of the Astral Realm to give us intellectual stability, wisdom, and psychic grounding. The association with stability therefore makes this realm a place of restriction and of preservation of the status quo. The symbols found here come up from the realm below, the underworld, and relate directly to these two functions. Thus, Earth is also the element of death and the grave. The cave or dolmen entrance to the underworld is found here, as well as the place of grounding symbolized as a stone circle or forest grove.

The Realm of Air: This realm gives us the sensations of smell and taste, both associated with the air of breath. It gives us our intellectual capability when it intersects with the lower Astral Realm, allowing logical reasoning and thought as well as the ability to communicate. Because of its mental correspondence, it is possible to access the Akashic Records through the Realm of Air. The memory of past lives and events both personal and universal are contained here—hence its association with knowledge. This may be symbolically seen as a great building, a library, which can be accessed by the traveler when the time is right.

The Realm of Fire: The element of Fire is traditionally associated with sight. Our drive and our "spark" come to us from the Astral Realm through Fire. It is the element of raw and uncontained energy, with potential for both creation and destruction. The related symbolism reflects this. The magical sword or athame is forged by smithcraft, so it is not surprising that sometimes the traveler finds a forge with the smith hard at work. The smith can reshape you to travel to other realms by destroying the old self and creating a new one within the fire of the forge.

The Realm of Water: Physically, this realm gives us the sense of hearing and is responsible for the manifestation of all our senses in the other elements. This is the element of emotion. In the Astral Realm, emotions manifest positively, while negative emotions are repressed into the underworld. Because of this, it is the most commonly used elemental realm by which to access the underworld. Commonly found symbolism includes the well, the lake, or the river. While wells and lakes may be used to descend into the underworld, rivers are often used to mark the boundaries between the different realms, as they mark psychological crossing points.

The Outer Realms

The Realm of the Divine: This is what is referred to by Jungian psychologists as the *superconscious*. The occultist knows it as the Higher Astral. It is found above the Astral Realm. It is the Realm of the Divine, the unknowable force that is the intelligence of the universe itself. In Druidic terms, it is *Ceugant*. To understand it, think of "heaven" and "God" as in fact the same thing. Cabalists would call this *Ain Soph Aur*—the unknowable. It has no form as such, until it descends into the realms below, where it takes on the forms that human consciousness has assigned to it. For example, in passing through the Astral Realm it becomes what we know as a god or goddess. It cannot manifest without this mediation first taking place. Hence, deities have associations with the elements, the underworld, et cetera. It is an unattainable realm, which means we cannot enter it in our current state of consciousness, although a gifted traveler or psychic may catch a glimpse of this realm. This is the place our souls ultimately reach after death, before reincarnation. The Buddhists refer to this realm as Nirvana, and seek to rejoin it rather than reincarnating.

The Realm of the Ancestors: This is the collective unconscious, where the many images of Jung's numinous archetypes are stored. It is positioned below the underworld. This is the true Realm of the Dead and the ancestors, and in many myths it can only be accessed by dying, by crossing the river of death itself. A good example is the Greek myth of the river Styx. The Realm of the Ancestors has been portrayed in many ways, as Helheimr to the Norse and Annwn to the Druids. The Greeks saw it as Tartarus, the abode of Hades. It is important to recognize the culturally different ways to view it, as it is easy to confuse this realm with the underworld. Like the Realm of the Divine, it cannot be accessed directly from the Realm of Experience. Its passage through the other realms shapes the images originating from it, just as happens with the Realm of the Divine. It is possible to stand at its gates and see some of the images within it, but it can be dangerous to attempt to enter it. In the flood of imagery that would overcome your senses, you would literally risk losing your mind. In all cultures, this is a realm of danger, death, and horrific images. The sign on its door has always read "Keep out!" or face challenges to your sanity.

Guides and Guardians

The Astral Guardian

This guardian is our Higher Self, the aspect of our being that exists on the higher astral level, the Realm of the Divine. It is that part of our soul that is permanently connected to the unknowable divine. It is linked strongly with the crown center, particularly when this center has been opened. Its purpose is to protect us spiritually and psychically from intrusion. It tries to guide us through our lives by encouraging our spiritual and karmic development. In Cabalistic and Western magic, it is often referred to as the *Holy Guardian Angel*. In magical practice, the objective was to join with it, to obtain unification of the higher and lower selves. This still applies in all true occult practices, including Witchcraft. Its symbolism may take the form of a deity when someone dedicates himself or herself to serve a specific god or goddess. It is our *primary life-guide* (for more on this see pages 172–173). It may even manifest through the anima or animus if the individual's spiritual potential has been repressed. Any exercise to find the Astral Guardian will normally involve exploring the higher areas of the astral and calling the guardian to descend to meet you there.

The Astral Guide

The role of the Astral Guide is to show us around the Astral Realms that are safe to access at any given stage of our spiritual development. It therefore tends to be encountered only in the Astral Realm and higher levels of the elemental realms. It can be seen as a lower aspect of the Astral Guardian, and can manifest in human form or as a totem animal. In shamanic magical practices, one can ride totem animals to explore the worlds. It is important to realize that totem animals are not power animals: totem animals have a completely different role, one restricted to the Astral Realms. They generally take the form of the animal or mythological creature that a person's ego aspires to be like, such as a dragon, unicorn, lion, eagle, et cetera—but usually winged creatures. It is important to realize that the Astral Guide will be clothed by your ego in this realm, and that you will be unable to see its true form until you have performed an underworld descent to understand your own ego.

The Guardian of the Mysteries

The role of the Guardian of the Mysteries is to protect the mysteries from those who are unready to experience them. It guards both the entrance to the underworld and the gate to the Realm of the Ancestors. Its form will always be terrifying, to scare the seeker and thereby warn of the dangers beyond. It challenges the seeker with a question or a riddle. If not answered satisfactorily, the seeker will be turned back until they are ready to proceed. To continue anyway is to face its wrath! In the Greek mysteries, the Guardian was Cerberus, the monster sometimes seen as male (a three-headed dog), sometimes as female (a hybrid of lioness, lynx, and sow), who challenged everyone approaching the gates of Hades, the underworld.

The Underworld Guide—the Psychopompos and the Power Animal

This guide performs a similar role to the Astral Guide, but it helps the seeker explore the Shadow Realm (the underworld). In modern Wicca, Cernunnos—the Horned God and Lord of Death and Resurrection—performs this role. In Northern Tradition, Odin or Woden fulfills the same role. In the mysteries of Greece and then Ptolemaic Egypt it was Hermes, in the forms of Hermes and Anubis, respectively.* All these images of the psychopompos have animal aspects about them: Hermes was the father of coven-hoofed Pan, Cernunnos is part stag, and Anubis has the head of a Jackal. Odin/Woden is the exception, but as two wolves and two ravens escort him, the animal aspect is still there. In shamanism, the psychopompos is traditionally the power animal. As mentioned earlier, it is important to understand that the power animal is very different from the totem animal. The power animal is generally a real mammal or bird, and very rarely a reptile. Before any exploration of the underworld, the psychopompos should be actively sought by descending to find it via the id and the Realm of Experience. In seeking it, a bridge is made between the collective unconscious of human and animal. The animal recognizes the id in the seeker as its own and comes to meet the seeker; the same will apply to the psychopompos as a deity-form. Thus, when you seek a guide to the underworld, the Underworld Guide finds you. Once revealed, the Underworld Guide needs to be connected with regularly. It is traditional in shamanism to exercise your power animal, often by dancing with it. The same applies to the Underworld Guide—whatever form it takes. It is able to act as a guide in the underworld because of its association with

---

* According to *Isis in the Graeco-Roman World*, they were sometimes combined in the Graeco-Egyptian mysteries as Hermanubis.

the individual's id and with the Shadow, which is the area where many impulses from the id are repressed.

The Four Elemental Guardians

Every Witch who calls the quarters effectively has invoked the elemental guardians. They are the same "Lords of the Watchtowers"[3] that are invoked in traditional Wiccan practice. These are the spirits, the higher forms of the elements themselves, whose role is to control the raw form of the element—hence the need to invoke them in ritual when using elemental-based magic. What is rarely talked about is the fact that they can also act as guides to their own realms. They may manifest in several different guises. They may relate directly to their gendered association, a maiden for Water, a mother for Earth, a young male warrior for Fire, and an old wizard figure for Air. But they can be just easily represented by other forms such as mythological creatures (e.g., a dragon for Fire, et cetera.). It will depend very much on the individual, as most symbolism does. These guardians can be met at the entrance to each elemental realm as you ascend the Spiral Path. If you try to enter their realms and you are not ready, they will challenge you with a question before allowing you to pass.

The Spiral Path

The Spiral Path is a pathway that starts from the bottom realm, the Realm of the Ancestors, and ascends through each realm spiraling clockwise as it goes. After leaving the underworld, it then proceeds to spiral past the entrance to each of the elements starting with Earth and then proceeding through Air, Fire, and finally Water. At the last elemental realm, it becomes the "bridge" to the Astral Realm. After passing over the bridge, the path divides into two, a left-hand path and a right-hand path. Between these two paths exists the Tree of Life, with its roots passing down into the Realm of Experience and finally into the underworld and Ancestral Realms. Its trunk goes upwards and branches into the higher Realm of the Divine. The right-hand path takes you into the Astral Realm, while the left-hand descends, anticlockwise through the elements again, and into the Realm of the Underworld. It is at this junction where the Astral Guide can be met.

Exercise One: Ascending the Spiral Path

This practical visualization exercise in exploring the cosmology of the other worlds can be done in a coven or group setting. It can also be done individually, but one would need someone who can read out the following path-working, or one would have to memorize the realms and the path-working.

This exercise is designed to give you a taste of the realms. It lays the ground rules for the exploration of these worlds as you walk between them. Be aware that everything that you meet here is real, although clothed in imagery generated from your own unconscious mind and from that of the collective unconscious. All entities should be treated with the reverence they deserve. If you treat them as real, they will act as real. Be aware that many of the symbols we have talked about may appear slightly differently than you expect. Do not be put off by this. This is normal. We each clothe these experiences in the symbols that we understand. Just allow yourself to flow with the experience.

You first need to get yourself comfortable in a quiet, warm room. Breathe rhythmically and deeply for several minutes before you start (you may want to use the same breathing technique used for opening the chakras). Try to block out all the memories and activities of the day that seem to intrude upon your thoughts. Visualize yourself in darkness, quiet and alone:

"You are in darkness. You are standing, your feet on a path of stones and pebbles. You can feel them beneath your feet and hear them crunching against each other.

"Slowly you can make out points of light emerging above your line of vision—the stars twinkling in the heavens.

"As you breathe in, you can feel the cold air of the night in your lungs. You start to slowly make out images in the darkness.

"Ahead of you, you can make out a path winding upwards and to the right, through a forest of dense trees.

"Above the tree line, you can see a new sickle moon rising, lighting the path ahead of you that ascends, always to the right, into the darkness.

"You breathe in, and you can feel the cold air of the night in your lungs. Slowly you start to make your way up the path, heading toward the sickle moon set amongst the twinkling stars.

"You can hear the crunch of pebbles beneath your feet, and hear the rustling and calls of the animals of the night as you commence your journey.

"As you slowly round the first bend, you can make out two points of light in the distance and a shadowy figure between them.

"You breathe in, and you can feel the cold air of the night in your lungs. As you look up, the moon has grown fuller, and is now reaching almost a quarter, set amongst the twinkling stars.

"As you continue your journey along the path, you can see the figure more clearly. It is standing between what now appears to be two torches.

"You come closer and closer, until finally you stand before the Guardian of Earth. The guardian asks you a question. You reply, and then you continue on your journey up the path, always to the right.

"You breathe in, and you can feel the cold air of the night in your lungs. As you look up, the moon has grown, and is now reaching almost a half, set amongst the twinkling stars.

"As you slowly round the second bend, you can make out two points of light in the distance and a shadowy figure between them.

"You can hear the crunch of pebbles beneath your feet, and hear the rustling and calls of the animals of the night as you commence your journey.

"As you continue your journey along the path, you can see the figure more clearly. It is standing between what now appears to be two torches.

"You come closer and closer, until finally you stand before the Guardian of Air. The guardian asks you a question. You reply, and then you continue on your journey up the path, always to the right.

"You breathe in, and you can feel the cold air of the night in your lungs. As you look up, the moon has grown, and is now almost three quarters full, set amongst the twinkling stars.

"As you slowly round the third bend, you can make out two points of light in the distance and a shadowy figure between them.

"You can hear the crunch of pebbles beneath your feet, and hear the rustling and calls of the animals of the night as you commence your journey.

"As you continue your journey along the path, you can see the figure more clearly. It is standing between what now appears to be two torches.

"You come closer and closer, until finally you stand before the Guardian of Fire. The guardian asks you a question. You reply, and then you continue on your journey up the path, always to the right.

"You breathe in, and you can feel the cold air of the night in your lungs. As you look up, the moon is now almost full set amongst the twinkling stars, and in the distance you can hear the quiet trickling of water.

"As you slowly round the fourth bend, you can make out two points of light in the distance, and a shadowy figure between them.

"You can hear the crunch of pebbles beneath your feet, and the sound of water now seems to be louder. Its roar fills the forest.

"As you continue your journey along the path, you can see the figure more clearly. It is standing between what now appears to be two torches, and behind them you can make out a bridge crossing over the river that you have been hearing.

"You come closer and closer, until finally you stand before the Guardian of Water. The guardian asks you a question. You reply. The guardian points to the bridge beckoning you to cross into the next world.

"With the sound of the roar of water in your ears, you cross the bridge, the torrent of water beneath you. You feel the material the bridge is made of beneath your feet and make your way to the other side.

"You breathe in and you can feel the cold air of the night in your lungs. As you look up, the moon is now full, set amongst the twinkling stars.

"You can hear the crunch of pebbles beneath your feet, but otherwise all is quiet as you continue the journey along the path.

"The path seems to straighten, and very slowly you begin to make out something ahead that seems to block the path.

"As you move closer, you realize it is the Great Tree, the Tree of Life itself. It seems to grow larger and larger as you approach it.

"You are finally standing in front of it. As you look up, you see the tree seemingly disappear into the heavens. Its great trunk is almost three times the width it would take for your arms to enfold it.

"You can see that the path divides into two in front of the Great Tree. One path goes to the right, always curving on to the right and up, the continuation of the path you are already on. And one path goes to the left, always curving downwards in that direction into the darkness of the night.

"Looking down you see the great buttressed roots disappear into the ground, and you notice a hole that is big enough to squeeze through if you dare—the entrance that would take you to the cave where your Underworld Guide resides.

"You become aware of a presence. As you step back from the tree, you become sure that you are not alone. You are not. From behind the tree, a figure appears. Under the light of the moon, you can make out the figure's face and clothing.

"The figure is your guide to this world. You ask them their name. They tell you, and explain their purpose for being here at this time to meet you. They tell you that they will meet you here again whenever you wish to explore this realm.

"But now it is time to return. Time to return to the world of illusion hidden in the normality of everyday living. Return. Return. Return to the place where you started, the place where this all began.

"Now open your eyes."

After completing this exercise, you may feel light-headed. If you do, this is an indication that you need to be grounded (see the grounding and chakra-closing exercises found on page 151). It is not unusual in such exercises for things to happen at a different pace from that of the person reading the path-working aloud. If this happens, go at your own speed and allow things to happen in your own time. Unexpected things may also happen. One of the entities you meet—possibly one of the elemental guardians or even your guide—may give you a gift. In shamanic terms, this is a *totem*; an object of power that connects you to the realm it originated from. If the elemental Guardian of Air gives you an object, it will be associated with the element of Air, et cetera. There are many things it could be: a precious stone, a flower, or even a feather. If you receive such a gift, you should try to find a physical token of the same object, as it will help you connect with that realm in future magical working. Many practitioners of shamanism carry a small bag for such objects. It is commonly known as a spirit bag, and is traditional in many cultures. In ancient Irish lore, it was known as a crane bag, while Native Americans might call it a medicine bag.

The Creation and Use of the Astral Temple

Constructing and using an astral temple has always been an integral part of the Western magical tradition. The Order of the Golden Dawn, the Ordo Templi Orientis, and all the magical orders of the twentieth century made it a major part of their magical practice. The first time the idea of such an astral construct was publicly published was in Dion Fortune's *The Sea Priestess* in 1957.* Prior to this publication, the practice was a closely

---

* Dion Fortune's Moon Temple is unusual in many ways, as it connects all the realms of the Axis of Consciousness in one place. Over the years, Janet has regularly performed the Journey to the Moon Temple with dramatic results. It has not been unusual for the spirits of passed loved ones to appear, as well as personal messages from the gods and goddesses.

guarded secret. Dion Fortune's work became an important part of the Gardnerian Wiccan corpus. Over the years, her Moon Temple of Isis has gained more and more form. It has become a permanent construction of symbolism on the astral level. Much of this is due to the fact that her writings are still published and read by Witches and occultists in general, which has the effect of giving more power to the construct. The method for creating an astral temple is no different from that of consecrating a magical item and creating an astral double for it. The major difference is that a physical token is not necessary, although a painting or piece of sculpture may be used for this purpose.

In a working magical coven that has built up a gestalt or coven mind, such a temple may have already been created, although the coven may not be aware of it. The more the coven works in a consecrated Circle, the stronger the temple will become. This also applies to solitary Witches who create their own personal astral temples. The coven may give form to their temple by deciding what it looks like, what materials it is constructed of, and (as previously mentioned) even have someone draw a sketch or paint the joint interpretation of the temple. This piece of art can then become an important centerpiece of the physical Circle when they are working, mounted on the wall behind the altar. Once this is done, they can access the temple by ascending the Spiral Path into the Astral Realm to ask the Astral Guide to take them there.

The visualization of the temple should be carried out regularly, both as a coven and individually. The temple will gain more power and form on the astral level this way. It is important that all the coven members agree to visualize the same temple. The astral doubles of the magical tools of the coven should be visualized there, as well as other symbols such as the statues of the gods and goddesses used by the coven. Once the coven members are happy that the temple has been built, it can then be used magically.

One uses the temple magically by visualizing the performance of magical rites within it. An advantage of this is that the coven does not actually have to physically meet in the same place to carry out a ritual. Coven meetings can take place on an astral level in the astral temple. The coven members just have to have a quiet place in which to visualize and meditate upon the temple.

The astral temple's primary purpose in the Western magical tradition is to invoke gods and goddesses directly, and to interact with the Astral Guardian. It acts as a gateway for these entities to enter directly from the Realm of the Divine. Speaking from our experiences with the temple, we can say that it is much easier to connect with Deity directly on this level than on the material. You just have to verbally call them within the temple, and if they are ready, they will appear.

Covens that use astral constructs all speak of having similar experiences. We have heard many stories from individuals and covens who have met within the temple at a predesignated time. When they have talked to each other later in the material world, their stories about their experiences have been uncannily similar, even down to what they talked about. These are common occurrences.

NOTES

1 Quoted in K. Wilber's *The Spectrum of Consciousness*, page 24. William James (1842–1910) was an original thinker in and between the disciplines of physiology, psychology, and philosophy.
2 Ovid and Varro mention Hekate being 'drawn down,' and separately mention her worship at crossroads.
3 "The Lords of the Watchtowers" are a common teaching in the Gardnerian and Alexandrian Traditions. They are usually invoked by using the Invoking Pentagram Ritual of Earth in these traditions (see figure 7, page 206), rather than by visualizing the Guardians themselves.

8

Sorcery:
The Magical Art of Witchcraft

Real magic is energy-based, not ceremony-based.
—SKIRNIR FREYASSONN[1]

T he word *sorcery* tends to cause a negative reaction, mainly due to the stereotyping that has occurred in fictional literature and films. The average person's mind holds images of wizards with flames coming from their fingers, and enchantresses glamouring knights in shining armor. The word *sorcery* is therefore unpopular among neo-Pagans, who find that this fantasy portrayal of the word has demeaned it in some way.

By the Middle Ages, sorcery had come to mean alchemy and high magic, which was a form of magic based on Judeo-Christian rather than pagan thought. The word *sorcery* has origins in the French word *sorcier*. It is traditionally used in that language to describe a witch. But even this word has its origins in an older word from which we derive the word *source* or *to source*. This suggests the idea that sorcerers or witches sourced their power from the divine Spirit. This is important as it is no different to the way contemporary Eurasian shamans claim to derive their magical power directly from the "spirits."[2] A good example of this in ancient Pagan practice is the Norse runes, which are actually a system for representing the different energies of the universe that were magically directed by the *vitki* (magician). The Welsh and Irish Celts had a similar system called Ogham, where the energies of the universe were symbolized as trees. In this chapter and the next, we present a combination of certain received traditions like these with new innovations developed in response to the requirements of our time.

What is this energy? From the perspective of the Witch, it is the very energy of life itself. When someone interested in Witchcraft comes to us, we have a simple test. We get them to close their eyes and, with their palms up, ask them to put their hands out in front of them. We then ask them if they wish to see some magic. How they react to what happens next is important. When they open their eyes, they discover that we have placed a simple houseplant in its pot on their outstretched hands. We look for the recognition in their eyes, that magic is not separate or super-natural, but is life itself.

The idea that magical power and the energy of life are one and the same is not new. It is well known in the spiritual practices of Taoism, and more importantly to us, in the Indo-European magical practices of Hinduism, commonly known as Tantra.* It has appeared even in science fiction, which can be perceived as modern mythology.† Almost everyone is aware of the idea of "the Force" in the *Star Wars* films. The Jedi Knights are, by any definition of the word, sorcerers! This puts the stereotyped images more into perspective. When we see the wizard with flames coming from his fingers, we are seeing power, the controlled use of energy, coming from his fingers—his aura. In the glamoury of the enchantress, we are seeing the use of both the aura and the energy centers in the body to create a perceived image eliciting an appropriate response.

So what is the difference between power and energy? Energy is the raw unmolded material, as opposed to power, which is controlled energy put to use. In her first two books, *The Spiral Dance* and *Dreaming the Dark*, Starhawk talks about power in several ways.[3] Her discussion applies to magical energy as well. *Power-over* is the manipulation of another person's energy in order to control him or her;‡ whereas, *power-from-within* describes the Witch's role as one who helps individuals come into

---

* We would like to point out that this word is often misused to mean purely sexual magic. The correct word for this is *Shaktiism*.

† Much science fiction has story lines based on old mythological precepts. *Star Wars* is one example given, but also the series *Star Trek: Voyager,* which follows the pattern of Homer's *Odyssey*. These stories also follow the theories put down by Joseph Campbell in his *Hero With A Thousand Faces*. Science fiction is a modern development of mythology. So it's not surprising that so many Witches are science-fiction fans!

‡ The continual use of power-over practices within Wicca has also contributed to the dogma-rebellion and dogma-acceptance patterns that continue to occur in the Wiccan movement (see chapter 2, pages 39–40).

their own power. This is a perfect description of a priestess or priest. While we agree with Starhawk, we would like to add another complementary perspective. Ultimately it is not our power, as it derives from the *divine* itself and will eventually return to it.

The energy of life is dynamic; it does not stand still. The energy of the aura and the seven chakras is no different; it is transient, always moving. It is like running water. You may try to hold on to it in your cupped hand, but it will eventually seep through your fingers, go back into the earth, and make its way back to the great sea that it came from. It is not possible to hold on to it. So to make any magical use of it, it becomes necessary to work with the flow and ebb of this energy, allowing it to flow in the direction it wants to flow. In traditional Anglo-Saxon magic this is conceptualized as the idea of *Wyrd*, where this flow is also seen to affect the whole course of your life, in microcosmic/macrocosmic fashion (for more on this see pages 164–166). This philosophy has strong similarities to the ideas found in Eastern Taoism. To work against this flow, to coax the creative energy into a direction it would not naturally go, can be perceived as the misuse that Starhawk refers to as "power-over." In popular terms, this is commonly known as black magic, although we consider this a misleading term, as magic and energy are neither black nor white.[4] Because this energy is effectively on loan to us, we therefore have a responsibility to use it wisely and ethically, or face the karmic consequences.[*]

Being of divine origin, its use connects us with the gods and goddesses in a more direct way. By practicing magic correctly, we are using this divine energy and allowing it to direct us in its use. By doing so, it will (eventually and in the fullness of time) bring us face to face with the mysteries, as "the first thing that magic changes is the self," whether we intend it to (see pages 46–50, 209–210).

The Chakra System of Magic

Madame Blavatsky and the Theosophy movement almost certainly introduced the Hindu/Buddhist chakra system into Western occult thinking at the end of the nineteenth century. In Indian philosophical thought, the chakras (or chakrams) have been known since at least since the seventh century, the time of the first transcription of the Vedas. An early form of the system probably existed well before this date, and there is some circumstantial evidence that a proto-chakra system was known throughout

---

[*] It is important to note that these Karmic consequences are not the Judeo-Christian idea of "divine retribution," but a natural process of rebalancing in accordance with magical law (see Appendix A).

the earlier migratory Indo-European culture. This would have brought this bodily energy system into pre-Christian Germanic, Celtic, and Greek mystical thought.

The symbolism of the caduceus in Greek myth bears a striking resemblance to the chakra system. The serpents may represent the path of kundalini and the places where they cross represent the chakra centers. The caduceus is also the symbol of Hermes, who, as Hermes Trismegistus, is equated with Anubis as the Guardian of the Mysteries. This symbolism of the caduceus was cited by the Theosophy movement as evidence of a similar system in Europe, and notes on this relationship were first published in C. W. Leadbeater's *The Chakras—A Monograph* as early as 1927.[5] Thus many Western occultists started working with chakras around the turn of the nineteenth and twentieth centuries.

Within Western occultism there has always been the doctrine of "don't mix traditions." A belief that it is dangerous to mix magical systems has resulted in the idea that Western philosophical thinking does not always readily combine with Eastern. This dogma has its origins in ceremonial magic rather than pagan philosophy, which has always been ready to adapt to new ideas due to its polytheistic philosophy (see pages 36–38). Regardless of whether you believe the evidence for the existence of a Western system of energy points of Indo-European origin, it did not stop occultists from working with them. It soon became apparent to them that the chakra system, and the energies it represents, is as real as the physical organs of the body. In some magical orders they were an important part of their mystical doctrine, but their use was kept well hidden. Aleister Crowley and his Ordo Templi Orientis used them extensively, but Crowley refers to them only fleetingly in several of his works as "the Seven Seals." In his poem *AHA!*[6] he describes opening "the great gate," the access to the astral levels through the crown chakra:

> There are seven keys to the great gate,
> Being eight in one and one in eight,
> First, let the body of thee be still,
> Bound by the cerements of will,
> Corpse-rigid; thus though mayst abort
> The fidget-babes that tease the thought.
> Next, let the breath-rhythm be low,
> Easy, regular, and slow;
> So that thy being be in tune

With the great sea's Pacific swoon.
Third, let thy life be pure and calm,
Swayed softly as a windless palm.
Fourth, let the will-to-live be bound
To the one love of the Profound.
Fifth, let the thought, divinely free
From sense, observe its entity.
Watch every thought that springs; enhance
Hour after hour thy vigilance!
Intense and keen, turned inward, miss
No atom of analysis!
Sixth, on one thought securely pinned
Still every whisper of the wind!
So like a flame straight and unstirred
Burn up thy being in one word!
Next, still that ecstasy, prolong
Thy meditation, steep and strong,
Slaying even God, should He distract
Thy attention from the chosen act!
Last, all these things in one o'erpowered,
Time that the midnight blossom flowered!
The oneness is. Yet even in this,
My son, thou shalt not do amiss
If thou restrain the expression, shoot
Thy glance to rapture's darkling root,
Discarding name, form, sight, and stress
Even of this high consciousness;
Pierce to the heart! I leave thee here:
Thou art the Master. I revere
Thy radiance that rolls afar,
O Brother of the Silver Star!

(First published in *The Equinox*, vol. I, no. III, 1910)

Other occultists of this period warned against their use, including not-ed occultist and author Israel Regardie, but this was more of a warning against mixing the chakras with other magical systems, such as Cabala. This would certainly be inadvisable, although it has not stopped Cabalists from adapting the idea of energy centers into Cabalistic rites, such as the

Middle Pillar Exercise, due to the lack of an extensive body/spirit system in Western occultism. Francis King and Stephen Skinner even adopt chakra symbolism in the form of the tattwas, the symbols representing the chakras. In *Techniques of High Magic*, they use the tattwas of the four lower chakras to represent the elements, plus a fifth—Akasha—to represent Spirit.[7] They conveniently leave out the symbols for both Ether (the throat center) and mind (brow center), as they do not fit into general Western occult thinking.

Chakra is Sanskrit for "wheel" and is used to signify the idea of a turning center of energy within the body. To the gifted psychic, chakras manifest as revolving discs of light emerging from the body, sometimes described as funnel-shaped when viewed from the side. These centers are normally arranged along a vertical line within the human body. It is important for anyone studying them to realize that there is more than one descriptive system; this will well help to prevent confusion while researching the subject. Different systems quote different numbers of centers, as well as positions and functions. These range from seven major chakras up to ten, and up to twenty-one minor chakras. The most commonly used system is the original seven-centered one, and we feel this is the best system for Witches to concentrate on until they sufficiently understand the nature of the energy they are working with.

The chakras act as connection and transferal points for the energy of the body. It is vitally important for any student of the occult to understand that the chakras are not objects, but expressions of the flow of energy. Just as the elements exist in the physical body, so they also simultaneously exist in the other three auric bodies (see pages 144–146). The first four lower chakras are dedicated to the elements. The next three upper chakras are for the purpose of generating the aura bodies. The result of this is a complex interwoven system of energy, which is sometimes seen by the clairvoyant as a web of colored energy enmeshing spinning colored vortices.

The energy does not exactly spin out from each chakra as at first suggested. Rather, the force actually pours into each center at its rear and is then pushed out by the spinning motion at right angles to itself at the front of the body. This action has been described as the same effect as when a bar magnet is pushed into the field of an induction coil, resulting in an electrical current that flows round the coil at right angles to the direction of the magnet.[8] One effect of this action is to cause the formation of "petals" of the undulating primal energy as it passes through the chakra. The number of petals within each center increases as you move up from the root center, with the exception of the brow center (see pages 140–141).

In most individuals, the chakras remain in a semidormant state and each center is only opened more fully when its action is required in everyday life. Normally, only three to five centers are clearly open at any one time; they enlarge as spiritual development increases. When all the centers are opened simultaneously in perfect balance and have reached their full development, each center spins in the direction opposite to its two adjacent chakras. This effect has been likened to the transferal of energy by series of cogs.

This action is responsible for moving two flows of energy, one positive, one negative, up and down the whole system, from the root center to the crown center, when the centers are consciously opened in various spiritual exercises, such as yoga. This flow of energies at its most powerful is the mystical kundalini, the serpent fire, which the Eastern yogis attempt (though only with full understanding and control) to raise through the other chakras to bring about psychic enlightenment. If aroused early in the unprepared, the kundalini is potentially highly dangerous, and we recommend that those interested in these practices find a competent instructor.

One interesting aspect of the system is its relationship with the physical body's endocrine system.* Chakric meditation seems to act as a color-coded trigger system for controlling these glands and the release of their hormones. There is certainly a correlation between the action of each chakra and its corresponding endocrine gland. A good example of this is the solar plexus center, which is governed by the element of Fire. This center is responsible for governing the body's vital energy. It can be no coincidence that it is positioned over the adrenal glands, which are responsible for stimulating energy for the body's "fright and flight"† reflex.

Visualizing the Chakras and the Energy Flow: The Bathtub Analogy

Most descriptions of the chakras can be quite complicated and often hinder a true understanding of what the chakras are, particularly when it is

---

* The endocrine system is a series of ductless glands in the body responsible for releasing hormones directly into the bloodstream.

† "Fright and flight" reflex is the release of adrenaline and noradrenalin into the bloodstream in times of danger, resulting in increased awareness and energy levels for the purposes of physical protection.

necessary to visualize them. One of the most reliable ways of doing this is the visualization we give below. This is best done in a semimeditative state, with eyes closed in a relaxing atmosphere.

First visualize a bathtub, and then visualize it in the shape of a person. Imagine there are seven plugholes, and place them appropriately in the positions of the seven centers.

Secondly, fill the bath with water. Imagine the water spiraling down the plugholes in a clockwise fashion. Now visualize this spiral flow alternating at each chakra: the root center turns clockwise, the sacral turns anticlockwise, and so on up the body.

Thirdly, now imagine this process in reverse, as if watching a film backwards, with the water spiraling up out of the plugholes and into the bath. Now take away the bath, but keep the water there so that you have a figure of a person made of water.

Finally, imagine the water coming up out of each plughole is the appropriate color for the chakra. We often suggest that you visualize appropriately colored drops of ink being dropped into the center of each chakra. Now imagine the water flowing out from the front of each center, and then being pulled into the other centers from the back, to be pushed out and on again at the front.

What you are now visualizing is the flow of energy around the aura as it comes out of each center, resulting in a cascading flow of color around the body. By visualizing the chakras in this fashion, it is possible to understand the way energy flows up and down the body, and how the aura is generated. It is also more obvious what happens if the energy flows faster through one center than another: it begins to pull in more colors and converts them to its own.

The Seven Major Centers

1. The Root Center (Vedic name: Muladhara): Earth

This is the seat of the mystical kundalini, which in Hindu culture is traditionally believed to be a goddess.[9] There are differing views about its actual position. If the body is in the lotus position, it is certainly at the base of the spine (the fourth sacral bone). There is also the view that the normal position of this center is at the base of the feet. This makes sense to us, as it is the center that links us with the earth. While dowsing, this center picks up energies within the earth, and allows dowsers to detect what they are searching for. It is normally seen as a rosy red color when at rest, and fiery orange-red when active. It is divided into four segments or petals, these represent the four elements in the material world.

As the center is principally related to the element of Earth, it is responsible for the disposal of unwanted, impure energies that may pollute the aura and the other chakra centers. It is therefore of vital importance in the act of grounding. Within the physical body, it governs the spinal column and the urinary system, including the kidneys. This chakra is also associated with physical sensations like pain and pleasure.

2. The Sacral Center (Vedic name: Svadhistana): Water
This is positioned in the genital area. Early Theosophists and practitioners of Laya Yoga, a form of yoga that focuses on the raising of kundalini, worried that concentration on this center would result in the awakening of sexual feelings, they replaced this chakra with the minor spleenic center, which was described as several inches off-center and to the left of the others. Sexual impulses were considered inherently "black" in nature, as much of the Theosophist literature of the period testifies.

This chakra appears orange in color and relates to the element of Water. It is traditionally divided into six petals (the four elements plus "above and below"). It has obvious associations with sexual love, as it controls the flow of energy to the reproductive organs and the endocrine glands in the gonads. Psychologically, it is associated with the emotions, and it is actively involved in all forms of intimacy, interpersonal feelings, and one's emotional well-being.

3. The Solar Plexus Center (Vedic name: Manipura): Fire
Early Western literature gave a blend of several shades of green and red for this center, and divided it into ten petals, but modern writers tend to portray it as yellow, as do many psychics and healers. We also prefer yellow for this chakra, as yellow better fits the color sequence for all the chakras.

Because of its association with Fire, it is sometimes referred to as the "survival" center. Physically it is related to the digestive system and the adrenal glands (although some relate the endocrine glands to the first center). This center therefore governs the lower gastrointestinal tract, including the stomach, liver, and gall bladder (probably because this is the system responsible for producing the body's energy).

4. The Heart Center (Vedic name: Anahata): Air

This center relates to the heart, which in Western culture has been traditionally associated with love and the emotions. This chakra is responsible on the etheric level for our capacity for empathy with the pain and pleasures of others. Because of this relationship with compassion, it is of great importance for those involved in the healing arts to study this center in depth. This center is also responsible for absorbing the energy of love that we receive from others, thus boosting our self-esteem and increasing our ability to return that love.

For those on the spiritual path, this chakra is the first center to deal with the concept of "self," as it gives us the ability to really understand our true selves." For this reason, some have placed this center with the higher chakras despite its elemental nature. On the physical plane, it governs the heart and the associated vagus nerve and circulatory system. This center is also positioned in the same area as the thymus gland, connecting its actions to the immune system of the body.* It is related to the element of Air, and modern practitioners tend to see it as green or turquoise in color. Early Theosophical works gave it a golden color and divided it into twelve petals.

5. The Throat Center (Vedic name: Vishuddhi): Ether

This is the first of the upper centers; it is positioned at the throat. It relates to the concept of Ether, and is therefore the center responsible for generating and connecting us with our etheric body. It is positioned over the larynx and has obvious associations with communication and speech, the power of the word, listening to others, and taking responsibility for what we say.

Physically it is related to the respiratory system, the upper alimentary canal, and the vocal apparatus. The throat center also affects metabolism, due to its relationship with the thyroid and parathyroid glands. All traditions agree on its blue color. It is divided into sixteen petals.

6. The Brow Center (Vedic name: Ajna): Mind

This is the mystical third eye; it is positioned on the brow. It rules the mind and is responsible for generating the mental body. It is well known as the center that controls clairvoyance and psychic experience. For this reason, some refer to it as "the doorway to eternity."

---

* Until recently, doctors believed that the thymus went dormant after puberty, but recent research now suggests that it remains active, stimulating the production of white blood cells when required.

Within the physical body it affects the ears, eyes, lower brain, and nervous system. It is positioned perfectly over the pituitary and hypo-thalamus glands, which control the whole endocrine system. Again, there is no dispute among traditions about this center's color, which is violet or indigo, although there is some dispute regarding the number of petals. There are two differences in thought. According to C. W. Leadbeater, there are ninety-six petals,[10] but according to most Hindu and Buddhist traditional writings, there are two.

From the perspective of the seeker of the mysteries this chakra has two petals, as the brow chakra governs the psychological processes. The idea of two lobes therefore gives us polarity: positive/negative, right brain/left brain, yin/yang, et cetera, and of course, Jung's concepts of anima/ani-mus, and ego/Shadow, which are of prime importance in understanding the mysteries (see pages 46–50).

7. The Crown Center (Vedic name: Sahasrara): Spirit
This is the final center, known as the "crown" because of its position at the top of the head. It is the ultimate link with the person's astral body, and is where the soul enters. It is therefore governed by Spirit. It is the abode of what is often referred to as the Higher Self, or Holy Guardian Angel. This is the Astral Guardian, which monitors and protects us when we venture into the spiritual realms (see page 122).

This center's color varies, depending on the individual's spiritual de-velopment. It is generally visualized as white, which is made up of all the colors of the spectrum. In a spiritually developed person, it becomes quite large. When fully open, it covers the whole head—producing the classical halo effect. This effect is also produced by its staggering 972 petals.

In oriental pictures and statues this chakra is often shown quite promi-nently, as it is in early Christian iconography. This is considered the highest chakra, as it connects the individual to Divinity, which is Kether (the crown) in Cabalistic terms, or God and Goddess in general Pagan terminology. In the physical body, it controls the nervous system and the higher functions of the brain.

An Eighth Center
Spiritualists tend to work with an eighth center for which they have no name. This is the center Aleister Crowley refers to in his poem *AHA!* It is located from eighteen to twenty-four inches above the crown center. This puts it outside of the physical body but within the aura. It is said to act as an intersection between the body's aura and the soul's energy. As such,

it can be considered an extension of the crown center and related to the remnants of the pineal gland.* We suggest it is, in fact, the crown center as manifest in the spiritual body, and not a separate center.

Opening the Chakras

Opening the chakras is an essential exercise if you are going to work with magical energy. Many Witches accustomed to working group magic (in a Circle) and raising the cone of power, find this quite easy. We would recommend using the following opening and closing exercise on a daily basis until you are adept at the processes involved. It takes about twenty to thirty minutes. We would also recommend having somebody present who is sensitive and able to see the chakras the first few times you do it. Your helper can confirm when the centers are open. With practice it takes less and less time to open your centers, and you will eventually find that you can discard this exercise completely and open them by willpower alone.

The first step is to find some place quiet and comfortable to sit. The best position to sit in is the well-known lotus position used in yoga, as it has the effect of bringing the Muladhara, or root center, into line with the other chakras. If you are not supple enough to use this position, sitting cross-legged or kneeling will have a similar effect. The important thing is to stay comfortable for a reasonable period.

The next step is to breathe regularly. There are various breathing patterns used, but we have found that breathing out for seven seconds, holding for two seconds, breathing in for seven seconds and finally again holding for two seconds, is the most effective. It is important to breathe from the base of the lungs by expanding the stomach first, and then the ribs. It will take a while to get used to this, so give yourself time to master it. Then visualize that you are breathing in light. (Initially this should be white light.)

Energizing the chakras, one by one, is the third step. Continue the breathing pattern that you began with—which should be natural and rhythmic by now. If you are sitting on the floor, visualize the root center at the base of the spine as a red, glowing, spinning ball. As you breathe in, visualize the color of your breath as the same color as the center (in

---

* For a long while it was considered to be an inactive organ, but now it is believed to be responsible for controlling the various biorhythms of the body. It works in harmony with the hypothalamus gland, which directs the body's thirst, hunger, sexual desire, and the biological clock that determines our aging process. It has long been thought by mystics that it was the "seat of the soul."

this case, red). This should have the effect after several minutes of making the chakra expand while spinning faster and glowing brighter. Finally, imagine the energy from the center you have just energized moving up to the next chakra (in this case, the sacral center), while changing the color of the light you are breathing to that of the new chakra (in this case yellow). Again, it should take several minutes to energize this chakra, which should behave in the same way as the first center. You then simply repeat

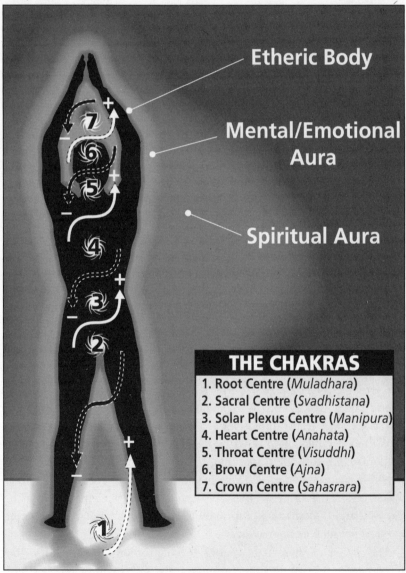

Figure 5 The Chakras and Aura

the process until you reach and energize the third eye (brow center). Then visualize all the colors from each of the energized chakras moving swiftly up to the crown center at the top of the head. Allow the energy, which is now white, to leave the top of the head like a fountain. Let it bathe and purely your aura, removing any "dirty colors" while brightening the existing ones.

The Aura

The Aura is the visual expression of the seven layers of energy that surround the physical human body. There is one for each chakra, but in practice most only manage to see three of these levels: the etheric, the mental/emotional, and the spiritual. The other four are related to the elemental centers that manifest the physical body. The inability to see all the different levels is mainly due to cultural perception. Western thought tends to confuse the mental/emotional body, although in fact it is not distinctly divided. Some advanced psychics are able to see all of the seven levels within the aura, but most are generally only able to see the three main levels we have mentioned below.

The various levels of the aura also act as a psychic shield, and a form of interface for communication with other organisms. It can indicate the emotional and mental state of individuals, as well as how spiritually developed they are. Every living organism has an aura, and with practice it is quite possible to see it. The easiest aura to see is that of a tree at dawn or twilight. It normally manifests as a misty grey field around the topmost branches. In humans, the aura is generated by the action of the chakra centers spinning. The result is that three distinct levels of the aura exist, layered like the skin of an onion (see figure 5).

The Etheric Body

The grey misty area closest to the body is generally referred to as the etheric body, which normally extends about one to three inches over its surface. The term Ether refers to a state between energy and matter. Gifted psychics often describe the etheric body as being composed of energy lines forming a sparkling translucent web along which sparks of bluish-white light move. This gives a pulsating effect. The first four chakra centers generate it—these being related to the elements of Earth, Air, Fire, and Water. This is important to realize when doing any magical work, as we shall explain later.

The action of these four centers in conjunction with the fifth (the throat center relating to Ether) results in the formation of this body of the aura. The etheric body vibrates at the same frequency as Spirit, and acts as a vehicle for it. It therefore helps to shape and anchor the physical body, which is why it hugs the surface of the body so closely. For this reason, it is sometimes referred to as the etheric double. Its main purpose is to feed the body with life force, or prana.

The Mental/Emotional Body

The second part is the mental/emotional body, which is generated by the sixth chakra. It is made up of even finer energy than the etheric body. Unlike that body, it is normally ovoid in shape. How far it projects depends on the immediate mental and emotional state of the individual. The aura will withdraw closer to the body of someone who enters a room full of strangers. When that person feels more comfortable with the others, it will begin to return to its normal size.

The aura of an extroverted person can project out as far as several feet, but that of an introvert may remain always close to the body, almost withdrawing into the etheric body. A trained psychic sees this part of the aura as made up of a variety of colors. These, like the size of the aura, indicate the mental, emotional, and (occasionally) the physical state of its owner.

The Spiritual Body

The last body, and the least easy to see—even for a sensitive, is the spiritual body. This connects with the last of the chakras, the crown.

In a spiritually developed person, it can extend from the body for some distance. It is said that the spiritual body of the Buddha Gautama could be seen for six miles! This part of the aura exists on the astral plane, and is the individual's connection with the world of spirit. The individual's consciousness moves in this body, combined with the mental/emotional body, during astral travel in the higher planes. But during out-of-body experiences on the material plane, it is only the mental/emotional body of the aura that detaches from the physical body. This can happen involuntarily during sleep, and on very rare occasions results in what is often referred to as lucid dreaming. This occurs during the phase known as rapid eye movement (REM) sleep by scientists (for more on this see page 182).

Because of the etheric body's responsibility for continuing the life functions, it remains attached to the body until the moment of death. Like the mental/emotional Body, there are colors present, but these indicate the character and personality of the individual rather than just his or her present emotions. After physical death, the consciousness leaves the physical body and withdraws into the astral.

The Auras and Chakras in Magical Work

It is important for a Witch to have a true understanding of what is happening with their body's energy system even when they perform some of the most basic acts of Wiccan practice. In fact, all of the magical practices utilized in Wicca stimulate the chakras and the aura, while using their flow of energy as a source of power. We believe that for a Witch, to use an analogy, it is not enough "to drive the car," but it is also necessary to "understand how the engine works." The application of the knowledge brought about from studying the chakra system and the aura, grants this understanding better than any other system we have come across, as it is intrinsically a holistic system, incorporating both a physical and spiritual understanding of occult practice.

When setting up a temple (the most common magical practice in Wicca), we can see the chakras and aura at work:

1. **Consecration of Salt and Water:** Blue energy is visualized, cleansing these elements. It derives from the throat center and concept of Ether. The color for this chakra, of course, is blue.
2. **Casting the Circle:** The Circle is visualized as a globe of blue energy coming down the arm into athame or sword. This energy is, again, coming from the throat center. Blue is seen as both a protective and a cleansing color because it strengthens the etheric body.
3. **Calling the Elemental Watchtowers/Use of the Pentagram Ritual:** This actually opens the appropriate chakra in the participants. For example, if you call the western, Water quarter, you will also open the sacral center.

It is noteworthy that the system at work here relates directly to the chakras. When calling the quarters, for example, the centers are opened in sequence: east—heart/Air, south—solar plexus/Fire, west—sacral/Water, north—root/Earth. We do not believe that this is a coincidence, as the previous act of using the throat center to cast the Circle would open this chakra too, just as the act of concentration and visualization would open the brow center. To finish, the invocation of Deity would open the crown center. What we see in the Circle casting and calling of the quarters in general magical practice is a ritualized act of opening the chakra centers and extending the aura for protection.

The etheric energy from the throat center is the most common form of energy used. In the act of consecrating salt and water, it is used for purifying and activating these two elements (salt representing Earth). The consecration results in the formation of an astral double, a thought-form on the higher planes, from the life force itself (prana). In consecrating a magical tool, all four elements are used in sequence. This is based on the occult idea of the four elements creating Spirit. The energy from the four elements does, of course, come from the appropriate lower chakra, activated by the symbolism used. In reality, it is actually creating life force, or Ether. It is this which creates the astral double, as there must be a reflection of all life on the astral planes: "As above, so below," in reverse, so to speak. This is symbolized in the Celtic cross rather than the pentagram, which represents Spirit controlling the elements rather than the creation of Spirit.

This use of the four elements and Ether is also important in other magical acts such as creation of thought-forms or spell work. In thought-form creation, the process is the same as consecration except that mental/emotional energy is added to create an entity. A common way of creating thought-forms is using a jar filled with samples of the four elements: consecrated Water, incense (Air), candle wax (Fire), and Earth. Traditionally "life" (etheric energy) is then breathed into it, and the user gives the thought-form a name, appearance, and charges it with an objective. These latter actions give it energy from the brow center responsible for mental/emotional activity. The result is the creation of an entity on an astral level.

It is also worth looking at energy-raising rituals to understand what importance the bodily systems play. The cone of power is raised by the use of the energy from the coven. This is generated by physical activity such as dancing. This increases mental/emotion energy flow as well as etheric. Chanting also increases energy as it increases flow from the throat center more fully, the center related to communication and *pranic* flow. Circle casting is not just done for protection: it is also cast to "maintain the energy raised within thee." It acts as a barrier to hold the combined aura of the coven, as individual auras of the coven members not only increase but merge with each other. The Circle symbolically represents the group's aura and to what limit it can extend on the physical and etheric levels. Such rituals, of course, strengthen the coven mind, as the use of Ether creates an astral double of the coven on the higher levels.

Practical Exercises

The following are exercises designed to help the Witch feel the flow of magical energy. You will first of all need to be aware of which of your hands produces energy, and which hand receives it. One easy way to find out which is which is to clasp your hands together and then to see which thumb is on top. Normally this is the primary hand, and we should point out is no way related to whether someone is right or left handed. Some find that if they repeat this exercise several times the thumb changes. This is not unusual, and means they can use either hand. Since magic generally goes clockwise in the magic Circle, the left hand usually gives energy and the right receives it. This is important to know because if you send and receive with the opposite hand you will need to practice using both hands. There is a commonly used phrase related to the use of aura energy in magical or healing work: "energy follows thought" or "where thought goes, energy flows." It is possible for the mind working (of course) through the brow chakra to direct the energy flow from the hands. To help understand the magical use of energy, we have included two exercises.

Exercise Two: Two-Person Exercise

This exercise is very useful in helping to form the magical polarization between working partners.[11] The first stage is for both of you to open your centers (see pages 142–144), and sit comfortably facing each other. You may sit either on chairs or cross-legged on the floor. The important thing is that you are of roughly equal height. You should each place the palms of your hands facing each other at chest height. You and your partner's palms should be about twelve inches apart. It is important that your hands do not touch at this stage, as the object is for each of you to feel for the other's aura. After a period of time sitting in this position, you should both begin to feel the energy emitting from the minor chakra centers in the palms of your hands. This normally feels like heat to most people, but some individuals may perceive it differently.

Once both of you have felt the flow of energy, you should signal to each other, and then simultaneously close your eyes. Very slowly the two of you should move the palms of your hands toward the other person's hands, slowly entering each other's aura, until you touch fingertips to fingertips. You should then visualize the energy flowing from your heart center in a circuit going clockwise, from your left hand to your partner's right hand, through your partners heart center and back, through your partner's left hand, to your right hand.

Two-Person Energy Exercise

After a period of time visualizing and sitting in this position, you may get the sensation that your partner's hands are moving ever so slightly in a circular motion. You should try to follow these movements—but on no account should either of you try consciously to lead these movements. For you are feeling the flow of energy within your partner's aura as it emerges from his or her chakric centers.

At this point, you and your partner should try to see what effect concentrating on various significant words, colors, and concepts have on the flow of energy. For example, concentrating on the word "love" will probably increase the flow of energy because of its associations with the heart center, which is being used in this exercise. This is the perfect opportunity for you and your partner to find what triggers the flow of energy for you personally and for you to develop the correct frame of mind for healing. Developing this will enable you to flow with the energy of the coven in magical work. You should repeat this exercise using the crown center and the root center. If using the crown centre, bring the energy down and through the heart center and, likewise, if using the root centre, bring it up and through the heart center.

Exercise Three: Group Exercise

This is really an extension of the two-person exercise and is useful for attuning the whole coven to each other's energy and for understanding such processes as raising the cone of power. This should preferably be done in a previously cast magic Circle. The coven sits in a Circle and, where possible, sits alternating male and female—although if this is not possible, it will not make any major difference. The Priestess or Priest, or whoever directs the exercise, talks everyone through the opening of the chakras. When this is completed and everyone is happy with the results, all the members of the coven hold hands, left palm down, right palm up. The person directing the exercise then tells them to visualize blue etheric energy flowing from one person to the other in a clockwise direction. They encourage the coven to visualize the energy coming down from their crown chakra (white/silver/gold), through the brow (violet) and to the throat centers, where it changes to blue, and then down and around the heart center (color remaining unchanged from blue). It then goes down through their left hands. At the same time they receive energy from the person to their right. This increases the energy flowing around the Circle. When the person directing the exercise feels the energy has built up enough, they encourage everyone to push their hands out the center of the Circle at chest height, and then visualize the energy flowing

Group Energy Exercise

from their fingertips where it forms a glowing ball, spinning and growing as they feed it. The color of the energy can be changed as it is passed around the Circle. The easiest colors to change into are the colors of the chakra centers that the energy has already passed through.

At the end of the exercise, the energy can be dealt with in two ways. The Priestess or Priest can "throw" the energy in the same way as is done with the cone of power (once a worthy recipient of the magical energy is decided upon), or the energy can be taken back into the coven and grounded. We would recommend the former method, until the coven members are all thoroughly adept at grounding themselves.

Closing Chakras and Magical Grounding

It is important to ensure that your chakras are closed after you have finished any form of magical work, particularly after the above exercises. This is commonly called "grounding." Leaving them fully open can result in a loss of vitality, higher risk of disease, and mental stress. Most people who are not grounded describe a feeling of disconnection from the world, a feeling of light-headedness. The easiest way to close the chakras is to eat. This is the purpose of the Cakes and Ale/Wine ceremony found at the end of most Wiccan rituals, as the ingestion of food closes the chakras, while replenishing any energy loss. (Modern Witches are renowned for their fondness for chocolate!)

One other method commonly used is to place the palms of the hands flat on the ground to remove any excess energy left in the system. This is then visualized as going into the ground. This procedure is commonly used while visualizing the root center.

If you are new to magical practice, or to doing any form of intensive magical work, we would recommend the following technique: visualize the energy draining back down from one chakra to another. Once you have drained the energy from each chakra to the one below it, you visualize a shutter closing it from vision. You repeat this center by center. When you reach the root center, remember that it is the only one you leave open all the time—because it acts as the body's grounding point and helps to prevent mental and psychic overload.

NOTES

1 Pseudonym for a little-known Anglo-Saxon practitioner. He regularly lectures on traditional English magical practices. Taken from his London talk of July 2003.

2 Jane and Fridman Namba, *Shamanism: An Encyclopedia of World Beliefs, Practices and Cultures*, vol. 1., p. 547.

3 *The Spiral Dance: A Rebirth of the Ancient Religion of the Great Goddess*, chap. 3, p. 61; chap. 7, pp. 136–150; chap. 8; and *Dreaming the Dark: Magic, Sex, and Politics*, chap. 1, pp. 1–14.

4 This idea of there being two forms of magic—black and white—is derived from monotheistic thinking. This is a concept examined carefully by Isaac Bonewits in his seminal work *Real Magic*, where he talks about magic being many colored.

5 The Reverend C. W. Leadbeater's work has become the standard source material on chakras for most writers on the subject. Unfortunately, it is full of the Victorian prejudices of its time, resulting in this information being relayed into modern works—for example, the position of the root center being at the anus or perineum due to the belief that the physical universe was, by its very nature, corrupt. This is a belief not held within the Hindu/Vedic religious belief system.

6 Published in *Magick*, page XXIII.

7 This use can be found in chapter 6, pages 54–59 of *Techniques of High Magic*.

8 This action is clearly described in Leadbeater's work, as well as in recent editions on chakras, including Anodea Judith's *Wheels of Life*.

9 According to Anodea Judith in *Wheels of Life*, "all the Chakras were originally first associated with the Goddess Kundalini. She is described as a sleeping serpent coiled three and a half times around the first Chakra at the base of the spine. Her name comes from the word *kundala* which means 'coiled.'"

10 The Reverend C. W. Leadbeater lists ninety-six petals in his work *The Chakras—A Monograph*. His rationalization for this number of petals relates to energy rather than symbolism.

11 In Wicca, magical polarization was traditionally between couples: a linking of the chakras between two people on an astral level. The act of polarization creates increased magical energy between a couple. In later magical development, the individual polarizes with his or her own anima/animus complex with the same effect. This is an essential part of the mysteries.

9

The Wheel:
Cycles of Time and Fate

Change is the constant, the signal for rebirth, the egg of the
phoenix.
—CHRISTINA BALDWIN*

Many years ago we had a strange experience that caused us to seriously question the nature of time. Like most people, we had always seen and perceived time as linear, but this experience challenged that deeply ingrained idea. Gavin had learned hypnotic regression as a technique from a Buddhist he knew in Portsmouth, and had been regressed by her several times. Janet wanted to explore some of her past lives, so he went through the process of taking her back. First Gavin relaxed her, putting her into a light trance state. He then took her slowly back, initially by asking her what happened this day last week and then last month, last year, et cetera, until he started working on memorable events, such as birthdays, Christmas, et cetera. Finally, Janet was taken back beyond birth. At this point, things did not go as we had expected.

Janet began to recall a past life. She described sitting in front of an expectantly waiting crowd. She described them singing and chanting, and she described slowly entering a trance state. "What are you doing here?" came the sudden retort from a voice that was definitely not Janet's! "Be

---

* Christina Baldwin is a writer and lecturer on the subject of spirituality and the spiritual journey. She has several books to her name including *The Seven Whispers: Listening to the Voice of Spirit* (New World Library, 2002) and *Calling the Circle: The First and Future Culture* (Bantam, 1998).

gone foul spirit!" A rapid question-and-answer session opened up between regressed and regressor. Gavin tried to work out exactly what had happened, as Janet, or rather the seeress, became more agitated! In the end, Gavin decided the safest course of action was to bring Janet back to the safety of the living room, so he slowly brought her out of the trance state. She had no memory of the events.

There is no doubt in our minds that this incarnation of Janet's was that of a seeress, a prophetess, possibly in Northern Europe,* who entered trance for the benefit of her community (see page 179). We keep an open mind on what had happened, but we believe one possible reason why the incarnation started to question Gavin was that she perceived him as an unfamiliar entity or spirit. We believe this happened because Janet was in a trance within a trance, so to speak, which opened up a bridge between two lines of time, one past, one present. At this time, Janet knew nothing about trance practices—except, of course, Drawing Down the Moon, with which she was very familiar. This experience was to lead us into a completely new field of study, some of the fruits of which can be found in this book.

From the moment humanity first became sentient and self-aware, we have been preoccupied with time. By dividing it, logging it, cataloguing and pondering on it, we have attempted to control the uncontrollable passage of birth, growth, decay, and death, which in turn have come to represent time. This need to control time comes out of fear and apprehension about tomorrow, stimulated by our primordial need for survival. It is so strong that one of the first science-fiction novels ever published was about time travel: H. G. Wells' *The Time Machine*. The idea of time travel continues to be a favorite subject amongst science-fiction writers and pulp sci-fi on television because of our inherent fascination with the passage of every second, minute, and hour.

Many aspects of magic have been about this attempt to control time. The magic Circle is cast in the direction of the sun, for the first unit for measuring time was the passage of the day into night. Each quarter has become not only associated with a time of the day, the position of the sun, but also a season (north to winter, east to spring, south to summer, and west to autumn). As many Witches can testify, our perception of time changes when we are in the magic Circle. For some, it seems to speed up; for others, it seems to slow down. To quote from one ritual: "This is a time that is not a time, in a place that is not a place, on a day that

---

*   This is the practice of Seith, or Seidr, that we have mentioned previously in chapter 7.

is not a day, between the worlds and beyond."[1] Time is, at the end of the day (excuse the pun!) about our own perceptions. There are physical markers: the movement of the sun dictates our whole perception of time, but we decide what markers to use, and this is very much guided by our spiritual beliefs.

From antiquity, time was always connected to the steady movement of the stars, planets, and the sun. The great Greek philosopher Plato confirms this association in his major work on cosmology: the *Timaeus*. He identifies time with the movement of the celestial bodies: the cosmology of "wheels within wheels," or the "crystal spheres." Although Plato's student Aristotle tried to separate time from our movement through space, it was the Christian scholar St. Augustine who finally started to separate the two in people's minds at the start of the Christian era. He considered time to be purely subjective, an internal sense, and outlined this belief in his work *Confessions*. He wrote, "What, then, is time? I know well enough what it is, provided that nobody asks me; but if I am asked what it is and try to explain, I am baffled."

Divination, prophesy, and soothsaying are all magical arts associated with Witchcraft. They are attempts to foretell the future and to discern our fate within the rigors and uncertainty of time. Janet has noticed over the years that the number of customers coming to her for tarot readings increases at times of social stress and world upheaval. In recent years, this has been particularly noticeable during times of war.

Foretelling the future was important to the spiritual practices of the ancient world. In ancient Greece, the Pythoness of Delphi would sit over a chasm believed to be the entrance to the realm of the dead. She would sit on a tripod over a chasm and inhale the fumes that rose from the abyss below her. Her consciousness would be overcome, and she would enter trance and communicate in cryptic images to the gathered dignitaries. It was believed that she was inspired by one of the serpents of the staff of Apollo, the deity to whom she was dedicated. Similar processes can be found throughout Europe, although the method of inducing trance is different. The practice of Seith and of Drawing Down the Moon are both methods of true divination, for they enable contact with the divine to understand the future. From a sociological viewpoint, it can be said that these practices came about to allay people's fears and apprehensions, allowing them to function with less stress in the world around them. Prophets thereby assisted the requirements of survival not only for the individual but also of the society they lived in. They promoted order and structure within the society and thus became a method of social control.

It is interesting that the staff of Apollo is none other than the same caduceus carried by Hermes, who as Hermes Trismegistus is the psycho-pompos, the guide who takes us to the mysteries. The staff can represent not only the energy centers of the body (see page 134 and figure 5, page 143), but also the axis mundi of the spiritual cosmology (see pages 114–115 and figure 4, page 118). It also bears a startling similarity to the basic structure of DNA, which biologists now know causes our aging process.* Something to consider is this: is it also a map of time? Our usual belief is that time is linear and we move only in the direction of the future. This is opposed to ancient thought, which observed the circular movements of the heavens, stars, and planets, and concluded that time is cyclical.[2] This is also why the standard week has seven days, each with a planetary association. Our ancient ancestors believed that time would repeat itself, but this was a spiritual rather than a scientific belief.

For anyone on the spiritual path, it is impossible to separate our perception of time from our spiritual practices. Many believe that the main purpose for religion's coming into being was to allay our fears of death.[3] We say that religion's main purpose is to prove that there is more to our future than just death, oblivion, and nothingness. Our spiritual perception of time tells us that life and time are cyclical and that our soul will return. This enables us to realize that there truly is meaning to life.

The Eight Sabbats

The Witches' year is traditionally divided into thirteen lunar periods called Esbats and eight solar festivals called Sabbats (see figure 6). Each week is divided into seven days, one for each visible planet, plus the sun and moon. This is repeated in the day, which was also traditionally divided according to the planets in medieval magical thinking. The origins of the modern Pagan year can be found in the folk festivals of Europe, as well as in academic works of the nineteenth and twentieth centuries. There are many books on these festivals, indicating their importance in the theology of modern Paganism. With her late husband, Stewart, Janet wrote one of the most influential works on the subject, *Eight Sabbats for Witches* (see Bibliography); it remains one of the standard source books for information on this subject. It is not our intention to repeat that material, but to supplement it with more spiritual insight. Yet it is still necessary to run through the basics of the eight festivals of the Witches' year.

---

*   It is interesting to note that the structure of DNA was discovered because of a dream by one of the scientists.

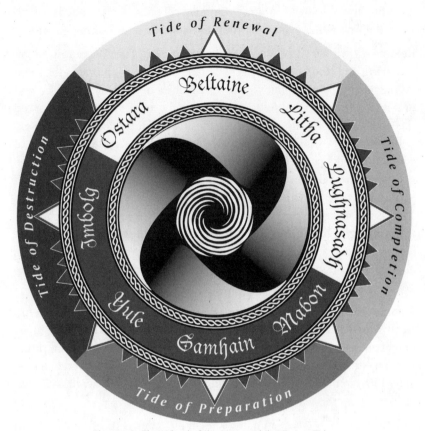

Figure 6 The Wheel of the Year and the Power Tides

Imbolg: (February 2) Also known as Oimlec and Brigantia. Christianized as St. Bridget's Day and Candlemas. Imbolg means "in the belly," a reference to the seed growing in the ground. It is the quickening of the year, the first fetal stirrings of spring in the womb of Mother Earth. Agriculturally, it was the time when the ground was prepared for planting. In Wiccan ritual practice, it is marked by the banishing of winter and the welcoming of the Goddess into the cycle of the year. A traditional Irish chant proclaims, "Bríd [Bridget] is come, Bríd is welcome."

Spring Equinox: (on or near March 20) Also known as Ostara, after the Anglo-Saxon goddess of spring—Eostre. Christianized as Lady Day and Easter. In the Mediterranean practices associated with this festival, there were strong sacrificial mating themes linking it to the mysteries, particularly those of Cybele, which involved the death and resurrection of her lover Attis. It is clearly apparent why Christianity chose to place Easter near this festival (on the Roman Catholic calendar, Easter Sunday is always the first Sunday after the first full moon after the spring equinox).

Beltane: (April 30) Also known as Bealtaine, May Eve, Walpurgis Night, Cyntefyn, and Roodmas. In Wicca, Beltane very much embraces the same theme as the spring equinox—the resurrection of the Oak King, the god of fertility. In traditional folk custom, the lighting of the Bel-fires marked this occasion. It was also a traditional festival of unbridled sexuality. Sexual rites were an important part of the agricultural cycle, as a form of sympathetic magic to fertilize the crops for the coming harvest. These rites continue today in folk custom as May Day, with the erection of the phallic maypole (for more on the symbolism of the maypole, see pages 114–115). Aspects of this tradition continue in Wiccan ritual, such as in the jumping of the Baal Fire and the celebration of the Great Rite, which reenacts sexual intercourse either symbolically or actually. Beltane was also traditionally the time for "greenwood marriages," which were temporary unions.

Summer Solstice: (on or near June 20) Also known as Litha, Alban Hefin, and Christianized as St. John's Day. The solstice marked the sun at its height, with the nights now beginning to draw in earlier. In Wiccan ritual, it is the end of the rule of the Oak King, and his death. The Goddess now gives birth to the Holly King who rules from this point onward, symbolically marking the waning of the year.

Lughnasadh: (July 31) Commonly known as Lammas (Loaf Mass). This is traditionally the harvest festival celebrating the end of harvest of cereal crops, such as wheat, barley, et cetera. In times of old, it was the time of sacrifice in thanks for the food crop, which would sustain the tribe over the coming year. Once, it may have been an act of real human sacrifice. But even before the advent of Christianity, it changed into a symbolic act, and as a symbolic act, it continues in modern Wiccan ritual.

Autumn Equinox: (on or near September 20) Known as Mabon in Wicca, as well as Alban Hefed. After autumn equinox, night starts to become longer than day. It is the second harvest festival, when berries appeared on bushes.

Samhain: (31 October) Halloween, All Hallow's Eve, Calan Gaef. This was the time of year when domesticated livestock was either brought into the homestead for feeding and protection, or slaughtered and salted for the winter months. It is the latter that gives it one of its associations with death, as well as the fact that most deaths occurred at this time of year, due to the change in weather conditions. It is also the third harvest festival when fruits, such as apples, were ready to collect from the trees. In agricultural pagan practice, it is the New Year, the time to honor the ancestors. This is done in Wiccan ritual by calling back the dead, and then celebrating this connection with the past.

Winter Solstice: (on or near December 20) Yule, Modranacht, Alban Arthan. This was the original New Year in the hunter-gather cycle, the occasion when the days started to become longer. For the Anglo-Saxons and the Norse, it remained so, even with the advent of agriculture. It became known as Modranacht, the "night of the Mother," when the Goddess gave birth to the God of the New Year. This is one of the principle reasons Christianity originally placed Christmas on this date. In Wicca, it marks the birth of the Oak King.

The Witches' Wheel of the Year

Pagan Name	Common Name	Date	Saint/Holy Day
Imbolg (Oimlec)	Candlemas	February 2	St. Bridget
Ostara	Spring Equinox	Approx. March 20	Original Easter
Beltane (Bealtaine)	May Eve	April 30	St. Walpurgis
Litha	Summer Solstice	Approx. June 20	St. John
Lughnasadh	Lammas	August 1	Lady Day Eve
Mabon	Autumn Equinox	Approx. September 20	St. Michael/ Michaelmas
Samhain	Halloween	October 31	All Saints/All Hallow's Eve
Yule	Winter Solstice	Approx. December 20	Original Christmas/ St. Stephen, St. Nicholas

The Solar Festivals—the Hunter-Gatherer Cycle

The first festivals recognized by man were the solar festivals, particularly the equinoxes. For some Witches this may be a revelation, but for anyone living in Ireland who has explored the landscape, this is patently obvious. The first hunter-gatherers who came to Ireland settled and started to build the monuments, the passage tombs, and mounds, which exist on many of the hills of Éire today. Most of these monuments are lined up to the equinoxes rather than the solstices. Slieve na Callaighe (the "Hill of the Witch") in County Meath, Four Knocks in County Lough and the great passage tombs of Knowth and Dowth in the Boyne Valley are all aligned to the spring equinox. Sites such as Brú na Bóinne (Newgrange) and Stonehenge in England, which mark the winter and summer solstices, respectively, are in the minority. This is really quite logical, for the equinoxes are the easiest to recognize, due to their equal length of day and night. It is a powerful time magically, being a balance of polarized energy. Their recognition by ancient peoples would have divided the year into two; they may even have perceived the existence of two years, each six months long.

We can theorize that the Goddess of Life and Fertility ruled spring and summer, starting on the spring equinox, while the God of Death and the Hunt ruled autumn and winter, beginning on the autumn equinox. Even today, some Witches still divide the year between these two deities. The God of Death and the Hunt was, of course, the Horned God of Witchcraft: Cernunnos or Herne (see pages 231–232). His importance would have been self-evident to a culture that relied on hunting during the winter months to survive when access to plant food-sources had come to an end. His worship ensured the success of the hunt, and he was believed to have taught man the first skills of hunting, the first male mysteries. Modern Witches refer to this festival as Mabon, a reference to the Welsh Celtic male deity who rode on horseback and was believed to hunt with a hound of unsurpassed ability.

The Goddess of Life and Fertility ensured the arrival of the spring, the warmth of the summer, and the fertility of crops and plants. Her arrival marked the beginning of the pastoral year. From her came the fertility of the tribe and the power of the tribes' women to bear children. She was the first Mother Goddess and, as such, was responsible for teaching the first female mysteries. Modern Pagans have named the spring equinox after Ostara, a goddess of fertility. We derive the word *Easter* from this goddess.

The solstices began to take on more importance as early agriculture developed. It became necessary to mark the midsummer and midwinter positions to calculate the right times to harvest and plant. Eventually, the lunar cycle was to take precedence over these festivals, but they were still important as they marked the points where the year started to wax and wane.

The Fire Festivals—the Lunar Agricultural Cycle

What are commonly referred to as the Celtic fire festivals date back prior to both the Celts and the Northern European peoples. They date back to the first agricultural practices of our early ancestors. They have become associated with specific dates in the modern calendar, since they were absorbed by Christianity as saints' days. Hence, they tend to have several names. For example, Lughnasadh is also commonly known as Lammas, or as it was originally known before being shortened in speech, Loaf Mass—the Christian name for this harvest festival. We think the festivals of Imbolg, Beltane, Lugnasadh, and Samhain were originally lunar celebrations, falling on new, full, or waning moons. Until quite recently, crops were planted according to the phases of the moon. As agricultural festivals, this would have been reflected in the time the celebration. This can again be found in the Old English church calendar, where the festival closest to Imbolg was also known as Plough Charming Day or, more importantly, Plough Monday.* Monday is, of course, the day related to the moon. These were practical festivals as well as spiritual ones. They related directly to the everyday survival activities of the farming communities that celebrated them.

Each month was directly related to an entire moon cycle. Moon cycles can be twelve or thirteen in a year, as one moon cycle is 29.5306 days. Each moon had a different attribution.†

Names of the Lunar Months

January	Snow Moon
February	Death Moon
March	Awakening Moon
April	Grass Moon
May	Planting Moon
June	Rose Moon
July	Lightning Moon
August	Harvest Moon
September	Hunter's Moon
October	Blood Moon
November	Tree Moon
December	Ice Moon/Long-Night Moon

* This is a traditional Anglican (Church of England) festival, although now rarely performed.
† It is important to remember that there are several systems of names for the lunar months.

Many of the names of these "moonths" relate directly to the festivals that fall in them, particularly Samhain and Lughnasadh; Blood Moon relates to the need to butcher livestock before the winter, and Harvest Moon relates to the harvest festival of Lammas. Beltane falls on Planting Moon, indicating that the festival would have been a celebration of the completion of this agricultural task and the asking for blessing on this act. Imbolg would have been Death Moon; a name that may seem odd at first until you take into account that Imbolg is about rebirth from death, and the time of the year when humans and animals die from the hardships of winter.

One theory we have developed is that the lunar cycle and the fire festivals were originally directly related to each in the following way: Imbolc would have been held on the dark moon/new moon toward the end of January or beginning of February. This is logical, as the Goddess was hidden from view, and preparation of the soil traditionally takes place at this time. Beltane would have been on the new moon, marking the beginning of summer. Lughnasadh, the harvest festival, was traditionally held at full moon, the time of completion and birth. Samhain would have originally fallen on the waning moon—the moon now associated with the Crone—at the end of October or when it fell in the first couple of weeks of November. The Christian church placed the lunar-orientated agricultural fire festivals on saints' days, and in one stroke managed to remove the worship of the moon and the Goddess from the calendar.

Many Pagans and Witches are, in fact, still worshipping on these saints' days rather than the original dates for the fire festivals. Many covens find themselves working on the closest weekend due to the commitments of work and modern living. There is nothing wrong with this, as in a fast, modern world it is necessary for Witches to be adaptable. These festivals, related to the activities of man as well as astronomical cycles, may be flexibly observed. Even the lunar associations are now a side issue, as few modern farmers sow, plant, or harvest according to the moon. In practice, this means that a good Witch needs to look at the activities of the countryside (or even the town) for guidance as to when to hold the festival. We do this ourselves. We wait to celebrate Lughnasadh (the harvest) until the crops are in—an eminently more sensible way of doing things when you think about it. We teach our students that if they want to know what a seasonal festival is all about and conduct a ritual with appropriate symbolism, the answer is to "look out the window" and draw your inspiration from nature, not a book!

The inclusion of the Oak King/Holly King cycle into Wicca is really quite modern, with Robert Grave's *The White Goddess* and Sir James Frazer's *The Golden Bough* as the major sources. Prior to its inclusion in Janet and Stewart's Book of Shadows, and then into *Eight Sabbats for Witches*, its use was nonexistent within the standard Alexandrian Book of Shadows or within any of the copies of the Gardnerian Books of Shadows that we have seen.* It was included because it worked—for it was based on an observable cycle within nature. Additionally, to quote Stewart, there were "very little bones" in the existing Sabbat rituals. From a progressive viewpoint, we see no reason why others cannot do similarly, looking at the cycles of nature where they live and adapting their seasonal festivals appropriately.

In *The Witches' Way*, Janet and Stewart pointed out that the seasons in the Southern Hemisphere (and therefore the seasonal festivals) are 180 degrees out.[4] This is now completely accepted by the Pagan communities of Australia and New Zealand. The debate now is focused on the position of the elements and Circle casting.† The question is, should the Circle be cast anticlockwise, the apparent direction of the sun when looking toward the equator from the Southern Hemisphere? Should the element-to-direction correspondences be changed? Should north now be associated with Fire because the sun is now in the north at midday, and likewise, should the south be associated with Earth? The existing cardinal/elemental point correspondences in the Northern Hemisphere have had these attributes because of the sun's position at various times of day (see pages 113–114, 237). From the viewpoint of the mysteries we would say that it is necessary to look to nature rather than dogma, and to change appropriately. Others would disagree, arguing that these associations are set in stone on the astral level. We do not believe this to be true. Our counterargument is that the occult law of "As above, so below" applies here, implying that the physical movement of the heavens in the Southern Hemisphere would be reflected on the astral level if you are working in that hemisphere.

This flexibility of location does bring up another issue. How relevant is it to work an agricultural cycle in a location where that actual cycle does not exist? It seems logical to us that any connection with nature means connecting with the natural environment around you. We believe

---

* We have little doubt that since the 1960s, much of its material has been incorporated, either from the primary source or as handed down "traditional" material.

† This is a debate fuelled by several talks and articles by Julia Phillips, a well-known Wiccan writer and lecturer. She outlines her argument for the quarters being also affected by the Southern Hemisphere in the online magazine *Shadowplay* # 25, http://www.shadowplayzine.com/Articles/between_the_worlds.htm/.

that, for example, it is pointless to work with symbolism such as the Corn King if corn does not exist as a crop in your location. We feel it would be better to echo the local environment in your seasonal workings. By doing so, you will connect with the season cycle on a deeper level by recognizing *as above, so below* (see Appendix A).

Spirituality, the Mysteries, and the Power Tides

The Power Tides

By connecting to nature directly, we realize that we are physically affected by these cycles, particularly those of the sun and moon. If you have ever come across anyone who suffers from "winter blues"—or as it more correctly known, seasonal affective disorder (SAD)—you will be aware of the effects the yearly cycle can have on us. SAD is, in fact, not a disease or a disorder, but a memory of the time when our metabolism—the speed of our bodies—slowed down due to the decrease in certain frequencies of light during the autumn and winter months.* This was necessary as food became in short supply; a slow metabolism requires less energy (food) to sustain it. In the modern age, with abundant food and warm houses, this is redundant, but in the past it was a necessary physical reaction needed for survival. Unfortunately, evolution has not caught up with some people, and they still have this mild hibernation reflex. They are directly affected by the power tides. What is interesting to note is that the most effective cure for SAD is *hypericum*, or as it is more commonly known, St.-John's-wort. Obviously our ancestors were aware of its effects, as St. John's Day was the summer solstice, the day when the sun was at its height.

The purpose of recognizing the yearly cycle in magical practice is to connect us with the ebb and flow of nature's energies, which are called the *power tides* (see figure 6). This is a highly important aspect of Witchcraft, as it firmly grounds Wiccan spirituality in the cycles of nature. Without connection to these energies, we would neither be able to connect with our own true selves nor with the gods and goddesses as manifestations of the divine. The cycles of sun and moon affect all other cycles of life, including the seasons, the tides of the seas, and (ultimately) the cycle of life on Earth itself, including humankind. From this we can see why such occult sciences as astrology became so important, as well

---

* SAD is caused by the lack of light during the winter months. Light is necessary for stimulating the production of serotonin, a neurotransmitter, within the brain.

as the later recognition of biorhythms, which gained popularity in the 1970s.* There are four power tides in the year:

Tide of Destruction: winter solstice to spring equinox

Tide of Renewal: spring equinox to summer solstice

Tide of Completion: summer solstice to autumn equinox

Tide of Preparation: autumn equinox to winter solstice

The ebb and flow of creative, transformative, and recessive energy are directly related to the equinoxes and solstices. It is at these times that they reach their peak. Some of the most magical times to work are when these powers are in a balance, an equal polarity, an equal state of yin and yang, not just in basic magical work but also in self-transformative work related to the appropriate energy. The four fire festivals are the celebration of the use of this energy in conjunction with the feminine energy of the lunar cycle for agricultural and fertility purposes. But the most magically important festivals to this cycle are the solstices and equinoxes.

The mysteries are therefore directly related to this energy, as well as the deities associated with each of the festivals. Each Sabbat is also named after a deity, for example, Imbolc is also known as Brigantia—the British name for the goddess Bríd. The spiritual attributes of the energy present were personified† as gods and goddesses. It is therefore possible to connect

---

* In the 1890s, a highly respected doctor from Berlin, Wilhelm Fliess, did pioneer work involving the twenty-three- and twenty-eight-day cycles of some of his patients—their biorhythms. The statistics he gathered led him to believe he had discovered certain rhythms that were fundamental to life. These rhythms related to the occurrence of illness, as well as emotional, mental, and physical agility. He developed two theories based on the principle that nature bestows "master internal clocks" on humans that begin counting at birth and continue until death, and that these clocks are responsible for regulating a twenty-three-day cycle that influences the physical condition while another regulates a twenty-eight-day cycle influencing the emotions. From a Pagan viewpoint, it is interesting to note that this twenty-eight-day cycle seems to be directly related to the cycle of the moon, particularly as the moon is said to govern the element of Water, the element of emotion. As interest grew in Dr. Fliess' theories, Sigmund Freud (as well as many other noted scientists) began showing an avid interest in the studies. In the 1930s, a very successful study was done that related accidents to the critical days in the cycle; these are the days when the cycles drop from highs to lows. Although there is plenty of evidence for biorhythms, many more mainstream scientists and doctors still debate their existence, but they certainly fit in with the cyclical nature of both the lunar and Power Tide cycles.

† The church, of course, slowly merged aspects of saints with those of deities, making it easier to absorb the lunar fire festivals.

with these energies via Deity itself and use this energy in experiencing the mysteries. Our ancestors saw the passage rites of birth, death, and life as magical rites. They would have orientated such rites to the power tides. Hence, Beltane was seen as a time of marriage and procreation, being at the height of the Tide of Renewal.

The Gods and Goddesses of Fate and Wyrd

Even today, we still personify time. The old Greek god Cronus, for instance, is still with us as "Old Father Time," holding his sickle and hourglass. He appears at every New Year, but few realize his true name or origins. At the stroke of twelve, he dies and Harpokrates (equated with Egyptian Horus) is born, the child of hope for the forthcoming year. Our need to personify time goes back even further than these primal deities. The Triple Goddess of modern Witchcraft—the Maid, Mother, and Crone—relates to the cycles of the moon. The waxing, full, and waning moons are also the Moerae, the Greek goddesses of fate. They were the daughters of Zeus by Themis. Clotho was the spinner of the web of life. Her sister Lachesis wove the threads. Finally, the last sister, Atropos, would cut the thread. Their will was carried out by the Keres, "the dogs of Hades." It was said that they would pounce on the dying at the appointed hour. This myth is almost identical to that of the Norns of the Norse and the Wyrd Sisters of the English. It has a common origin in Indo-European culture.

It was Wyrd (or Urd) who was responsible for spinning the thread of life, while Verdandi wove this as thread of fate, and Skuld would finally tear the thread. It was said that they were the guardians of the sacred tree of Yggdrassil (see pages 114–116). They remain with us today in *Macbeth* as the three witches, "these three weird sisters," and as the much-sanitized modern Wiccan concept of the triple Moon Goddess. The Triple Goddess does, of course, reflect time, but on the much smaller scale of one lunar month. The Moerae and Norns are eternal, reflecting the cycles of life. In both Norse and Greek myth, it was believed that even the goddesses and gods of the ancient world were at the mercy of the three fates. Even they could not escape the ravages of time. This is a prominent theme in the Norse/Icelandic poem "The Lay of the High One"[5] when Odin hangs on the world tree, Yggdrassil, to discover the runes. In this classic description of a shamanic initiation, Odin goes through the process of sacrificing the self by descending into the underworld through the Well of Urd. In Norse myth, the Norns guard the base of Yggdrassil. Odin corresponds with Wednesday in the weekly cycle. Wednesday is governed by the planet and god Mercury (in France, Wednesday is known as Mercredi—Mercury's day), who is, of course, none other than Hermes Trismegistus, the psychopompos of the mysteries. Here we have a clear link in mythology between the ideas of fate, time, and the classical idea of the mysteries.

Our modern word *weird* does, in fact, have its origins in the word *wyrd*. Wyrd is often used to describe our ancient ancestors' concept, which is similar to fate. We have all had "weird" things happen to us, for example, just when we require help in some way, someone appears from our past to miraculously help us. Possibly a series of events seem to strangely come together in such a way to cause a thing of monumental importance in our lives to come to pass. This is Wyrd at work. To our ancestors, our fate was not fixed. They perceived that our lives were like a web, a web of Wyrd, and that we slowly worked our way from the outside of the web to the center along the strand spun by Urd or Clotho, to the moment of our death, when Skuld or Atropos would cut the thread.

As we move forward on the strand to the center, the strand of development and growth, it is inevitable we will have to cross the weft of the web, woven by Verdandi or Lachesis, the concentric strands that she wove around the web. This signifies that there are some things we cannot avoid. They are generally karmic and carried over from previous incarnations. Some things in our lives are destined, such as meeting an acquaintance from a past life, be it a positive or negative experience. The general outcome of one's life is not fixed: for instance, what happens after you meet that person is in your hands! There are many different ways of reaching the center of the web. One can move sideways along a weft on to a different strand to the center. You can even move backwards, particularly if you do not learn an important lesson. You therefore become destined to repeat the pattern in a cyclical fashion until you break free from it. Sometimes this breaking free from a cycle can, in fact, be a form of initiation, and you can break a cycle that may have existed throughout many lifetimes. If we do not, the cycle is destined to repeat itself into our next lives, for the cloth on Verdandi or Lachesis' loom remains unfinished.

Our ancestors believed strongly in cycles. They saw cycles around them in the movement of the sun and moon. This idea is carried over in modern astrology, where it is believed that our lives go in a twenty-nine-year cycle called the "Saturn return." It is important to note that Saturn (as a god) is none other than the Romanization of the previously mentioned Cronus, the Greek god of time and fate. In astrology, the Saturn

return is believed to be a time when we come into our own as controllers
of our own destiny; an important goal of magical practice.

The Mysteries of the Wheel of the Year

We experience the seasonal tides both internally and externally with each
passing year from Imbolg—when we emerge from the womb, to Yule
(winter solstice)—when we return at death to the earth. Every spring,
like Persephone, we rise to greet our own new season of life from our
underworld of winter depression: we wake to new growth, optimism,
and an enthusiasm for our future challenges. By the time Mabon (autumn
equinox) is upon us, we become more aware of how our lives have progressed during the warm months of summer, digesting and storing away
for the winter months things to be worked on to better our future after
the winter solstice. We digest all those glorious memories of the long lazy
days of summertime, intuitively knowing that after the crisp frosts of
autumn when our senses become sharper, we inevitably have to face the
dark underworld days that lie ahead of us.

With each year, our awareness of self-identity becomes more complete. From the angst of teenage years when our bodies are budding and
our brains are still struggling to reach full maturity, to the early adult
years when the desire to reproduce takes precedence, we become self-
absorbed, full of free spirit and inner desires. By the midsummer of our
lives, we are formulating future security, learning from the lessons of
those early years. We have gained a modicum of wisdom and maturity.
The Crone of Wisdom from whom we desired to learn as we grew up
is slowly replaced by the Mother Goddess. This is the time of nurturing
years of our lives. Caring for our young and finding ways to provide for
their future adds to our personal library of knowledge and wisdom. A
healthy individual should by now have the confidence to have learned
from the mistakes inevitably made during those formative years and be
gracious enough to admit to not always being right.

As we enter our middle years, within ourselves spiritually, the Mother
is replaced by the Maiden Goddess, and a sense of freedom and peace
begins to descend upon us. Our offspring are nearly fully independent,
forming lives of their own, and we are once again free to explore our inner world. It is "time out" for us. The middle years are the time to harvest
the fruits of our lives and to enjoy a newfound freedom. We explore all
the possibilities that life now offers to us. We can look back on the mistakes we have made on our life journey. We will view some with sadness,
others we will find humorous, and like Persephone, we will throw caution

to the wind and laugh with joy at all life has to offer. Yet, deep inside, we are aware that the underworld cave is coming more into focus with each passing day. Like the Spring Goddess, we must eventually enter that cave and explore the great winter mystery: the mystery of death. To the Witch, however, this is not viewed with cold terror but more with a sense of déjà vu. We know that, like the sun at Newgrange during the winter solstice, light will penetrate the realm of Hades, and we will return to this earthly cycle to renew the mysteries within each of us. With each rebirth, we acquire more knowledge and spiritual strength; the cyclical mysteries of life and death are the very foundation stones that will be our guides upon the path of existence.

NOTES

1   From *A Book of Pagan Rituals* by Ed Fitch.
2   This is a view proposed by Mircea Eliade, one of the world's foremost authors on mythology and religion, known by most Pagans for his seminal work *Shamanism: Archaic Techniques of Ecstasy*.
3   A theory of the philosopher Frederich Nietzsche.
4   Chapter 25, pages 269–272 of *A Witches' Bible*.
5   From *The Poetic Edda*, also known as *The Sayings of Har*.

10

Priesthood: Connecting with and Serving Deity

We should take care not to make the intellect our god; it has, of course, powerful muscles, but no personality.
—ALBERT EINSTEIN*

It is the role of the priestess or priest not only to commune with the gods and goddesses as the manifestation of the divine, but more importantly to serve them for the benefit of humanity and the world. The priest or priestess has traditionally (throughout the world) been defined as someone who acts as a conduit for Deity—for the ancestral gods and goddesses of the people to talk through them to guide or help the people in some way. To quote the well-known Witchcraft writer Gavin Frost, the modern age presents us with "a religion that cuts out the middle man."[1] Witchcraft has become a religion that does away with the old Christian idea where only the priest connects with the divine. In this situation, the role of the Witch as a priestess or priest becomes more important, as it now becomes their responsibility to teach people how to connect directly with the old gods and goddesses of the people.

There is a difference between connecting and serving. While connecting with Deity should be at the core of all religious practice, serving as a priestess or priest of Deity is a vocation, a religious calling, and therefore not suited to everyone. Some might say that this is elitist thinking. But that argument confuses connecting to Deity with serving Deity as if they

---

* Better known as the physicist responsible for formulating the theory of relativity, Albert Einstein also saw the divine at work in the laws of physics.

were the same process. We would say they are not, as no one would accuse a doctor of being elitist for following his vocation, nor say that only he was responsible for your health and well-being. Any good doctor would say you are ultimately responsible for your own health. Likewise, the priesthood's role is to help the individual connect with the divine, but not to do it for them.

The Witches' role, we believe, stretches beyond the boundaries of what is referred to as "Pagan community." It has been the nature of neo-Paganism to be insular, due to fear of discrimination and prejudice. In some areas, this has resulted in the attitude that we should only be concerned with acting as priesthood within the coven and the Pagan community, and not beyond. This attitude is very much influenced by the doctrine of secrecy (see pages 28, 31–34) and the fear of prejudice and discrimination. Speaking from experience, when you connect with the divine, you cease to see the world with such limited tunnel vision. Even labeling oneself *Witch* or *Wiccan* becomes secondary to the idea of being a priestess or priest of a specific god or goddess. Connection with the divine enables one to realize how arbitrary religious divisions are. Many Witches and Witchcraft-based organizations have put their hands out in friendship to other religious groups, realizing that the divine is present in every perception of spirituality. Witches can now be found on ecumenical councils both in Europe and in the United States.* We are pleased to say that this has had an important beneficial effect, both for the Pagan community and the world in general.

The Witch must serve everyone in his or her community, not just the Pagans. We do this ourselves, as do many other Witches. Janet counsels local people with the use of tarot cards; Gavin acts as a healer when called upon. We have also found ourselves performing rituals for non-Pagans, particularly passage rites such as handfastings (wedding ceremonies). Sometimes these have been secular with very little in the way of religious overtones; sometimes these have even included some Christian symbolism if, due to a previous divorce, the couple have been unable to marry in the Catholic Church. We see all of this as part of our role as a progressive priesthood of Witchcraft. In recent years, we have found ourselves doing rituals for our community at local events such as a blessing for a twinning of two towns, and a harvest thanksgiving festival for our local Chamber of Commerce.† We see this as part of our roles as priest and priestess.

---

* The Aquarian Tabernacle Church based in Seattle, Washington, is very active in promoting Ecumenicalism in Wicca, as are several other Wiccan organizations.

† These are done under the guise of *Ancient Ceremonies Theatre*. We see no dichotomy in doing this, as theater's origins are in Greek ritual and ceremony.

By doing so, we are not only overcoming prejudice and creating a better understanding of what Witchcraft is about, but also truly serving the divine as priesthood.

We are certainly not the only ones doing this. It has become a trait of those who are progressive in their approach to Witchcraft. We would credit Starhawk as a progressive priestess in both her internal work with the Reclaiming Collective* and her political actions (whether you agree with them or not). Neither she nor the collective separate their magical lives from their everyday lives. They seek to serve the divine—the Goddess and God—in everything that they do. They have strong convictions, which can only come about from having strong connections with Deity. But it is always important to remember that as priesthood to different gods and goddesses we may end up serving in different ways.

Connecting with Deity

Connecting with Deity is one of the primary mysteries in Witchcraft practice. It is therefore both subjective and experiential. We also believe that you do not find your deity: your deity tends to find you. In this respect, it is very similar to "finding your power animal" in shamanic practice. The same process of "meaningful coincidence," which Jung would call "synchronicity," tends to occur.[2] First you are brought to the attention of the god or goddess concerned. This could be in ritual or in something you do in everyday life. A good example of this happened while Gavin was working on our previous book, *The Healing Craft*, and working on reclaiming the Hippocratic Oath as a Pagan oath. This caught the attention of the primary deity mentioned in the script, Aesculapius. We had several occurrences related to the deity around our home, including physical manifestation. Gavin did not continue the connection through any practice, mainly because he already had Freya as his primary deity to whom he was dedicated as a priest. But those experiences leave him able to work with Aesculapius in future.

The idea of taking a specific god or goddess for one's primary life-guide is important.[3] This is the deity you connect with fully, and becomes your face of the divine. It is this deity who will guide you through your work as a Witch and help you understand the nature of your spirituality,

---

* Reclaiming is a tradition of Witchcraft that began in the 1980s in Northern California, and by the year 2000, had adherents throughout North America and in parts of Western Europe. Reclaiming has no formal "membership." It is a community of women and men working to unify spirit and politics (abridged from www.reclaiming.org).

and as the name suggests, will act as guide for you in everyday life. For this reason it should be the one you dedicate to as a priestess or priest, as their servant, if you decide to do so. We should point out that this is a reciprocal arrangement. The deity needs you as much as you need them. You are not their slave. Consider yourself their employee—and remember that this means you have union rights! We have found that life-guide deities look after you, if you look after them.

You can recognize your life-guide because they possess aspects that relate to you in some way. Not surprisingly, many Witches find that they have goddesses who are linked to Witchcraft (see Appendix B). A healer may get a deity of healing if this is their calling, while a blacksmith may get a deity related to Fire or smithcraft. The deity may be linked to your mundane career or vocation. Bear this in mind, as you may be disappointed if you think you will necessarily get a goddess of Witchcraft! But we have found, more often than not, that there is an ancestral link between yourself and your deity.

The idea of ancestral deity is at the root of ancient pagan practice. Many of the gods and goddesses that we know have their origins in ancestral worship, a form of paganism we can still see practiced in Japan today as Shinto. This comes about through a deification process of an "honored ancestor." A good example of this is the Northern European god Odin. He was originally a tribal leader who gave his people a code of conduct to live by, the "Havamal" or "Sayings of Har," as well as the runic language that Pagans are more familiar with. Initially, he became a mythical hero mentioned in song and prose by the Skalds—the Northern bards. Offerings would have been made to him, strengthening the process. The result is that he became deified, not just in the minds of his people, but on an astral level. This was a process well-known to the Romans who tried to accelerate it for political reasons on several occasions: initially by granting godhood to the Emperor Augustus and then to later emperors.

We have found that strong genetic links with the primary life-guide tend to come to the seeker. In our case, both of us have a mix of origins for our ancestors, but the strongest is our English (Norse/Anglo-Saxon) origins. It is hardly surprising then, that we have made a link with our goddess Freya. There may also be links through reincarnation. You may have not had the genetic link in this life, but may have had one in a past life, as we have found with those using Egyptian and Middle Eastern deities.

The gods of the locality may also make a claim. We once did a talk in a shop in New York City on this subject. A young lady wanted to know why she had made a connection with an orisha (Santeria spirit/deity-form), which was now an important part of her life. She had no genetic or past-life connection as far she knew. It left us initially dumbfounded, and we were unable to explain why this had occurred. We believe that this orisha had been drawn to her through her locality, for she lived in an area of New York City where there are many practitioners of Santeria. The invocation of the orishas had, over a long period of time, installed them as *genius loci*, the deities of the land or area. We actually owe a debt of thanks to that young lady, as she made us think carefully about why this had happened and made us challenge our preconceptions. It has made us examine the possibility that a localized deity-form may be able to take on this role as life-guide to a priestess or priest.

Generally, we find that primary life-guides fit into one of three categories—although it is not unusual to find a deity that fits into two, and very rarely, all three:

- **Primal:** These are deity-forms that represent natural forces both macrocosmic and microcosmic (e.g., the sea, the wind, or even the natural human drives; e.g., sexuality, and fertility).

- **Ancestral:** Deities that you are genetically linked to, as well as the deities of craftsmen and craftswomen—those deities that manifest human skills. The goddesses of Witchcraft fit into this category (e.g., Aradia), as do the gods and goddesses of smithcraft (e.g., Bríd).

- **Genius Loci:** Translated this means "the spirit of the place," in other words, deities who are connected to a specific place. They may also *be* the locality, for example, the goddess Boann is the River Boyne, and the goddess Pele is the volcano Kilauea.

Once you have found a primary life-guide (or rather, once the deity finds you) you need to research it, both intellectually and psychically. There is plenty of material written about the many gods and goddesses who exist but they may not always be correct. You will also need to connect with them psychically by using some of the techniques below.

Reinforcing the Bond

It will take time for you to be certain that you have found your god or goddess. Be aware that this can take years! As with Gavin's experience with Aesculapius, it may not necessarily be the only god or goddess you have an experience with. You may connect with others, intentionally or unintentionally, if you decide you need their help for specific magical work. This does not necessarily mean that they are your primary life-guide.

We give here techniques to help you not only connect with your god/ goddess but also to reinforce that connection:

1. Make a shrine or altar, inside or outside your home. It needs to be decorated appropriately to the deity, so some research will be necessary. Regularly leave offerings appropriate for the deity on the shrine. (Janet regularly leaves flowers of specific colors on our shrine to Freya every Friday, her day of the week.) Offerings of other sorts may also be required. Make sure you "feed" your god or goddess, leaving offerings of their favorite drink and foods, particularly if you are asking for assistance of some form.* They will also be more than happy to tell you what they need!

2. Every god or goddess has his or her own festival date. Some of them fall on the traditional Wiccan calendar of eight Sabbats, others don't. Make sure you are aware of your deity's festival and the customs related to it. Always make sure that you leave some sort offering on that date, even if you can't mark it with a full ritual or celebration.

3. Meditate on your god or goddess. Visualize them in front of you. Talk with them: ask them questions and ask them for guidance. This is one of the first stages of learning the processes involved in deity assumption or Drawing Down the Moon. Remember that your god or goddess is there to guide you through the difficulties in your life. Listen to their guidance.

4. Dress appropriately in everyday life, as well as in ritual. You may naturally find the inclination to dress in a certain way. For example, followers of the love goddesses (Aphrodite, Venus, et cetera) tend to dress provocatively. Wear the colors associated with your god or goddess, even if only on a scarf. Most goddesses of Witchcraft have black associated with them, which is why Witches usually wear black. This is often a subconscious decision. Deities of healing prefer their acolytes to wear white, while some deities have taboos on certain colors. Make sure that you have researched this fully, so as not to offend.

5. Work magically with the culture of that deity. Understand its specific symbolism, magical practices, and mythology. It makes no sense to work in a Celtic style of ritual if you are working with a Greek deity— ritual is language, therefore, use the language your deity understands. It is important to note that you do not have to work this way all the time, but only when you are working with your god or goddess.

---

* This is a common practice in Santeria with the feeding of orishas. The same principles apply to Western deity-forms.

6. Be aware that there will be some deities that you will not be able
to work with once you have dedicated to your god or goddess. For
example, followers of the Norse god Thor will not be able to work
with Loki, as this would be offensive to him. Make sure you know the
mythology surrounding your deity.

Priesthood—Dedicating to Deity

Once you are certain that you have found your life-guide, consider the
need to dedicate to them as their priestess or priest. This is a serious commitment. We cannot understate this in any way. We would recommend
that at least a year should pass, if not more, between finding your life-
guide deity and dedicating your life to them as their priestess or priest.
What makes being a priestess or priest of a deity special is the level of
commitment and the nature of the relationship. A deity is for life, not
just for Yule! When you dedicate to your god or goddess, you agree to
let them direct your life completely. You are committing yourself to being their servant. Likewise, they commit themselves to look after you. As
we can testify, you never do without. But you get what you need—not
necessarily what you want. It is a reciprocal arrangement. You are giving
them "the tiller" of your life, rather than just asking them for directions
as you would have done before. They will now intercede directly without
asking and will put you in the direction that they feel is necessary for
you to serve them. We always warn that these can sometimes be negative
rather than positive experiences. The question in the Wiccan initiation—
"Art thou willing to suffer to learn?"—becomes highly relevant in such
circumstances.

The results of dedication to a specific deity are life-changing. How
you view and relate to the world can dramatically change. Becoming a
priestess or priest of a deity is one of the mysteries in its own right, as it is
closely connected with the Wiccan second-degree initiation. It can therefore take you on a descent into your own underworld, your Shadow, to
face the darker aspects of yourself that you would prefer to ignore. There
is no place for personal ego in this process. For this reason, we would
not recommend this dedication until you have already been through this
mystery. Otherwise, you may find yourself being used by Deity in a way
you could not have foreseen. (We have seen deities use their dedicated
priestesses and priests as negative examples for the benefit of others.)

Any dedication should be done in the cultural fashion of that deity, as
previously mentioned. You may also want to have a new set of robes as
part of the dedication ritual, as well as a piece of jewelry that is connected

with that deity: one that you consecrate and wear permanently after your dedication. The ritual can be simple: purifying and anointing yourself, making an oath to serve the god or goddess you have connected with as their priestess or priest, and then adorning yourself with the new robes and newly consecrated ritual jewelry. It can be done privately or as part of a coven ritual. If possible, it is always useful to try to find someone else who has been through this form of dedication, even though it may not be to the same deity. Their advice will be invaluable.

The service you give to the deity as their priestess or priest will differ according to the god or goddess you have agreed to serve. A priest or priestess of a healing deity will devote their life to healing, while a priest of priestess of a deity of smithcraft, such as Bríd, may make beautiful things as part of that devotion to them. Bear in mind deities rarely have just one aspect, so you may find yourself learning new skills. It is also not unusual for the priestess or priest to take on some of the personality traits of the deity that they serve, particularly if they are drawn into them during ritual.

Drawing Down the Moon and the Assumptive Process

In both modern and older pagan traditions, the ultimate expression of connection and service to a deity is to "assume" the deity in trance. The term and practice of *Drawing Down the Moon*, as found in the Gardnerian and Alexandrian Traditions of Wicca, are firmly rooted in Charles Godfrey Leland's *Aradia, or The Gospel of the Witches*. There is little historical doubt that such a rite existed in Etruscan religious practice, but little is known about the psychological processes involved and what effect they actually had on the priestess. We can be sure that the ritual used in modern Wicca probably has little in common with the original Etruscan practice. In the modern Wiccan rite of Drawing Down the Moon, there are elements of ritual high magic and Cabala. For example, the Fivefold Kiss is said to be the enactment of the Center Pillar Ritual,[4] which performs the same role as opening the chakras. Regardless of its mixed origins, most Wiccan priestesses can attest that it works and has become the central ritual of Wiccan rite—the communion with the Goddess through the priestess.

Janet and her late husband, Stewart, created the rite of "Drawing Down the Sun," the male equivalent of Drawing Down the Moon. They felt a need for sexual balance. They created the ritual and first published it in *The Witches' Way* in the early 1980s following discussions with Doreen Valiente. Doreen then went on to produce a "Charge of the God" to supplement her earlier work. There is no reason why a man cannot assume a male deity-form, just as a woman does the Goddess. It is seen all the time in religions such as Vodoun, and according to Ray Buckland (who has studied their practices for many years), it is also not unusual for the loa to manifest contra-sexually (a female loa "riding" a male adherent and vice versa), something he told us he once witnessed.* There should be no surprise in this, as spiritual mediums have always been able to do the same thing.

Generally, Drawing Down the Moon is an act of prophesy that can work in several ways (or may progress through several stages) according to the priestess' adeptness.

1. The Priestess may meet the deity in a trance state in another level of reality, such as the astral plane, and then receive important, but sometimes cryptic, messages from them. This is a prophetic act of clairvoyance or clairaudience.†

2. The deity speaks through her, she feels the deity enter, but she retains her control and memory of the entire event.

3. The deity-form completely overwhelms the priestess, sublimating the priestess' personality completely. She loses complete control and memory of the events that transpire.

We do not know which of these the priestesses of old experienced, but we do know from our own experience what is happening today, which we feel is of more importance from a progressive perspective.

From illustrations of the time, there is evidence that the Etruscans used much more hypnotic techniques in their rites than we do today. One such illustration on a piece of pottery shows the use of a bowl to reflect the moon into the eyes of the priestess. On one occasion, we mimicked this ritual with surprising results. While the full moon was reflected into Janet's eyes by Gavin and flashed (he tilted the bowl up and down), he also invoked the Goddess Diana. She came through Janet, taking over her whole demeanor as well as changing her voice. She then went on to

---

* Zora Neale Thurston says in *Tell My Horse*, "Baron Samedi delights in dressing his 'horses' in shabby and fantastic clothes like Papa Guede. Women dressed like men and men like women. Often the men, in addition to wearing female clothes, thrust a calabash up under their skirts to simulate pregnancy. Women put on men's coats and prance about with a stick between their legs to imitate the male's sex organs" (224).

† As in Norse/Anglo-Saxon Seith, sometimes a priestess may have no contact at all in this first stage. What in fact happens is pure prophesy with the priestess relaying the cryptic messages derived from images that she perceives.

prophesize for everyone in the Circle, one by one. This was no different than her experience with the traditional Alexandrian and Gardnerian style of Drawing Down the Moon, except that a specific deity was
invoked and a different technique was used. For in Doreen Valiente's
"Charge of the Goddess," the invocation is not aimed specifically at one
deity, but at the broader archetype of the Great Mother. We believe
this indicates that Doreen Valiente was well aware that the Gardnerian
method for invoking the Goddess was not intended to bring through any
one goddess in particular.

Drawing Down the Moon is an act of mediumship. This description
covers all the stages mentioned previously that are commonly experienced by Wiccan priestesses. But the possession of the priestess in trance
by a deity has a specific name: the *assumptive process*—the assumption
by a recipient of the deity-form's personality. The assumptive process is
not only found in Wicca. Traditions using it can be found across the world
in many other cultures. The first to come to mind is Vodoun, in which
participants of a ritual may be "ridden" by a loa. But it can also be found
in other traditions close to home, such as ancient Norse and Anglo-Saxon
culture with their practice of Seidr or Seith.* This Northern European
practice is witchcraft in the true sense of the word, and would no doubt
have been practiced in England. It is where the words *sooth* and *soothsayer* originate. In Seith work, the seeress or seer is traditionally seated
on a small hill if outdoors, or on a high chair if indoors. They descend
into the underworld by means of hypnotic chanting while visualizing the
route to the underworld. The spiritual cosmology used is well recorded
in the "Voluspa" or "Song of the Seeress" in *The Poetic Edda*† (something
we have already talked about more fully in chapter 7).

After the descent, the seer or seeress then enters the gates of Helheimr, the underworld, Jung's Shadow. It is here that they recount what
they see to those present, who may ask questions about the future. What
they see is generally in symbolic form, just like a dream. For example,
"I see you walking along a wall with a drop on either side, but you are
close to the end of the wall and will soon be able to walk on firm and safe
ground again." It is generally left to the person receiving the information
to translate the cryptic imagery.

---

*   *Seith* is the word our modern words *sooth* and *soothsayer* derive from.

†   *The Poetic Edda* was written in the thirteenth century. It has the most complete
description of an act of Seidr/Seith prophesy, as well as the most complete description of a pagan cosmology, described by a seeress herself.

In recent years, trailblazers such as Diana Paxson have reconstructed the practice of Seith.* We are honored to have been present at such an event. Although there is no mention historically about deity-forms assuming the seers or seeresses, this very quickly began to occur with quite dramatic results. The gods and goddesses had a voice again and wanted to use it!† The process parallels Drawing Down the Moon as found in Wicca, but with a Northern European slant, but unlike Wicca's Drawing Down the Moon, a cosmology is actively applied in the process.

As Janet can attest, no instructions were given for Drawing Down the Moon when she trained within Alex Sanders' coven. No visualization or trance techniques were taught, nor was any advice even given. The technique relied purely on the dogmatic following of ritual with no understanding of the metaphysics involved. When it was successful, the priestess got either one of the two results we have described: a descent into the underworld to gather symbolic information, or a trance possession—an act of mediumship. We believe the latter should be the desired result of Drawing Down the Moon. The former should be an intermediate stage, and the first experience of those who are new to the technique.

The Metaphysics of Deity Assumption

When a priestess or priest has successfully had the moon (or sun) drawn down on them, they generally describe the same feeling. They are sitting in the back of their mind, seeing and hearing everything that is going on, while the deity speaks through them. They often feel as if they are descending in an anticlockwise spiral. Those witnessing the rite often comment that they see what appears to be a physical change in the face of the priestess, seeing their face shape-shift into that of the invoked god or goddess. There can also be a change in voice and, noticeably, in temperament. This clearly describes an overlaying of the priestess' or priest's aura or mental/emotional body with that of the deities.

For this to take place, several things must happen. The first is that the chakras have to be opened. In the traditional Wiccan ritual of Drawing Down the Moon, this is done by the Fivefold Kiss, which is carried out by

---

*   The biggest exponent of this practice in neo-Paganism has been Diana Paxson of Berkley, California. She has toured the United States giving demonstrations of this Northern European form of prophetic trance. She has been a major influence in our work in the areas of Wiccan trance work.

†   There is no historical evidence that deity assumption occurred in Seith or Seidr practice. In recent years, some practitioners have discouraged this process because of this lack of historical evidence.

the magical partner of the priestess. This rite should have the opening effect on the chakras, but we now use a Sevenfold Kiss* to ensure their full opening during this rite. This also assists in creating an exchange of polarized energy, emanating from the throat center (Ether) of the priest performing the rite to the priestess the moon is being drawn down upon.

There are three chakras that specifically need to be open during this rite if it is to be successful: the root center (Muladhara), the brow or third eye (Ajna), and the crown center (Sahasara). The root center ensures that there is grounding, so that there is a free flow of energy during the process. If this is not opened, then there will be no flow of energy and the deity's aura will not flow into priestess' aura. It also keeps the actual priestess grounded and able to witness what is happening, hence most priestesses or priests describe the feeling of "stepping back" within themselves as already described. If not, they will have problems realigning their own aura's mental/emotional body after the deity has left.

The brow center is the key to the whole process. It not only generates the mental/emotional body, but (more importantly) it is the center responsible for psychic connection. It enables the achievement of the trance state, but only when it is fully opened.

The crown center, the chakra that generates the spiritual body, is the gate through which the deity's mental/emotional body descends into and overlays the priestess' own aura. It is here that our Astral Guardian resides (often referred to as the "Holy Guardian Angel"). This aspect of our Higher Selves prevents unwanted entities from gaining entry, which would result in what is commonly called "demonic possession." In all our experiences of trance techniques, we have never seen this form of possession occur.†

In the usual rite of Drawing Down the Moon, polarized energy draws the deity-form through the priestess' spiritual body and into the mental/emotional body. In normal Wiccan practice, this is done by the priest's use of the invoking Triangle of Water, where he inscribes a downward point-

---

* This goes in the order of feet (root center), genitals (sacral center), abdomen (solar plexus center), upper chest (heart center), mouth (throat center), forehead (brow center), and top of head (crown). During the kissing process, the person performing the rite breathes prana into the appropriate center.

† Such forms of possession only normally occur in people who are already psychological disturbed. "Demonic possession" is a symptom, not the cause, of the problems the person has. The possession takes place owing to disconnection with their Higher Self on the astral level. The entity that comes in simply fills the existing void.

ing triangle on her chest, traditionally using a wand. But if the person is in balance with their own anima/animus complex, then this exchange of polarized energy will not be necessary, as they will be able to generate it themselves through their own chakras. This is what happens in ecstatic, shamanic techniques, where ecstatic dance and rhythmic drumming are used. This technique not only opens the chakras, but also increases the energy of the aura, making it more accessible to the deity.

It is also important to understand what is happening from the viewpoint of brainwave activity.[5] This is normally measured by electroencephalogram (EEG). In our everyday waking lives, our brainwaves are in a state that psychologists called *beta*, but when we relax, our brainwave activity slows and enters a stage called *alpha*. The two most important brainwave activities relevant to the process of deity assumption are theta and delta. When a priestess goes into the lighter, prophetic trance states we mentioned earlier, she enters a theta brainwave state—the next slowest stage from alpha (which normally occurs just after we enter a sleep state), but if she goes deeper, she enters the lowest brainwave activity stage, known as *delta*. As previously mentioned on page 85, this is the same state that we enter in lucid dreaming during rapid eye movement (REM) sleep, when we, of course, connect to the astral levels.

Studying the processes related to the aura and chakras (see chapter 8), brainwave activity, and spiritual cosmology (see chapter 7) make it possible for us to clearly understand what is happening in the rite of Drawing Down the Moon, and allows us to create techniques that assist in the process of deity assumption.

Ways of Assisting the Process of Deity Assumption

1. Invoking. Start by calling a specific god or goddess by name. The first deity you assume should really be (but may not always be) the one to whom you are connected or dedicated as a priest. This will be the easiest one to bring through. Once you have worked with this deity, you can move on to being open to others, as you will have experienced the feeling of the process. This is important, as it is a subjective experience, and no two priestesses or priests have the same experience.

2. Using visualization techniques. The priestess or priest visualizes descending downwards to the left, while the invocation to Deity is called. At the end of the journey, she visualizes the god or goddess standing in front of her, and asks the deity to enter into her. To use

The Use of Masks and Veils

this method, it is necessary to have an understanding of spiritual cosmology, particularly the use of the Spiral Path (see pages 124–128). This method can be practiced beforehand in meditation, up to the point of calling the deity.

3. Using masks. This is an ancient technique used in ancient forms of shamanism dating back to the Stone Age. This is where the myth of shape-shifting comes from. A mask or veil, as well as appropriate dress, removes the everyday persona of the priestess or priest and replaces it with a magical one. This is particularly effective if the mask is of the face of the deity being invoked. By using this method, the ego can be sublimated, so it ceases to be a hindrance to the process.

4. Using rhythmic music. Drumming is a traditional method for causing trance states, or as Michael Harner calls them, shamanic states of consciousness (SSC).[6] Music with a strong rhythm of about 220 beats per minute stimulates theta-wave activity. Tapes or CDs of drumming music can also be used if drumming is not practical. Tapes for this purpose are now easily available from occult bookstores.

5. Chanting. Another ancient method. Instead of having just the magical partner invoke the deity, the whole coven does it with the use of a chant (*"Name-of-deity*, come to us!"), repeated rhythmically as the coven circles around the Priestess or Priest.

The God or Goddess Arrives!

What happens after Deity has entered the priestess or priest depends on both the deity concerned and the particular coven. In normal Wiccan practice, the deity speaks through the Coven Priestess, who may recite The Charge of the Goddess or something similar. Emphasis may be put on specific aspects of The Charge by inflection or by the addition of extra speech. The deity then prophesizes in a general way and directs the magical work of the group. After this, the deity slowly leaves the priestess. If the deity remains for a longer period than expected, it may be necessary for the magical partner to ask her to leave the priestess. This should always be done politely. It is also not unusual for the priestess to feel physically drained, particularly if the assumption has continued for a prolonged period. The usual cure for this is food, especially foods high in sugar. It is also common for the priestess not to retain any memory of what was said during the experience. What is happening is the same as when we lose the memories of a dream; the dream is fresh in our memory first thing in the morning when waking, but by midday we have only fragments of it left. This is hardly surprising, particularly if there is full assumption, as the mind will be in delta-wave activity, the same level of brain-wave activity found in REM sleep. There can also sometimes be a residual effect in the priestess where some of the goddess' mental/emotional body may be left behind, and some of the deity's personal traits intermittently reappear in the priestess. This can sometimes last, in our experience, for several days—particularly if the priestess is not grounded correctly through her root center.

There are other variations and departures from the standard Wiccan practice that work. One of these is for the deity to go around the coven, one by one, prophesizing to each individual. There is also no reason why members of the coven should not individually ask questions. When we have done this, we have prepared for it by having a chair for the priestess to sit on during the rite. One can also make libations, offerings, and requests to the deity. To do this, though, it is necessary to invoke a specific deity rather than do a generalized Goddess invocation (as is the norm in Gardnerian and Alexandrian Wiccan ritual).

When the deity has manifested through the priestess, it should be treated with respect. As we have said, it is a personality in its own right. It will consider itself a guest in your Circle, but will still expect to be treated with reverence. Be prepared for it to act according to its personality; on several occasions we have had people shocked by the behavior of the god or goddess who has come through. Expect a deity of love and fertility to act in a flirtatious way, and a god of a beer to go on a drinking binge! After the ritual, always remember that this is not the fault of the priestess or priest hosting the deity. They are not the ones responsible for the behavior of the deity.

But what happens if the Goddess or God called doesn't come through? Don't be downhearted. This is a spiritual discipline that takes time to learn. It also may be an indication that you need to do more study of the processes involved. This is not something you can learn overnight, and some may never be able to draw Deity into them in this way. Finding the right technique for you may be a process of trial and error. Drawing Down the Moon is a spiritual experience that, by its very nature and regardless of the metaphysical explanations we have given, is a subjective experience.

NOTES

1 Gavin Frost, *Drawing Down the Moon*, Margot Adler, chap. 2, p. 23.

2 Jung defines *synchronicity* as "a meaningful coincidence in time," but specifically to the connection with Deity: "The coincidence of a certain psychic content with a corresponding objective process which is perceived to take place simultaneously." From *Synchronicity: An Acausal Connecting Principle*.

3 This is our own definition. In the Spiritualist sense, it is no different than the Holy Guardian Angel.

4 The Center Pillar Ritual is the opening of the energy centers related to the Cabalistic Tree of Life (see figure 1). They are opened starting from the feet: Malkuth, Yesod, Tiphareth, Da'arth, and Kether. In *The Witches' Craft* (pages 24–31) Raven Grimassi points out that these are also known in Freemasonry as the "Five Points of Fellowship."

5 Research taken from W. C. Dement, *Some Must Watch While Some Must Sleep* (New York: W.W. Norton, 1978) and J. P. J. Pinel, *Biopsychology* (Needham Heights, MA: Allyn & Bacon, 1992).

6 Professor Michael Harner is considered the "father of modern shamanism." His core shamanism techniques were published in his work *The Way of the Shaman*, the first book of its kind.

11

First Steps on the Path: Finding a Progressive Teacher or Coven

Let us watch well our beginnings, and results will manage themselves.

—ALEXANDER CLARK*

Janet initially became involved in Witchcraft to get someone out of it. But this was in 1969, and things were very different. Even though the anti-witchcraft law was repealed in Britain in 1951,† there was no protection under European law,‡ and the general public found it the very difficult to cope with the idea that Witchcraft and Paganism were not connected with Satanism, let alone the concept that they were religions. Witchcraft therefore remained underground, which resulted in two major hurdles for anyone trying to find a way in. The first one was finding a coven, as there were no Pagan magazines or other forms of advertis-

---

* Film and Broadway actor. Died 1995.
† The Witchcraft Act of 1736 was repealed in 1951, following the prosecution of Helen Duncan, a spiritualist medium, in 1944. She was from Gavin's hometown of Portsmouth, and had, unfortunately, been too accurate for the authorities, informing a mother of her son's death at sea before the Navy could. She was considered a threat to national security.
‡ *The European Declaration of Human Rights* (1991), articles 10, 11, and 14, now guarantees European citizens the freedom of religious belief and practice, as does the United States' First Amendment. The United Nations' *Universal Declaration of Human Rights* (1948), article 2, does likewise.

ing widely available, and the second was learning how to find genuine Witches, ones who were not out to exploit you.

There were a couple of ways of finding covens at that time. One of these was to approach an occult bookstore to see if they knew of one. The other was knowing someone who knew of the existence of a coven. Even up to the mid-1980s this was still a problem, as Gavin discovered. It was still a situation where you were more likely to find egotists, who were more interested in exploiting others for the purposes of self-aggrandizement, rather than in teaching magical or spiritual practices.

Janet was introduced to the Sanders and their coven through a friend who was reading June John's *King of the Witches,* a biography of Alex Sanders. She went along with her friend because she was worried about her. At the time, Janet was a Sunday school teacher with a strict Christian upbringing. But this was not her first excursion to see some Witches, as she had previously gone along to visit an all-girl coven in Tooting, South London—a group Janet still refers to as "the red-knicker coven" because of a strange rule requiring the members to wear red lingerie during ritual. This seemed to confirm in Janet's mind that Witches were very strange people indeed! When Janet's friend said she was going to see Alex and Maxine Sanders, she decided she better go along too! Janet was quite surprised at what she found. Here was a spiritual path she could relate to. Rather than dissuading her friend from joining the coven, she joined herself. Ironically, the friend she went to protect decided it wasn't for her after all. Within a year, Janet had met Stewart Farrar, and she left with him to form a coven after receiving third degree. Such a quick elevation to this level would be considered unacceptable today, but was not unusual in the 1960s and '70s.

Gavin's introduction was very different. His mother had been very open about religion, in spite of being a lapsed Catholic convert. She encouraged exploration of all forms of spirituality, as well as the unknown and the supernatural. She openly visited mediums on a regular basis. He had originally been interested in several different religious paths, and had "pick and mixed" from them: polarity from Taoism, reincarnation from Buddhism, and polytheism from Hinduism. For a while he regularly visited his local Spiritualist temple for healing, as well as exploring Spiritualist doctrine. He considered his beliefs his own and was shocked to find, after getting a copy of Doreen Valiente's *An ABC of Witchcraft,* that his own unique belief system was the same as that of Wicca.

Over the years, Gavin read more and slowly met others in his home-town who were interested in Wicca. More books were being published about Witchcraft at this time, and more people were showing interest. Eventually, in the early to mid-1980s, he ended up in the woods one Samhain (Halloween) with a group of friends celebrating the festival. Af-terwards, Gavin felt uneasy. The ritual had not gone that well, the Circle hadn't been cast properly, and those present had seen inexplicable things in the woods. He set about looking for people with experience, or so he thought!

At this time in Britain, things were still closed off. There was no con-tact network for Witches or Pagans that covered the whole of the country until the end of that decade, and there were still few magazines being published. *The Wiccan,* the journal of the British Pagan Federation was still a piece of A3 paper folded in half, which only gave a few contacts for covens in London and thereabouts. The first group Gavin came across was a magic group working out of the back of an occult shop. It was not a Wiccan group, but a mix of Earth magic, ceremonial magic, Spiritualism, and various new age practices. It was from this group that the person who introduced him to Seax-Wica came, and helped him and the others form a coven. All the members of this subsequent coven went through several bad experiences with self-proclaimed "experts" and "teachers" who were more interested in control than in expanding the knowledge of the coven members. The climate of the time encouraged such individuals to thrive. Regardless of the setbacks, Gavin continued to look for an es-tablished coven to train with, while continuing to educate himself on the occult. Eventually, with his then-current partner, they formed their own coven, which ran successfully for many years. Hive-off covens still exist to this day in the south of England.

Neither of us regret the experiences we went through in trying to find a coven. "You have to kiss a lot of frogs before you find a prince," to quote an old saying. We tend to look at these as learning experiences we had to go through to understand Witchcraft properly. But that was then, and the situation today is very different.

The Attraction to Witchcraft

There are several reasons why people are attracted to Witchcraft. Many have the experience of "coming home." This has been voiced to us on several occasions and seems to be a common experience. This is mainly due to the fact that Witchcraft is a natural spirituality, with free expres-sion as a central part of it. Some become disillusioned with mainstream religion and seek to find something that fulfills their need for mysticism. This important part of Christianity seems to have been lost over the last century. Over the years, we have had contact with several Jewish and Christian Witches, who saw no dichotomy in being a witch as well as Jewish or Christian. It may seem odd to some that it is possible to be two religions at once, but this is not unusual in Eastern culture where fusions of such religions as Hinduism, Buddhism, and Shinto are common.

The need to find an explanation for a psychic or occult experience also draws people to Wicca. Witchcraft offers both a good grounding in psychic and occult practices and a logical explanation of such phenom-enon, which cannot be found so easily elsewhere. We have initiated at least one person who was a ghost hunter, and it was his need to find an explanation of his firsthand experiences that drew him into Witchcraft.

Teenage rebellion is also common factor. In recent years, television and movies have made this factor even more influential. Many young people go through the phase of challenging the norms and values of their parents and society. Teenagers who played with Ouija boards and tarot cards were almost a cliché when we first came into the Craft. Now it is the gothic/vampire image that is commonly seen at Pagan festivals. There is nothing wrong with this. It is part of growing up, and we are the first to admit that this element was (and still is) in us when we first became interested in Witchcraft. We expect the same is true of some quite well-known figures in Wicca today.

Many are attracted to the idea of the coven: a small group of people with a similar philosophy. This attraction has very much come about because of the breakdown of the extended family in modern culture. In the past there were large families with at least three generations interact-ing. Now we have the nuclear family consisting only of two generations, parents and children, which splits when the children come of leaving age (see page 77). The need to belong to a "family" group with its own iden-tity is a strong human instinct. Tribalism can even be seen in the youth culture that has developed since the 1960s. The coven fulfills this need, and many run on this line with the Coven Priest and Priestess acting as surrogate "parents." In fact, one of the greatest compliments a Coven Priestess can receive is when she is referred to as "Mom"!

We have also come across people attracted to Witchcraft because they have needed healing, be it physical or (more often) psychological. This is called "wounded healer syndrome." It is a concept known to anyone who is involved in the healing arts. It was known to the ancient Greeks, who

personified the concept as the crippled god of healers: Aesculapius. It occurs when a person who needs healing confuses this need with a desire
to become a healer. There is, in fact, nothing wrong with this, as the best
healers are those who can empathize. A good example of this is in rape
counseling: only someone who has been through this traumatic experience can really help others through it. Quite simply, the best healers are
those who have been healed. But the "wounded healer" process can only
take place if the person recognizes their need for healing.

Of course, the reason for someone's interest in becoming a Witch can
be a combination of any of the above rather than just the one. But none of
them are a reason to turn away anyone who is truly interested. It is easier
today to find out about what Witchcraft is than at any time in recent history, and the subject of Witchcraft has become more publicly acceptable.
But for anyone who seriously intends to take up the path of Witchcraft, it
is important that they understand why they are attracted to it, and what
the motivations behind this attraction are. They have to ask the question,
"Why do I want to be a Witch?"

By the turn of the millennium, both in the United States and the
United Kingdom, Pagan contact networks had been in existence for over
a decade. The number of books published on the subject has more than
doubled, and there are even glossy magazines on the market now. Finding a coven has never been easier. In the past, you took what you could
find, and you had little choice about what tradition or type of coven you
joined. Now the seeker not only has this choice but can also decide to go
solitary.

In the past, solitary Witches were not accepted, on the grounds that
they had received no formal training. To be fair, it was a good point, as
at that time there was not the same amount of material on Witchcraft
available as there is today. The publishing industry and the Internet have
changed this situation considerably, and we see no reason why a Witch
shouldn't train him or herself. There are now support groups for solitaries, training courses, and even instructional videos. There are disadvan-
tages, of course, for there is much you can learn about ritual and magic
from experienced people and the solitary Witch misses out on this. Most
of the solitaries we have met have learned just as much as they would
from a coven, although the process takes longer, and there is a greater
chance that they give up. We do recommend that those who wish to become a Witch try, wherever possible, to find a good experienced coven
to train with, but sometimes this is just not possible when one lives in an

area where there are no reputable Witches* around. It is better to train yourself as a solitary than join an incompatible coven.

Finding a Way In

So what happens if someone has decided that they want to start on this path and want to train with a coven, find an experienced teacher, or get support as a solitary? As we said earlier, this is much easier today than in the past, and there are several options open for the seeker to explore. We regularly find ourselves answering mail from seekers trying to find a teacher or coven, and the options we list below are our most common answers:

1. **Local Occult/New Age Bookstore:** It's not unusual for training groups, covens, support groups, and networks to advertise through these shops, normally with postings on the notice board. You may also talk to any of the staff or the owner, as they tend to know what's going on in the local area and can point you in the right direction. In our experience, they are always happy to help, as they are normally involved in some form of occult practice. It's also very common for them to be running some sort of group from the back of the shop, particularly if it's an occult bookstore. You may also find that they run workshops, lectures, and have guest speakers at the shop on a regular basis.

2. **Magazines and Periodicals:** There are several Pagan and Wiccan magazines around nowadays (some of these are listed in the back of this book under Appendix D). They always have a section for advertisements and contacts, normally categorized into covens, training courses, local moots (open meetings), and local events such as open festivals. Of course, you don't see many such magazines on your average newsagent shelf, although some are beginning to appear. You will find them in occult/New Age bookstores however.

3. **Local Moot/Support Group:** These are open Pagan meetings, not always specific to Witchcraft, but you can almost guarantee there will be a few Witches present. The useful thing about moots is that you can meet members of potential covens, or teachers, in an open, noncommittal environment, which is good for both parties. Organizers of moots are always quite happy to point you in the direction of whom to talk to at the moot and they often act as go-betweens for

---

* Our view of what a "reputable Witch" or coven is, is a Witch or coven that is ethically based—and that does *not* mean one that necessarily has the "correct lineage" or initiations.

magical groups, teachers, and potential members. Most moots have their own mailing lists, and can be found advertising on the Internet, as well as on the notice boards of occult bookstores. Moots act as excellent support groups for those who wish to follow the solitary path; they give a feeling of fellowship often not experienced by the solitary, but without the commitment of a coven.

4. **The Internet:** The amount of information on the World Wide Web on Witchcraft is quite staggering, and covens were quick to realize that they could anonymously advertise on this medium. Many covens, and even traditions, have websites outlining their practices, beliefs, structure, et cetera. This means you can quite literally shop around for the coven that suits you, although you may not necessarily find that your local coven advertises. There are also other sites (such as The Witches' Voice; see Appendix D), which have contact pages for covens worldwide. For the solitary, of course, the web offers an unlimited source of training material, and there are numerous online support groups for solitaries.

5. **Open Organizations:** There are several organizations around that are happy to accept members purely by application. Many of them require a declaration that the potential member has Pagan beliefs or ethics. They normally run some sort of contact service, as well having a magazine, website, and mailing list, and they organize events such as conferences (e.g., The Pagan Federation, the Covenant of the Goddess, et cetera.) They also tend to vet covens that advertise through them, and will refuse to list them if there are complaints against them. Such organizations can be found advertising in Pagan/New Age magazines, as well as in more mainstream, newsagent-shelf-type astrology magazines.

Approaching a Coven or Teacher

There are no hard-and-fast rules as to what happens next after you have found someone you want to learn with—as anyone who runs a coven tends to have their own personal rules on such things. If you met them personally at a moot, or an open gathering, it is up to you to approach them. Don't do this straightaway: attend several moots over a period of time and try to get to know them. You may find that you don't like them or don't agree with their ideas or philosophy. You need to make sure that they know that you are genuinely interested in learning about Wicca, but don't try to impress them, because you won't. Most good Coven Priestesses and Priests know a yarn when they hear one. Try to find out their views on things that might be of concern to you before asking about coven membership.

If at a first or even second meeting of an open meeting you are approached by a coven leader and asked if you are interested in joining their coven, walk away! Proselytizing is considered to be one of the few Witchcraft sins. There has always been a rule that you don't actively recruit but allow the seeker to find you. We still feel this holds true, along with the Hindu saying: "When the chela (seeker) is ready, the guru (teacher) will appear." We have found that coven leaders who proselytize do so more for their own needs rather than the needs of the potential member. The same rules apply if you are mailing a coven about membership. You should never receive a mail saying that you have been accepted without first having some sort of interview.

Asking the Right Questions

Interviews are normally the second step toward becoming a member of a coven, regardless of how you've contacted them. It gives the coven leaders a chance to meet you more formally and find out if you're serious. These normally take place at the home of the Coven Priestess and Priest, but they may also meet you at a neutral venue where you can talk quietly. Other coven members may also be present. Expect to be questioned about how you got interested in Witchcraft, what your religious beliefs are, and what you understand a coven and a Witch to be. Be honest! If you don't know the answer to a question they ask, be unafraid to say that you don't know. It is important that you be yourself. They aren't interested in what you know; they are interested in what sort of person you are, whether you will fit in with the rest of the coven, and if you have a willingness to learn. They should tell you what they expect from their coven members. This will include the level of work they will expect you to undertake, how they expect you to behave, et cetera. They should also tell you the origins of the coven, and how it is organized.

This is also your opportunity to assess your potential teacher. Are they genuinely interested in you and your spiritual development, or are they more interested in getting another coven member? Do they give you a chance to talk, express any concerns, and ask questions? These are all important questions to ask yourself. Any good coven leader is interested in you as a person, not as a coven member, and will therefore attempt to get to know you. They will also allow you to do most of the talking, and will prompt your questions if necessary. Beware of coven leaders who talk at you. This is not a good sign for things to come! They should allow you to ask questions and be comfortable with giving you the answers that you need. Beware of coven leaders who "fudge" answers they don't know. A good teacher will always admit if they don't know something.

It is always useful if you bring with you a list of the books you have read and have some idea of questions you want to ask them. Don't be scared of asking the hard questions.

Sexual initiations and skyclad work (naked in ritual) are the most common concerns for would-be initiates in our experience. Some covens still have sexual initiation, although nowadays such covens are rare, as the practice is becoming less acceptable to mainstream Witchcraft. There is nothing wrong with sexual initiation, as long as the initiate is made aware of this practice within the coven right from the beginning, and that such practices are safe, sane, and consensual. If you don't like the practice, you can look elsewhere. The same applies to going skyclad, which tends to be more common, particularly among more traditional Gardnerian and Alexandrian covens. Find out right from the beginning the practices of the coven, particularly their ethics. It may save you, and the coven that you are considering joining, a great many future problems. Again, don't be scared of asking such questions. You are more likely to impress a good teacher with your frankness than scare them off, as it shows you have thought everything carefully through.

If you are unhappy with the answers you receive, first try to get them clarified. If you are still unhappy, simply say that you don't feel this is the coven for you. Never join a coven if you have a doubt: you should be completely secure in your decision. A good coven leader will understand this. Not only will she be happy about it, she may even point you in the direction of a coven that might suit you! You should always part on good terms. We, as coven leaders, make a point of vetting potential members for a long period of time. We feel this is important for the integrity of the coven, as we don't want someone who is going to waste our time and cause problems because our coven doesn't suit them. But that doesn't mean that we necessarily believe Witchcraft isn't for them, and on many occasions, we have passed such individuals on to other covens better suited to them.

Control Issues

If things go well, the Coven Priestess and Priest are likely to say straight away that they will consider you, but they are unlikely to give you a firm yes or no immediately. You will probably be asked to informally meet the coven or even attend a Circle. Remember that these are people you are going to have to work with magically and psychically in an intimate environment, and they will also want to get to know you as well. This gives you a good chance to seriously look at the way the group is run and assess whether this is the group for you. With this in mind, we have included a list of considerations[1] when approaching a coven, to assess their practices and whether they are "a safe bet," so to speak.

1. How much control does the priest/priestess wield over the coven? Does this include the member's lives outside of the coven, including their sex and private lives?

You should look carefully at how much control the leaders of the coven have over the members. Witchcraft is not a cult, where its leaders affect the whole lives of its members. If a Coven Priestess or Priest tries to tell the members how to run their lives, then you should think carefully about joining—particularly if this is directed at the members' personal lives. A good coven leader doesn't make moral judgments related to a member's sexuality or relationships outside the covenstead. More importantly, they certainly don't see the members of the coven as potential sexual conquests.

2. Do the leaders of the coven claim to know everything? Do they claim to be infallible in their decisions, or even that their decisions are divinely inspired and therefore cannot be questioned? How are those who question treated?

Nobody knows everything. One thing a good Coven Priestess or Priest learns is that they never stop learning. Just because someone appears to have a lot of knowledge, this doesn't mean that they are wise, but that they have read a great deal! Wisdom comes from a combination of knowledge and experience. If you come across someone who says that they don't need to learn anymore, this is a bad sign. Such a leader is likely to be dictatorial and will take offence to questions, which they see as challenging their knowledge and, therefore, their authority. They may tell members to avoid or even not to read certain books or visit certain websites for this reason.

3. Is the coven run in a dogmatic fashion without creativity? Is it "by the book," so to speak, with the same rituals every Circle? Are new ideas discouraged and put down? Does the coven lack a sense of fun and humor, particularly if something goes wrong in Circle?

Witchcraft is fertility based spirituality and therefore sees the importance of creativity in everything. A coven that embraces the fundamental principles of Witchcraft, will therefore be creative in the way it works. There will be experimentation within Circle, and its members will be encouraged to experiment with ritual rather than dogmatically follow a system. Any dogmatic or doctrinal coven is likely to continually tell its members who show any creativity that they aren't doing things the "right way." Such covens tend to be stagnant and its leaders obsessed with tradition. A lack of sense of humor is a giveaway in such a coven. Mistakes by members are likely to be seen as failures rather than experiences to learn from. There will be little room for growth in such a group.

4. Do the leaders of the coven actively encourage its members to recruit? Do they poach members from other covens? Do they claim to be the only real Witches or coven in their area? Do they claim to have "the best coven"?

As we said earlier, proselytizing is unacceptable within Witchcraft. Sometimes leaders may get around this by sending out its members to recruit. This is still unacceptable and indicative of a cult-like structure within the coven. Coven Priests and Priestesses who try to steal members of other covens show a lack of security within themselves and in the coven they run. They may see themselves as being in competition with other coven leaders. This insecurity may manifest as elitism. There is nothing wrong with a Coven Priestess or Priest being proud of its coven achievements, but there is no competition in spirituality, and a good coven leader knows this. They know that the best way to build a coven is slowly, and that they will get more dedication from a coven member who comes to them in their own time.

5. Do the coven members pay for training, aside from the usual coven dues (donations toward covens costs such as candles and incense)? How do they rationalize this?

"You do not charge other members of the Craft" is one of the old laws dating back to Gerald Gardner. It still holds true within the coven setting. If you are specifically being charged for attending training Circles, this is financial exploitation. If you join a coven, you should expect to train for free, but don't expect the coven leaders to foot the bill for such things as candles, incense, and wine and food for Circle. Of course, many coven leaders run beginner's courses or even workshops outside of the coven, but this is different from running a coven.*

6. Are members discouraged from leaving the coven? Are ex-members demonized?

A good Witch knows that everyone must ultimately follow his or her own spiritual path, and a good Coven Priest or Priestess knows that this is also true for their own coven members. For this reason, a coven member should never be discouraged from leaving the coven. They may, of course, be offered other options in some circumstances, but they should never be told that they can't leave. There should be no paranoia or demonization of ex-members. This happens if the coven is worried that they might reveal a secret that might damage the reputation of the coven or its leaders. If they are worried about this, they probably have good reason to be, particularly if members are told to have no contact with ex-members. It indicates a problem within the coven.

7. Are members discouraged from being involved in outside activities, such as moots or open Circles? Is there a feeling of paranoia regarding outside groups and real or imaginary enemies?

Some covens, right from their conception, decide to remain secret. Its members may decide that they are quite happy with just being within the coven and may not wish to be in contact with the wider Pagan community. This is their personal decision. No coven should lay down a rule saying its members can't attend open Pagan events, meetings, or Circles. Leaders of such covens are worried that members may discover negative things about them, or compare what happens in the coven with what happens elsewhere. Paranoia and the idea of "enemies of the coven" are used by cults as a method of controlling their members, and if this is present within a coven, this indicates that there are more things going on in this coven than first meets the eye.

When you first meet a coven, be it informally or in Circle, the first thing that should strike you is how relaxed the members are with each other, particularly when the Coven Priest or Priestess is present. It should be a family atmosphere rather than that of a religious meeting. There should always be a certain degree of banter and humor going on. The members should always treat the leaders of the coven with respect. They give their time and energy freely to train the coven members, and

---

* They are not acting as Coven Priestess or Priest in these situations. There is no spiritual obligation between them and those attending their workshops, only the obligation to give "value for money."

deserve this respect. But it should be reciprocal. A good Coven Priest-ess or Priest returns the respect that they receive. In most covens that have been active for some time, the leaders tend to be seen more like parental figures than leaders.

You're In!

After being invited to several coven meetings, the Coven Priestess and Priest will decide whether to accept you into the coven. It is likely that they will confer with the other members of the coven on this decision, so be aware of this. The Coven Priestess and Priest may be happy with you, but if other members are not, you may still find yourself looking for another coven. Even when you are accepted, you still have the chance to leave if you are unhappy with the coven for some reason.

If you are accepted, then you have started with the first footstep on the path to becoming and understanding what a Witch truly is. As Stewart Farrar once wrote, "What makes a witch?" The answer he gave was, "A sense of wonder!" The long spiritual path of Witchcraft makes that sense of wonder one of the most rewarding aspects of being a Witch. The enhancing of your personal spirituality and the unveiling of the mysteries behind that spirituality will indeed increase your sense of wonder. Enjoy every step upon the path you have chosen to walk. Honor those who give of themselves to teach, be gracious in your dealings with others, and forgive those who you perceive as doing you wrong, for they are also teaching you. Remember that it is not the end result that is the wonder, but the journey itself, the quest for the Grail.

NOTE

1   These "considerations" originated from Isaac Bonewit's Cult Danger Evaluation Frame (first published in *Real Magic*), which we previously published in *The Pagan Path*. See http://www.neopagan.net/ABCDEF.html/.

Liber Actios

A Training
Manual

Liber Actios

A Training Manual

Learning without thought is labor lost; thought without learning is perilous.
—CONFUCIUS[1]

The purpose of the *Liber Actios* (*Book of Actions*) is to teach the Witch how ritual actually works. It is a suggested course of study that should take twelve months or more to complete. In many previously written books on the subject of Wiccan ritual, including our own, much emphasis has been put on exact words for rituals. Here the emphasis is on the feeling, understanding, and knowledge that are important to create successful ritual. To do this, it is necessary to have read the other chapters in this book, particularly the sections on knowledge-based ritual (see chapter 6), spiritual cosmology (see chapter 7), and on chakra and aura energy (see chapter 8). In this way, the student can learn ritual both as a skill and as an art form, while avoiding the dogmatic use of phrase. They can also add their own words and cultural overlay to any magical work (e.g., Celtic, Norse, Greek, Roman, et cetera) with a bit of research. Quite simply, this is a blueprint for creating your own unique Book of Shadows and personal (or group) magical tradition. This is in keeping with the ideals and Tenets of Progressive Wicca we have listed in chapter 2 (see pages 41–43).

Creating Your Book of Shadows

The Book of Shadows (BOS) is the Witch's magical diary and notebook. Of course, this is the traditional Wiccan name, but other names are also used, such as Book of Lights, Book of Light and Dark, Liber Umbrarum[2] (Black Book) to name a few we have encountered. What is important is its function as a record of what you are doing and what you have done. It is a magical notebook and diary combined. Traditionally, the BOS is passed on. In this way, knowledge could be accumulated over a period of time and added to by the new generations of Witches.

Most people imagine a leather-bound, black, dusty old tome of knowledge when you talk about the BOS. The reality is something different. Most Witches who have been around a while, including ourselves, prefer to use ring binders. These are popular, as you can move material around very easily, which is particularly useful if you wish to update rituals. There are some quite fancy ones for sale now, particularly from occult shops. In the last ten years, even the ring binder has been superseded: we are now in the age of the CD "Disc of Shadows" (DOS), with all the necessary material being kept on personal computers.

Your Book of Shadows is the first thing you need to acquire, even before being initiated. It may include the following material:

- **The Magical and Occult Laws** (see Appendix A). The first stages of a new Witch's training generally cover ethics, and magical and spiritual laws. In a coven, this also includes the Coven Rules and Craft Laws (see pages 81–82).
- **Magical and Spiritual Cosmology:** List and draw out a diagram of the realms. Mark out any paths you find between them as you explore them. Make a diary of your experiences within each realm.
- **Magical Exercises:** These include working with the elements and the other exercises included in this book, such as chakra exercises (see pages 137–138, 142–144). These should be included after you have done them—not before. You should include personal notes on your experiences: how you felt and what you visualized.
- **Rituals:** Circle casting, seasonal festivals (Sabbats), and other magical workings. Like the magical exercises, these should be included after you have done them—not before.
- **Correspondence Tables:** Instead of just copying out the correspondence tables as you have found them in this and other works, you should also include the correspondences you have discovered from

working with the elements in the exercises, and from magically working with the seasons and the power tides (see pages 164–166).

The Magical Tools

The most important magical tool that you have is your mind. Without
the skills and knowledge of their use, your other magical tools are useless
props. With practice, a good Witch should be able to cast a Circle or do a
magical act purely with energy and without any tools at all. Magical tools
exist purely as aids, which are particularly useful when you wish to focus
a group of people on a magical task or a complicated magical work. It is
true that a well-consecrated magical object exists on an astral level (see
page 147), but it is still just a tool, nonetheless.

The personal tool of the Witch is often referred to as the athame,[3] a
small knife blunted for safety purposes. It may have other names, such
as the sax, in the Seax-Wica Tradition. It can be decorated with magical
sigils as appropriate to your belief. It represents the element of Fire, just
like the sword (see pages 212–213), of which it is the smaller equivalent. It
is a memory of humanity's first truly crafted tool, the knapped flint, and
his mastery of the elements in creating it.[*]

There are four magical tools related to the elements, as previously
mentioned. Their purposes are related directly to the elements they represent:

- **Pentacle:** The tool for banishing through grounding, and for consecration to cause a physical/astral link
- **Wand:** The tool for invoking higher forms of Spirit, in other words,
  gods and goddesses
- **Sword/Athame:** The tool for invoking and controlling (through the
  use of will) lower forms of Spirit, such as elementals. It is important to
  note that its traditional use at the quarters is not to control the Guardians of the Quarters,[†] but the raw element they bring into the Circle.
- **Chalice:** The tool for evocation from within. For instance, the chalice
  is used to evoke the emotion of love and trust.

There are also two three other magical tools[‡] that are rarely discussed,
as such:

---

[*]   This is the reason it is equated with *will*.

[†]   In Gardnerian and Alexandrian practice these are referred to as the "Lords of the
      Watchtowers."

[‡]   With the four elemental tools related to the elements, it can be seen that all seven
      tools also relate to the chakras, as well as the accessible magical realms.

- **The Cauldron:** Represents Ether (see pages 144–145), life force.* It is placed in the center of the Circle during the raising of energy.
- **The Stang or Staff:** Represents the power of the mind: an extension of the power of Air. It is traditionally pointed at its bottom end so it can be pushed into the ground in the center of the Circle, where it represents the axis mundi[4] (see pages 114–116).
- **The Altar:** The altar represents the spirit of the individual practitioner(s) of the ritual, as well as of the divine. Normally it would consist of a small table with a cloth and a representation of Deity placed centrally on it. Outside, it could be a tree stump or even just a cloth on the ground. For a group or an individual, it should have on it representations of the sacred, such as a statue of the God or Goddess. Traditionally, it is placed in the north[5] or in the center of the Circle, although there is no reason it could not be placed at any of the other quarters if you are working with that quarter's element. On it should be the elemental tools, censer, candles, et cetera, as well as the athame ready for use.

Working with Your Aura and Chakras

It is a good idea to understand how your bodily energy system works before starting any of the following exercises, particularly those related to Circle casting and working with the elements. Read the chapter on sorcery (chapter 8) carefully, and start a regime of practice related to your chakras and aura:

- Open and close your centers on a regular basis for a period of a month, ensuring that you ground properly.
- Practice expanding and retracting your mental/emotional body on a regular basis.
- Be aware of how your chakra Centers and your aura react to the presence of others.
- After a period of time successfully opening your chakras, hold one hand in the other and visualize a circuit of energy flowing around from heart center to your hands and back to heart center. If you are working with a partner or group, work through the chakra exercises together (found on pages 137–138, 142–144).

---

* In Celtic myth, the cauldron was a symbol of rebirth, the return of the life force. A good example is the Dagda's cauldron.

Creating the Temple: Basic Magical Practice

The general method of creating sacred space in Witchcraft is to cast a Circle. There are generally three reasons for doing this before performing any magical work:

1. To put up a protective etheric barrier against spiritual intrusion.
2. To act as a vessel to prevent any magically raised energy from dissipating.
3. To create a sacred consecrated space that reflects onto the astral level.

A Circle can be cast for some or all of these reasons. The reason for casting the Circle is more important than any particular method of working. To perform any kind of magical working, the following are required:

- **Preparation:** Having everything you need to perform the magical task. This includes basic knowledge of ritual, magical tools, correct environment, et cetera.

- **Intention:** Being clear in your mind why you are performing ritual, and being able to focus on what you want to achieve. One should, for example, know what a quarter Guardian is if you will be calling one.

- **Visualization/Vocalization:** The ability to fix an image in your mind of the magical energy/spirit forms you are working with, and then verbally express what you are doing.

- **Action:** Implementing all of the above, including the correct physical actions for each magical tool—for example, an invoking pentagram using the athame.

These guidelines were originally summed up as the occult maxim "To know, to will, to dare and to be silent." This relates to the elements Air, Fire, Water, and Earth, respectively.

Casting the Circle

The first stage is preparation, as mentioned previously. You will require a quiet place where you can work undisturbed. Set up what you require:

- The altar with lit incense in a censer (or even just joss sticks), lit candles, and your magical tools, as previously described.

- Place lit candles in holders at each quarter. They may be colored for each element and quarter (see Appendix C for correspondences).

Sit in the space you are going to work in, and relax facing the northern quarter. Ground and center by visualizing yourself surrounded by the magical realms: the four elemental realms around you at each quarter, and the realms above and below (see page 117).

Pick up your athame from the altar, and hold it in front of you while facing the north. Think about why you are casting the Circle, what its purpose is, and why you are casting it.

Slowly draw the Circle by walking around the Circle clockwise. Visualize blue energy forming the Circle and creating a sphere surrounding you as you do this. This blue energy is, of course, etheric energy (see page 146–147, 150). Speak the reasons why you are casting the Circle. What words you use are not important, but the intent certainly is.

Calling the Quarters

The purpose of calling the quarters is to bring the elements into the magical Circle on a spiritual level. By doing so, you also assist in bringing them into balance within the self—"the first thing that magic changes is the self" (see pages 46, 209). For this reason, it is not the element that is called, but the spirit of the element, often referred to as the "Lord" or the "Guardian" (see page 124). It is a common mistake just to call the element itself. The spirit of the element regulates the flow of elemental energy into the magical Circle rather like a form of valve. This action protects the practitioner against elemental forms that may intrude on the sacred space being formed. This action also has the effect of opening the appropriate chakra related to that element (although the normal process of opening the chakras is from the root center up, we have found that opening from the heart center down in ritual, has the same effect (see pages 146–147). This action is generally verbalized as "witnessing and guarding the Circle."

We have used archetypes to represent these Guardians. These are, of course, how we see them. You may find that the Guardian you call may appear differently from the ones we have given below. There is nothing wrong with this, and we recommend that you work with the form that manifests for you. In fact, there is no reason why you cannot invoke deities to perform this role.* For example: east—the Dagda, south—Lugh, west—Bríd, north—Danu.

Traditionally in Wicca, the Lesser Pentagram Ritual of Invoking and Banishing (see figure 7) is used to call the quarter Guardians. This is only one method that can be used. You can also create your own ritual action to serve the same purpose. To give an example, we have created the invoking and banishing Celtic Cross (see figure 8). What is important is that

---

* These deities would, of course, be associated with the appropriate elements.

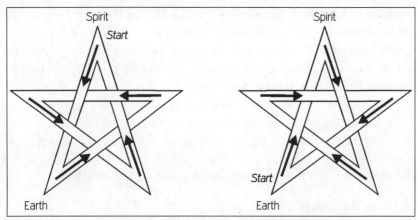

Figure 7 Invoking (L) and Banishing (R) Pentagram

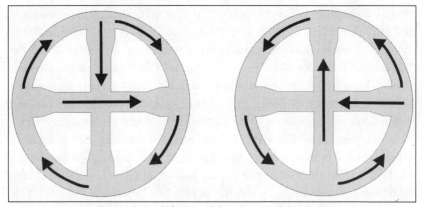

Figure 8 Invoking (L) and Banishing (R) Celtic Cross

it is reversible, so it can be used for banishing as well as invoking. Ritual stances can also be used (see figure 9), and we highly recommend these for the calling method used below.

- Go to the eastern quarter. Think about the Guardian of the element of Air. Vocalize this to reinforce your intention. Use a ritual action to reinforce the process. During this process, visualize the elemental Guardian. He is an old man, a sage or wizard, carrying a staff. He walks toward you and then turns to face outward. Become aware of your heart center opening.

- Now go to the southern quarter. Repeat the ritual process used above. Call the Guardian of the element of Fire and visualize him as a young man, a warrior with sword, walking toward you and then turning to face outward. Become aware of your solar plexus center opening.

Osiris Slain   *Osiris Risen*

Ritual Stance: Invoking

Osiris Risen   *Osiris Slain*

Ritual Stance: Banishing

Figure 9

- Now go to the western quarter. Repeat the ritual process as before.
  Call the Guardian of the element of Water and visualize her as a
  young maiden, fertile and bearing a chalice. She walks toward you
  and then turns to face outward. Become aware of your sacral center
  opening.

- Finally, go to the northern quarter. Repeat the ritual process. Call the Guardian of the element of Earth and visualize her as an older woman, a mother figure holding a pentacle or something else representing Earth. She walks toward you and then turns to face outward. Become aware of your root center opening.

After calling the quarters, stand in the center of the Circle facing north with legs slightly apart. Hold your arms out to your sides. Now visualize the realms around you. Vocalize this by saying something like:

"Before me is the Realm of Earth,
Behind me is the Realm of Fire.
To my right is the Realm of Air,
And to my left, the Realm of Water.
Below me are the realms of the underworld and my ancestors,
And above me the Astral Realms and the Abode of the Gods."

Banishing the Quarters
This reverses the process of invoking the Guardian of the element. Remember to use your intention, visualization/vocalization, and action.

- Stand in the eastern quarter. Visualize the Guardian protecting the Circle. Thank the Guardian for being present, and ask the Guardian to return to its realm if it wishes. Carry out the ritual action for banishing. Visualize the Guardian nodding to you in acceptance and walking away until it fades into the distance. Become aware of the appropriate chakra for the element closing. Repeat this process for each quarter, each Guardian, and each element.
- Now ground and center yourself. Ensure that all your chakras are closed (see page 151).

You may sense that a specific Guardian or Guardians have not left. If this has happened, do not worry. This means that there is some residual energy present related to that element. Allow the Guardians to leave when they have finished their task.

Finally, always remember when doing any form of invocation that the two most important magical words are *please* and *thank you*!

Working with the Elements
In most Wiccan and other magical traditions, working with the four elements is the first stage of practical training after learning the necessary meditation and visualization techniques (see pages 206–208). Traditionally,

the newly initiated Witch learned this when she was presented with the magical tools after initiation.[6] The next stage was to learn the correspondences of each element. Correspondences are a way of understanding how the elements are present in the world around us and how we can see them. It is, of course, an intellectual approach, and most Witches absorb this information from the many correspondence tables that are available in books. In fact, there are whole volumes dedicated to this function, such as Aleister Crowley's *Liber 777*, and other books that include detailed appendices, such as David Conway's *Magic: An Occult Primer* and Starhawk's *The Spiral Dance*. We have included some basic tables in this book (see Appendix C).

Mastery of the elements is important for two specific reasons. In the journey to experience the mysteries, balancing the elements within the self is essential to truly understanding them. Secondly, the elements are the key components used in all of the Witch's practical magical work, such as spell-craft and the creation of thought-forms. These two reasons cannot be separated from one another because of the simple occult law "The first thing that magic changes is the self." It is unavoidable that magical work will affect how the elements behave within the individual magical practitioner. It is therefore necessary to understand the elements not just intellectually, but also on the physical, emotional, and spiritual levels.

After learning about the correspondences and intellectual attributions of each element, it is necessary to feel the elements if you are to be one with them. They will "talk to you" and when they do, you will gain more knowledge about them "directly from the horse's mouth," so to speak. The first stage is always to connect with the elements physically in the natural environment. By doing so, you are connecting with each of them through the element of Earth. (As we said earlier, Witchcraft is traditionally said to be an Earth-based tradition of magic.) This step is followed by connecting with the elements on an astral level.

It is possible to access the elements by use of the Wiccan cosmology we have outlined in chapter 7 (see pages 118–122). By traveling up the Spiral Path (see pages 125–128) in a meditative state, you can ask each elemental Guardian for access to that realm and to guide you within its boundaries. What you see and experience in that realm will help you to understand that element. When we do such an exercise with our students, we take them to these realms and encourage them to explore them at their leisure, as by doing so, they will gain the benefits of connection with these elements in their everyday lives.

We recommend that certainly no less than a month should be taken to work on each element, and that all these exercises be carried out in a properly cast Circle.

Connecting with the Elements

The Element of Earth

Intellectual Connection: The traditional magical tool of the element of Earth is the pentacle. This is usually a round disc made of metal or wood with the pentagram, the symbol of Spirit over the four elements, graphically portrayed on it. It may also have other symbols related to specific Wiccan tradition, but these are superfluous to its function; what is important is its roundness, which represents the 360-degree view of the world we live in. There are alternatives to it. Some use a bowl of earth, and we have even seen an apple, freshly cut to expose the five-pointed star formed by its seeds. All are valid, as they express the physicality of the Universe, and the cycles of birth, life, death, and rebirth, which are at the center of our understanding of the mysteries. Earth is considered to be feminine in gender, and its archetype is the Mother to Crone in aspect, as it is considered to be "Mother" in its fertility and "Crone" in its death aspect.

Physical Connection: It is necessary to find a place that represents the element of Earth. Find a piece of woodland or forest that is quiet and where you know you will not be disturbed. After dark or at the winter solstice are good times, due to their associations with this element, but always put personal safety first. It doesn't necessarily have to be in the countryside. Many towns have parks where there are useful trees. Find a tree that appeals to you.

Connecting with the element of Earth

It should be large enough for you to sit with your back to it. Feel it, touch it with your hands. Put your face up against it. Try to feel what it feels. Now sit with your back to the tree in a cross-legged or similar comfortable position. Go through the process of opening your chakras (see pages 142–144). After your chakras are open, become specifically aware of your root center. Keeping your eyes closed, feel the ground beneath you through this center. You should become aware of the sensation of being able to pull heat up from the earth into your body. What else do you feel? Do you have any particular images come into your mind? Now put your hands into the soil around you and pick up a handful. What is it you are actually holding? What is its texture? What is "Earth" really made of? Finish by closing and grounding (see page 151).

Astral Connection: Follow the exercise on pages 125–128, Ascending the Spiral Path. On meeting the first Guardian, the Guardian of Earth, ask her to take you into the Realm of Earth. Allow her to lead you off the path into a forest or a similar place. She will then take you to a clearing where you find a stone circle, tree circle, or similar place (be aware it can be a different place for each person). This is a place of peace and tranquility, a place where you can go if you are stressed or facing problems. It is a place of grounding where you will find clarity of thought. It has obvious connections with the root center (see pages 138–139).

The Element of Air

Intellectual Connection: The magical tool of Air is the wand. Air is the element of the mind, governing the intellect, knowledge, and ideas. The wand is the perfect tool to represent this element, being traditionally made of wood. Air is the element that governs spiritual cosmology, which is, of

Connecting with the element of Air

course, an intellectual construct allowing travel and communication (both governed by Air) between the different realms of reality; hence the associations with Mercury (Hermes Trismegistus) who carries the caduceus (see page 134), which is a wand or staff. It is considered to be a masculine element, with the sage or wizard figure carrying his magical staff (such as Merlin) as its archetype.

Physical Connection: Find a high, windy place, preferably in the natural world, such as a hillside, cliff, or mountain—even a tall building where you can safely stand on the roof would be good. Dawn or spring equinox would be a good time to do this. Get comfortable, as you did when you explored the element of Earth, by sitting in a cross-legged position. Now open your chakras. Be aware specifically of your root center and your heart center. Breathe in deeply and listen. Now stand up, facing the wind, and open your arms wide. Visualize that you are breathing directly into your heart center. What do you hear? What do you feel? What do you smell? Let all your senses come into play. When you breathe in, where is the air going? What is it doing in your body? Finish by closing and grounding.

Astral Connection: Repeat the process similar to the element of Earth, but this time follow the path up to the next Guardian, the Guardian of Air. Ask him to take you into his realm, and allow him to guide you to a building with large doors. This is the Library. Knock on the doors and wait for entry. When the doors open, enter the Library and explore the contents. The Library is a useful place if you have questions about magical or spiritual matters, as the answers can sometimes be found amongst the books that sit on the shelves, but only if you look hard enough. You may find a large table with the book you need on it after visiting this place several times. This is your book, your Akashic Record. In it is recorded your past lives and built-up karma from those incarnations. But very few are able to read the whole of this book.

The Element of Fire

Intellectual Connection: Fire is the most active of the elements, being both creative—if handled properly—and destructive.* Its magical tool, the sword,[7] sums up its nature perfectly, as it is a weapon of destruction, forged in fire. Fire is the element of will and of desire, be it positive or negative. The sword has always traditionally been associated with law,

---

* Even this destructive aspect of fire is sometimes a positive aspect seen to be cleansing in nature.

so Fire also governs the will for justice. The sword is, of course, borne by the young warrior, an archetype that suits this element perfectly.

Physical Connection: Build an open fire outdoors, preferably at midday or at summer solstice. Sit in front of it, as with the other elements, but at a distance so that you can comfortably stretch your hands out toward it. Now open your chakras. Be aware specifically of your root and solar plexus centers. Keeping your eyes closed, put your hands out in front of you until you can feel the fire's heat on the palms of your

Connecting with the element of Fire

hands. What is it you actually feel? What do you smell? What do you hear? Now open your eyes. Look into the heart of the fire. What do you see? Are there any images forming in the flames? Finish by closing and grounding.

Astral Connection: Repeat the process as you did for Earth and Air, but this time proceed up the Spiral Path to the next Guardian, the Guardian of Fire. Ask him to allow you to enter his realm, and let him guide you into it. Let him take you to the smithy. You will hear it before you see it. You will hear the pounding of the hammer on steel, and smell the odor of the hot coals on the air. Watch the activities there, but do not enter the smithy; this is a place of both creation and destruction. Only enter the smithy if there is an aspect of your inner self that you wish to have removed from your personality, or reworked. This is the job of the smith who works here.

Connecting with the element of Water

The Element Water

Intellectual Connection:
The chalice (or cup) traditionally represents the element of Water. This vessel holds the chaotic nature of the fluid within, just as we contain the emotions within ourselves. It can also be seen to represent "the vessel of the universe"—creation itself. The chalice is the universe held in place by the spiritual, the Goddess energy of the divine, and her womb. Water is traditionally the element of "death and initiation," in other words, rebirth. Its archetype is therefore the fruitful and fertile Maiden.

Physical Connection: Find a river, a stream, or even a coastal inlet. Autumn equinox and twilight both have associations with this element. Go through the same process as you did in connecting with the other elements—getting comfortable and opening your chakras. Be specifically aware of your root and sacral centers. Breathe in and out rhythmically and open your senses. What do you smell? What do you hear? Allow yourself to drift with the sound of the water for a while, and allow images to form in your mind. Now open your eyes and carefully go to the edge of the water and scoop up a handful. What does the water do in your hands? What does it feel like? Finish by closing and grounding.

Astral Connection: Repeat the process as with the other elements, and allow the Guardian of Water to take you into her realm. She will lead you to a place of water, a stream, river, or even a well.[8] These are all access points to the underworld. By looking deep into them you can see, not only your Shadow and other aspects of yourself, but also future possibilities and events.

Exploring the Outer Realms: The Astral and the Underworld

After successfully exploring the elements, the next stage is a course of exploration of the Wiccan cosmology (see pages 119–120). Specifically, the Astral Realm and the underworld. There should be periods of rest between each exploration: we recommend at least a month. Exploration of these realms is a lifetime's work. The student should bear this in mind. The first stages are to find both your Astral and Underworld Guides.

Finding Your Astral Guide

This is already explained in Ascending the Spiral Path (see pages 125–128). Once you have found your Astral Guide or totem animal you simply ask them to show you around the Astral Realm. You should also ask your guide his/her name. This is important, as it is a way of calling your guide during future exploration of the realms. Once you have your guide, you can do the following things:

- If you have already practiced casting and creating sacred space on a regular basis, you will have already started to create an astral temple (see pages 128–130). Your guide will take you to your temple if asked, and if you haven't started this process, they will take you to the place best suited to create one.
- Within your astral temple, you can invoke your personal god or goddess.
- You can ask your guide to show you the different ways of accessing the various realms on the tree.

Finding Your Underworld Guide

This process is very different to finding your Astral Guide, although you initially use the same path-working technique described in Ascending the Spiral Path. Likewise, it is best if you have someone read it aloud to you. The only difference is that you stop at the Tree of Life and descend into the tunnel between the roots of the tree. You then descend from the Astral Realm into the underworld. On the way, you will pass through the Realm of Experience, the abode of your id, your animal self.

"Slowly, as you approach the base of the tree, you become aware of a dark patch between two of the larger roots. This circle of darkness grows as you get nearer to the tree, and seems to suck in the light around it.

"You can now make out that it is a hole; a large animal burrow. You crouch in front of it, and peer into its darkness. You realize that, with a bit of effort, it is large enough for you to enter.

"You push your head into the hole, then your shoulders, wriggling to get them in completely. The hole is tight, but not tight enough to prevent you moving your body and pushing yourself into it.

"You begin to push more of your body into the hole: Now your hips are in, and with a bit more effort, your knees, and finally your feet, leave the outside world.

"You are in darkness, complete darkness. You feel the earthy-smelling soil around you, and feel the tendrils of small roots touching your head.

"You push yourself down the hole, wriggling like a snake.

"Down and down you descend, down and down. Pushing with your shoulders, your hips, and your feet, down and down into the unknown.

"You descend further down into the darkness, down and down, down and down.

"You feel a root brushing your shoulder, but continue to descend, down and down, down and down, into the blackness.

"The tunnel you are in begins to feel tighter as you go deeper, but undeterred, you descend further, pushing with all your strength. Down and down, down and down, you go.

"The tunnel is now becoming so tight that you have to squeeze all the effort out of your muscles to move. Down and down, down and down, you go.

"Very slowly, you begin to make out a faint point of light: a grayness within the absolute blackness of the tunnel. You continue to head down, down and down, and nearer and nearer to this point of light.

"The tunnel has now become tighter, but the light has become nearer, and you push yourself toward it.

"You become aware that it is an opening to a dimly lit cavern, and you finally push your head through, and the whole of your body tumbles into the dimness that is beyond.

"You look around, and become aware that the light you could see was the phosphorescence of the cave walls. There is just enough light to see the ends of your arms and no more.

"Suddenly you become aware of a presence apart from yourself: the noise of movement but nothing else.

"You feel something brush past part of your body, and then a second later it happens again.

"Slowly, as your eyes adjust to the light, a shape begins to take form in front of you, and then it disappears into the dark shadows of the cave.

"Suddenly it is in front of you again, and you can make out the eyes of a living creature staring back at you.

"Then it is gone again into the shadows, but it returns. This time you can see not only its eyes, but also its shape—and you recognize what sort of creature it is.

"This happens several more times: the creature passing you, brushing against you, staring at you, and then finally disappearing into the shadows, and you become aware that it does not intend to return.

"You decide it is time to return with this experience. You find the entrance that you came into the cave through, and push yourself up into it.

"The tunnel is tight, but you push yourself up with your shoulders, hips, and feet. Up and up, up and up.

"Up and up, up and up, you go, retracing your journey.

"The tunnel does not appear as tight as it was, and you push yourself up. Up and up, up and up.

"The smell of the woods wafts down the tunnel, but you can see nothing but darkness. Up and up, up and up, you go.

"It has now become much easier to move in the tunnel, and you can see a bright point ahead of you. You push yourself up toward the light, up and up, up and up.

"The daylight is now much brighter, and you can now see the entrance hole to this tunnel. You push yourself up and up, up and up, toward it.

"Up and up, up and up, you go.

"Finally you push your head out of the tunnel."

"When you are ready, slowly return to this world by opening your eyes, and return to it with the experience of meeting your kindred animal spirit for the first time."

Although in traditional forms of shamanic working, you "dance your power animal" after finding it, we recommend that after you have completed this exercise, that you ground and center yourself. You may want to collect items that connect you with your Underworld Guide. These are often referred to as *totems*. They can be feathers, fur, small representations of the animal concerned, et cetera. You may want to create a small pouch to keep them in, and bring it out before doing any magical work so you make a connection with your Underworld Guide. This is particularly important when doing underworld descents.

Once you have found your power animal—your Underworld Guide— you can start to do the following:

- You can ask your Astral Guide to take you down the left-hand path of the Tree of Life into the underworld. This path is the reverse of the right-hand path. You will pass the elemental Guardians again on the way down, starting with Water, then Fire, then Air, and finally Earth. After Earth, you enter the Cave of the Mysteries.

- At the entrance of the Cave of the Mysteries, you call your Underworld Guide. On no account commence this journey without it. Ask the guide to show you around this realm. You can then explore the Underworld Realm and the mysteries.

Once you start to explore both the Astral and Underworld Realms, you will meet other entities, such as the Guardian of the Mysteries (see page 123). This guardian, along with your Astral and Underworld Guides, will prevent you from entering any realm you are not ready for, or experiencing anything before you are ready. They do this to prevent you from causing damage to yourself, so heed the advice or warnings that you receive from the guides and guardians that you meet on your journeys. They are real personalities, so treat them with as much respect as you would anyone who is teaching you.

NOTES

1   From the Confucian Analects (551–479 BC).
2   This term was used by Doreen Valiente in *Witchcraft For Tomorrow*. It is probably a more traditional term than *Book of Shadows*, as it can also apply to the grimoires of the Middle Ages.
3   The origins of the word *athame* are still debated. One view, remarked upon in Doreen Valiente's *ABC of Witchcraft*, was that it derived from *arthana*, a term found in *The Clavicle of Solomon*. Idres Shah claimed that its name derived from *al-dhamme*, an Arabic name meaning "blood letter" (from Ronald Hutton's *Triumph of the Moon*, page 273).
4   The stang is a traditional tool in Anglo-Saxon magical practice. Reference to its use can be found in several books, including *Witchcraft: A Tradition Renewed* by Evans and Valiente. Its use in modern Wiccan practice is connected to Robert Cochrane.
5   This placing of the altar in one quarter was adopted from ritual magic, where the altar is placed in the east.
6   The presentation of the magical tools is an important part of the first-degree ritual in Alexandrian practice.
7   According to Francis King, the Golden Dawn set up a blind related to the sword and the wand, exchanging them related to the elements of Fire and Air. The sword is traditionally associated with Fire, being forged in a smithy.
8   The well is believed to traditionally be an entry point into the underworld and a place of divination. This myth can be found in both Irish and Welsh Celtic mythologies (e.g., the Dagda's cauldron of rebirth, and Cerridwen's cauldron).

Appendix A

Occult/Spiritual Laws

The following is our own synthesis and simplification of the magical laws that we have come across over the years. For further information on the subject, we would suggest reading Isaac Bonewit's *Real Magic*.

1. The Law of Threefold Return

Also known as the law of cause and effect. This law states that anything you send out magically (or physically, for that matter) will return to you threefold: As ye sow, so shall ye reap. The threefold does not refer to it actually coming back to you three times, but coming back to you on three different levels: the physical level, the mental/emotional level, and the spiritual level. This law is an expression of exchange of energy on a more subtle level; therefore, it is important to ensure balance by returning favors or gifts in some way (see the law of balance). In runic lore, this is summed up as "a gift demands a gift" and is symbolized by the rune Gifu (the kiss).

2. Law of Cyclical Return

If you are unable to overcome a karmic obstacle, or unable to learn from the mistakes in your life, you will continue to face that obstacle until you learn how to overcome it. All other growth in your life will be stunted until you do so. This applies not just to this life—such a cycle can continue over several lifetimes. This is basically the law of karma and is connected to the previously mentioned law of threefold return.

3. Law of Polarity

In each thing, there is an opposite—for example, chaos/order, humor/grimness, positive/negative, male/female, yin/yang, et cetera. Both are inherently within the other, resulting in dynamic interaction and power (as in the oyster, where grit results in the creation of the pearl). It is for this reason that the use of such polarities is a source of power within magical practice.

4. Law of Attraction

Following on from the law of polarity, such opposites are attracted to each other. Hence male and female may find magical attraction within Circle (something that should not be misunderstood as sexual attraction). There is also another aspect of this law (sometimes known as the law of opulence or the law of synthesis), which states that if you wish to attract something, give away that which you already have of it. Quite simply, by bringing two forces together you create a third.

5. The Law of Balance

This law comes into play after the law of attraction. Opposite forces will always naturally fall into balance if left undisturbed. "The road to hell is paved with good intentions" is a good way of explaining what happens if this law is ignored. If you do magical work when none is needed, you may cause imbalance, resulting in the opposite of what you were trying to achieve (e.g., by doing good out of vanity rather than need).

6. The Law of Magical Accounting (the Karmic Bank Account)

When any magic performed rebalances the natural forces (see the above *Law of Balance*), a karmic payment is due. This payment can be taken in three different ways: it can be used to pay off any karmic deficit, it can be used to pay the universe for a request for magical assistance, or it can be stored in the personal karmic bank account to pay for future deficits (getting in the red). In the latter, it can be transferred after death to future incarnations. Such a karmic bank account accumulates interest. With a standing order or cosmic checkbook, it can be used to pay off karmic deficits as they occur.

7. Law of Triple Invocation

All invocations must occur three times to be successful. This triple invocation can either occur in the same fashion—for example, by saying, "I invoke you, I invoke you, I invoke you," or on three different levels—for example, by visualization, by vocalization, and by action. Regardless of technique, the triple invocation has the same effect—to send out the request on three levels: on the conscious, on the personal unconscious, and finally on the collective unconscious (astral) level.

8. The Law of Challenge
Everything that is experienced that is considered to be mystical, for example: prophetic dreams, visions, clairvoyance, et cetera, must be challenged to see if they are genuine psychic experiences. Experiences that are genuine stand on their own merits and are able to withstand such scrutiny; those that do not are potentially harmful if taken seriously, resulting in imbalance and a lack of grounding in the practitioner.

9. Law of Rebound
A superior force will always rebound a lesser force. Therefore, when approaching a guardian or entity on any level of the Astral/Elemental Realms, you will be challenged to your suitability to pass beyond them. If you are unable to pass them, it means that you are not ready and must return to continue your spiritual growth. This is particularly true when approaching the Gate of the Mysteries (see pages 53, 123, 218). To pass beyond a guardian, such as the guardian who guards the gate of death, is to experience a spiritual initiation.

10. The Law of Reflection
Most commonly expressed amongst occultists by the phrase "As above, so below." Everything on this material level of reality has its reflection on the higher astral levels. This is the basis of sympathetic magic. By using the elements (Earth, Air, Fire, and Water), it is possible to create an astral double and endow it with ability through consecration.

11. The Law of Knowledge (Including Self-Knowledge)
The basis of this law is that understanding brings control. Knowledge is essential for spiritual growth as well as for becoming adept at magical practice. The more that is known about a subject, the easier it is to exercise control over it; the more that is known about the self, the easier it is to control the self.

12. The Law of Names
A name, by common repetitive use, represents an object or person on an astral level. Therefore, the use of this name is a link to the object or person through the law of reflection. This is one of the reasons that the Craft name taken during initiation is kept secret, as such names are an

astral link to the bearer and could easily be misused. To know the name of something is to have control over it, particularly spiritual entities. A spiritual entity of good intention will always therefore disclose their name or intention to you.

13. The Law of Connection (or Unity)

Quite simply put, everything in the universe is connected. This means all events past, present, and future are linked. It is only our inadequate senses that perceive separation in the universe. Modern chaos theory postulates that a butterfly flapping its wings can alter the course of a far-off storm. Therefore, all magical acts will affect the whole universe in some way, however minor the effect may be perceived to be. This puts great responsibility on the magical practitioner.

14. The Law of Dichotomy and Paradox

All workable practices of magic have this aspect to them: the idea of the cosmic joker—or that the gods have a sense of humor (you may have noticed this in some of the laws). Magic only works because we believe it does; the moment we believe that it doesn't, then it will cease to work. This law allows effect to precede cause (time is not linear on the astral level). Several days after performing a magical working, an individual or group may discover that it had, in fact, worked several days earlier without their knowledge. It is closely linked to the law of attraction when the forces concerned are at odds with each other (e.g., grimness and humor). The application of this law can be found in such traditions as Discordia, which works on the aforementioned polarities.

Appendix B

Goddesses and Gods of Witchcraft

We have listed here a selection of gods and goddesses specific to the art of Witchcraft. It should be noted that many modern Witches worship other deities besides the ones listed. Due to the sheer number of such deities, we have tried to restrict the entries to those related to magic and sorcery.

Goddesses of Witchcraft

ARADIA: Medieval. Etruscan witch goddess, surviving into this century in Italy. Daughter of Diana (Etruscan: Aritimi or Tana) and Diana's brother, Lucifer (in other words, of the moon and the sun). Diana desired her brother, but he fled from her; so she turned herself into the shape of his favorite cat, which slept on his bed. She resumed her own shape while he was sleeping. When he awoke and found her, he was furious; but she charmed him with a song and seduced him, conceiving Aradia. Aradia came to Earth to teach the witches her mother's magic. She was unknown to scholars until Charles Godfrey Leland won the trust of Tuscany witch Maddalena and published the material she gave him in his 1899 book, *Aradia, or the Gospel of the Witches*. Aradia may, however, have spread wider than just Tuscany during the hidden centuries underground. The *Canon Episcopi*, a tenth-century Church condemnation of witchcraft, gives "Herodias" as a witch goddess name along with Diana, and *airidh* in Gaelic means both "summer pastures" and "worth, merit." There is some debate as to whether Aradia was an actual goddess or a Robin Hood-type figure, as indicated by Leland's description of her as the *bueno strega*, the "good witch," the protector of the poor, and the *daughter of Diana*—a description often used to describe a priestess in pagan times. It is very likely that Aradia was a priestess of her surviving cult.

ARTEMIS: Greek. Nature, hunting, and moon goddess; in Greek-speaking Asia, a mother goddess. Daughter of Zeus and Leto, and twin sister of Apollo—though a day older. Known as *Potnia Theron*, the Greeks assimilated her to a pre-Greek "Mistress of the Animals." Her Roman equivalent is Diana. Artemis probably absorbed a pre-Indo-European Sun Goddess, and her twinning in classical legend with the Sun God may stem from this. Bears were sacred to her, and she was associated with the constellation Ursa Major. Guinea-fowl were her birds. Doreen Valiente says her name may mean "High Source of Water" (*An ABC of Witchcraft*, 18)—the moon being regarded as the source and ruler of all waters, and of the oceanic, psychic, and menstrual tides. "Hence the moon goddess, by whatever name she was known, was the mistress of magic, enchantment and sorcery" (ibid.). Invoked by women in childbirth as Artemis Eileithyia. Protectress of youth—especially of girls. Invoked to bring good weather to travelers. She is depicted with bow and arrows, and often with a hound. One of her forms is Callisto. The many-breasted Artemis of Ephesus ("Diana of the Ephesians" of Acts 19), where her temple as a fertility goddess was one of the Seven Wonders of the ancient world, is much closer to her earlier mother function. Her cult there was said to go back to the Amazons. Festival: February 12, and the sixth day from the new moon.

BABA: Slavic. The spirit in the last sheaf of harvested grain; a woman bound to it would bear a child within the year. She degenerated to a frightening witch in folklore—Baba Yaga—who lived in the forest and scared people to death; she also rode the sky in a mortar, using the pestle as an oar. Skulls were put on fence-posts as a protection against her.

BEFANA: ("Epiphany") Medieval strega. Italian witch-fairy who flies on her broomstick on Twelfth Night (January 6) to come down chimneys and bring presents to children.

BENZOZIA, BENSOZIA: Basque. Mother goddess. As Bensozia, also a medieval witch goddess name, may mean "Good Neighbor," which is a common name for the fairies.

CAILLEACH BHEARA, CAILLEACH BUI, CALLY BERRY: Irish. **CAILLEACH BHEUR:** Scottish. (Beara is a peninsula on the Cork-Kerry border.) Lake and weather goddess who protected lakes from being drained. She dropped the cairns on the hills of County Meath from her apron, moved islands, and built mountains. Originally appeared as a triple goddess with Cailleach Bolus and Cailleach Corca Duibhne. As Cailleach Bui, said to have been a wife of Lugh. The *Book of Lecan* says she had seven youthful periods, married seven husbands (each of whom grew old and died), and had fifty foster children who founded many tribes and nations. In Ireland, a builder of mountains. In Scotland, a warner of storms and bringer of snow, overcome each spring by the appearance of Brighid,* she turned into a stone every April 30 and was reborn every October 31. Some scholars identify the Scottish form with Black Annis. One of the most ancient aspects of the Goddess in the British Isles. In Gaelic, Cailleach basically means a wise older woman, and may be applied to anyone from a nun to a witch. Interestingly, *caileach* with a single *l* means "chalice" in Irish—an essentially feminine symbol. In Scotland, the Cailleach was also known as the Carline.

CERRIDWEN: Welsh. Mother, moon, and grain goddess. Wife of Tegid Voel and mother of Creirwy ("Dear One"), the most beautiful girl in the world, and Avagdu, the ugliest boy. She had another son, Morfan, so ugly that no one would fight with him at the Battle of Camlann (at which Arthur and Mordred were slain) because people thought he was a devil. Cerridwen was said to have lived on an island in the middle of Lake Tegid. Owner of an inexhaustible cauldron called Amen (Awen), in which she made a magic draught called "greal" (Grail?) from six plants, which gave inspiration and knowledge. She intended to brew a potion in it that would make Avagdu brilliant in compensation for his ugliness, but Gwion (a little boy whom she'd left in charge of it) scalded his finger in the bubbling liquid and sucked his finger in pain—giving him the universal wisdom intended for Avagdu. Cerridwen pursued Gwion, both of them shape-changing: first she was a greyhound chasing a hare, then an otter chasing a fish, then a hawk chasing a bird. She finally caught and ate him when she was a hen and he was a grain of corn. As a result, she gave birth to Taliesin, greatest of the Welsh bards. This chase may relate to the initiation rituals of a Druid or bard. One of her symbols was a sow.

---

* The same folk myth appears in Ireland. Mackenzie probably took it from Ireland, or it originated on the Gaelic Scottish Islands.

Most of her surviving legends emphasize the terrifying aspects of the Dark Mother, yet her cauldron is the source of wisdom and inspiration.

DIANA: Roman. Equivalent of the Greek moon and nature goddess Artemis; Diana rapidly acquired all her characteristics. Originally from Latium, Diana was a goddess of light, mountains, and woods—and probably first a pre-Indo-European Sun Goddess. Associated with the constellation Ursa Major. One of her sanctuaries was at Lake Nemi, where her priest was an escaped slave who had to kill his predecessor in single combat to take the office—and then hold it in mortal combat against any would-be successor. Like Artemis, she was classically regarded as virgin, but probably originally a sacrificial-mating goddess. Under Christianity, she became the goddess of underground witches, whom the tenth-century *Canon Episcopi* condemned for believing they rode at night "with Diana, the goddess of pagans." In still-surviving Tuscany witch legend, Diana is the original Supreme Goddess and mother by Lucifer of Aradia, a name that also appears (as Herodias) in some later versions of the *Canon Episcopi*. Doreen Valiente suggests that one reason why the name *Diana* appealed to pagans was that *dianna* and *diona* were Celtic words meaning "divine, brilliant" (*An ABC of Witchcraft*, 89). British legend says Diana "directed the Trojan Prince Brutus, the founder of the royal line of Britain, to take refuge here after the Fall of Troy" (ibid., 91), and St. Paul's Cathedral in London is believed to be built on the site of a temple of Diana; there is a tradition that stags were processed up its steps until medieval times. Diana was regarded as the supreme deity by the Gauls as late as the fifth century, and was still worshipped by the Franks in the seventh century. The Gnostics identified her with Sophia. She was often portrayed as a mother with a child, and many of her temples were rededicated to the Virgin Mary. Festivals: May 26–31, August 13 and 15; on August 13, she was invoked to protect the crops against storms. Day: Monday.

FREYA ("Well beloved, Spouse, Lady"), **VANADIS** ("Ancestress-Friend"?): Norse, Germanic, and Anglo-Saxon. Fertility goddess, most revered of the Nordic goddesses. Daughter of Niord and Skadi, and sister of Frey. Originally of the Vanir (pre-Indo-European culture), in whose legend she and Frey were the children of Niord and his sister. The Aesir welcomed her and Frey and Niord and accepted them; but they rejected incest, so Skadi became Niord's wife in their mythology and his sister disappeared. Freya is sometimes confused with Frigg as wife of Odin, or in some stories, of

Od, who is sometimes equated with Odin. Frigg and Freya seem to have been originally the same goddess, or perhaps a Vanir triple goddess with Skadi; then to have developed as two, finally tending to remerge. Owner of a falcon-plumed robe in which she flew through the air, including to the underworld to gain information in her role as a seeress. She was a goddess of sexual pleasure, and was said to have slept with all of the Aesir and with her brother, Frey, as well as with giants and mortal men; her priests were regarded as her consorts. She is particularly called upon by women today who wish to regain the strength that Christian patriarchy has so long denied them. Medieval songs dedicated to her, called *mansongr*, or in German *minnegesang*, were suppressed by the Christians, but later troubadours and minstrels revived the tradition, dedicating their songs to the Virgin Mary. Said to have been a mistress of magic and witchcraft. Also a war goddess; commander of the Valkyries (originally her priestesses), she often fought alongside Odin; she claimed half of the dead slain in every battle for her hall, Folkvangr (Field of Folk), Odin taking the other half. She also received the souls of unmarried women. Loved ornaments and jewelry. She rode in a chariot drawn by two cats, and rode on a boar called Hildisvini ("Battle Swine") whose golden bristles showed the way in the dark. May have been priestess of a hawk-totem clan. Animals sacred to her included the sow, the cat, the falcon, the swallow, and the cuckoo. As Frigg, also the ram, the heron, and the spider. Although a goddess of Earth, she also had a watery side, and a dwelling in Fensalir ("Ocean Halls"). Her many names included Heidh ("Witch"), Horn ("Flax"), Gefn ("Giver"), and Syr ("Sow"). Her symbols were the spindle and the distaff; she was mistress of the crafts of the home. Associated with the zodiacal sign Leo. Friday was named after her. English place-names recalling her include Freefolk, Hampshire (Frigefolk in the *Domesday Book*, "Frigg's People"), Froyle and Frobury, Hampshire (both the latter Old English Freohyll, "Freya's Hill"), Fryup, Yorkshire ("the hop or marshy enclosure of Freya"), and Friydaythorpe, Yorkshire. Festivals: first Monday after January 6 (Saxon Plow Monday), November 21.

HABONDIA, DAME HABONDE, ABUNDIA: Medieval. A witch goddess name, doubtless implying "abundance."

HECATE: Greek. Originally Thracian and pre-Olympian, and probably even older. At the same time, a moon goddess, an underworld goddess, and a goddess of magic. Daughter of two Titans, Perses and Asteria, both symbols of shining light (a later tradition says Zeus and Hera). Took part in the Olympians' war against the giants. Dwelt in the underworld alongside Hades and Persephone. She protected flocks, sailors, and witches. Associated with crossroads, where her three-faced image was placed; offerings of food, called *Hecate's Suppers*, were left there on the eve of the full moon to propitiate her; one left them there and walked away without looking back, because no one dared confront her face-to-face. Of all the Greek goddesses, she was the most markedly triple. She was also absorbed into the Roman pantheon, where "Diana Triformis" consisted of Luna (Selene), Diana (Artemis), and Proserpine (Hecate). She was portrayed as three female figures, or as one human female with three animal heads—horse, dog, and bear, or sometimes three dogs. Like Herne in the North, she had the reputation of leading a Wild Hunt of ghostly hounds through the night. The night-calling owl was her messenger, and the dark yew and the willow, or osier, were her trees; witches' besoms were traditionally bound with osier; otherwise they were said to be useless. Her annual festival on August 13 (also that of the Roman Diana) was a propitiatory one to avert harvest-destroying storms. She is the Dark Mother, in both the positive and the negative sense. She can send demons to torment men's dreams, and drive them mad if they are not integrated enough to cope with her; but to those who dare to welcome her, she brings creative inspiration. In keeping with her depiction as a moon goddess, she has a son called Museos, the Muse-Man. For divination, the Greeks used "Hecate's circle," a golden sphere with a sapphire hidden inside it—the mysterious moon concealing the bright seed of understanding. Her symbol is the torch, which illumines the personal unconscious and reveals its secrets. In Caria (Western Turkey), she was the primary goddess; she had a sanctuary at Lagina. In Colophon, dogs were sacrificed to her, and she herself could shape-change into a dog. In Samothrace, there was a cave sacred to her called Zerynthos (from which she was also named Zerynthia) where dogs were sacrificed and mysteries performed involving orgiastic dances. It is interesting that Shakespeare has his three witches in *Macbeth* worshipping Hecate at a time when official propaganda had witches worshipping the Devil—growing up in the country, did he know better? Festivals: January 31, March 23, August 13.

HERODIAS: Medieval strega. Along with Diana, she is condemned as being worshipped by witches in the tenth century *Canon Episcopi*, and it is possible that the name is a variant of the Etruscan Aradia. The Biblical reference is from the story of John the Baptist's execution at the court of Herod (Matthew 14 and Mark 6), and many scholars believe her part in this is a later insertion.

HIR NINEVEH: Assyro-Babylonian. Goddess personifying the city of Nineveh. Roundly condemned in the Bible (Nahum 3:4): ". . . the multitude of the whoredoms of the well-favored harlot, the mistress of witchcrafts" [KJV].

LOUHI: Finnish. An enchantress who is capable of shape-changing and hiding the sun and moon. Rune 49 of the *Kalevala* tells how she sent a bear down to harass the people. She lives in Pohjola, the North, an area associated with magic.

MARI: Basque. Supreme Goddess, ruler of all other deities. Sometimes described as an Earth Goddess, but her attributes seem primarily lunar, as she is the patroness of witches and is a witch herself.[1] She lives in the depths of the earth but likes crossing the sky at night; so does her son/ husband Sugaar ("Male Serpent"). She rides the sky in a cart drawn by four horses, or in the form of a burning sickle or crescent, or engulfed in flames, or riding a broomstick in a ball of fire. The Basques appear unique in associating the moon with the color red and with fire, and Mari has strong fire symbolism. Sugaar also rides as a burning crescent, but to the Basques, the moon itself is always female (as is the sun and the earth). They respect her greatly, timing their woodcutting, sowing, and reaping by her phases. Mari's divinatory animal is the ladybird [U.S. ladybug], known as *Mari Gorri* ("Red Mari"), who is often asked to predict tomorrow's weather. Basques believe the light of the moon guides the dead to their resting place. Friday is Venus' day, and Friday night the witches' traditional meeting time. Mari is the patroness of all witches, and a witch herself, with oracular and magical powers. She often appears as an elegantly dressed lady, sometimes crowned with the full moon or a burning crescent moon. She is associated with Akerbeltz ("Black He-Goat"), whom Basque witches invoke and work with at their Sabbats, which are called Akelarre ("Field of the He-Goat"). She also rides a ram, around whose horns she wraps wool to wind into a ball. Other totem animals are the horse, the heifer, and the crow or raven. Mari changes her abode, spending seven years in Anboto, where she is known as Anbokoto Dama ("Lady of Anboto") or Anbokoto Sorgina ("Witch of Anboto"), seven years in Oiz, and seven in Mugarra. Other accounts say she spends time in Aralar, Aiztorri, and Murumendi.

SELENE: Greek (known as Luna to the Romans). Moon Goddess, daughter of Hyperion and Theia, and sister of the Sun God Helios and the dawn goddess Eos; though sometimes said to be the daughter of Zeus or of Helios. She was wooed and won by Zeus and by Pan.

TLACHTGA, TLACHTA: Irish. Goddess of witchcraft and the province of Munster. She died giving birth to triplets by three different fathers. Festival: October 31, Samhain Eve. Her sacred site is the Hill of Ward near Athboy, County Meath, where the first of the sacred Samhain fires was lit. She was probably a pre-Celtic sacrificial deity. The Church attempted to obliterate her memory, but she survived the Christian period by becoming merged with the daughter of Mog Ruith, the Arch-Druid of Ireland. This makes her sister of Tailtu, whose sacred site is not far from hers. Some texts say that, with her father, she opposed the coming of Christianity to Ireland and joined with Simon Magus in Italy to fight it. On returning to Ireland, she brought back the fragments of a stone wheel known as Roth Fáil or Roth Ramhach, which her father and Simon Magus had been using for magical demonstrations in Italy, and placed them near Rathcool, County Dublin, where they may still be seen. Her sacred animal is the cat.

Gods of Witchcraft

AKERBELTZ: ("Black He-Goat") Basque. Goat God, invoked by Basque witches at their Sabbats, which were known as *Akelarre* ("Field of the He-Goat").

CERNE: See *Herne*.

CERNUNNOS: Continental Celtic. The only known written name of the Celtic Horned God—appearing on the altar of Nautes, now in the Cluny Museum in Paris. Many other representations (such as on the Gundestrup cauldron) are clearly of the same god. The name appears to be a Romanization or Hellenization of Herne, a name that has survived in tradition and in place-names (q.v.).

FREY, FREYR: ("Lord, Spouse") Norse. God of fertility, prosperity, and peace. Equivalent of the Celtic Horned God. Son of Niord and Skadi, and brother of Freya. Originally Vanir; for his and Freya's acceptance by the Aesir (see *Freya*). Being an ithyphallic fertility god, he was very likely horned originally; in one myth of Ragnarok, it is said that he fought with antlers. His wife was Gerd. His hall was Alfheim, home of the Light Elves, given to him by the gods when he cut his first tooth. His horse was Blodhughofi ("Bloody-Hoofed"). His chariot was drawn by two boars,

Gullibursti ("Golden-Bristled") and Slidrurgtanni, and he often rode Gullibursti, who was said to be able to move over land and sea faster than a horse. Frey was probably originally chief of a boar clan of the Vanir before they merged with the Aesir. His other sacred animals were the stag and the bull (or ox). His magical flaming sword could fight of its own accord, and was the only protection against the fire demon Surt. His ship, Skidbladnir, summoned up wind as soon as its sail was hoisted; it could hold all the Aesir, but could also be folded up and put in his purse. In Sweden every year, his image traveled the country accompanied by a beautiful girl called "Frey's Wife," who also acted as priestess of his great temple at Upsalla. His titles included "Protector of the Gods," "Ruler of the Hosts of the Gods," and "God of the World." He was a sovereignty god; many kings who were regarded as his representatives were known as *frodhi* ("fruitful").

HERMES: Greek. Messenger of the gods, and god of intellect, communication, commerce, and travel. On occasion, also a trickster, bringing good luck to thieves. Originally (like Pan, who was said to be his son), Hermes was Arcadian, and in that form seems also to have been horned and goat-footed.[2] He was the psychopompos, conducting dead souls to the afterlife. Son of Zeus and the pleiad Maia. His many reputed lovers included Aphrodite, Hecate, and Persephone. His symbols were the caduceus, the winged cap, and the winged sandals. The Romans equated him with Mercury.

HERNE, CERNE: British and Anglo-Saxon. The Horned God, envisaged with stag's antlers. There are traces of him in both Celtic and Saxon tradition, where he was also revered as the god of ale, but like many of the gods of early hunting and agricultural cultures, he was pushed into the shadows by the later and more sophisticated pantheons, particularly those of warrior aristocracies. As Prionsias MacCana puts it in *Celtic Mythology*, "The Cernunnos cult would probably have survived longest among the lower orders of society, where custom died hard and orthodoxy was not easily imposed. Unfortunately this is virtually unknown territory, for it is only in recent times that the usages and beliefs of the common people received conscious recognition in written literature" (48). Cernunnos (q.v.) has become the generally used name for Herne or Cerne. The only substantial legend of Herne that has survived is that of Windsor Great Park, where he is said to lead the Wild Hunt mounted on a black horse and accompanied by red-eyed hounds. He was associated with a great oak that once grew there. There are many stories of his still haunting the Great Park—one as late as 1962, when a group of youths found a hunting horn there, blew it, and reported hearing an answering horn and seeing the Wild Hunt approaching; terrified, they ran off. His memory also survives in several English place-names in either the *H*- or the *C*- form—for example: Herne Hill, Herne Bay, Hern Drove, Herne Pound, Cerne Abbas, Upper and Nether Cerne, and the River Cerne. It has been suggested that the name Herne was adopted from the mating call of a doe for her buck—approximately *hurrrn*—on the natural assumption that if that was what she called him, that was his name.

LUCIFER: ("Light-Bearer") Roman. The Christian use of the name, from its only Biblical mention in Isaiah 14:12, is a misunderstanding of the passage, which does not refer to the Devil, but is a satirical metaphor for the tyrant king of Babylon, who occupied Palestine at that time (it is part of a song in the traditional Hebrew lamentation rhythm). In Tuscan witch legend, Diana, the first of all creation, divided herself in two; the darkness was herself, and the light was her brother, Lucifer. She desired him, but he fled from her as she pursued him round the heavens. Finally, by shape-changing into a cat, she got into his bed. He woke to find his sister beside him. From their union was born Aradia, the witches' teacher goddess.

MOSHTO: Romany. Sun God and Horned God of the summer. He is one aspect of the Great God, the other being Arivell, Horned God of the winter. Arivell was demoted by Christianity to a demon, possibly because Romanies call winter "the little death"; in fact, he is entirely beneficent. This one God in his two aspects was son of the Creator Goddess Anusia and the Great God Vista, and brother/consort to the Moon Goddess Doia-Bori. Moshto and Doia-Bori gave birth to the earth and all life on it.

ODIN, ODHINN: ("Fury, Inspiration") Norse. Chief god, god of war and poetry, and conductor of the dead. King of the Aesir, which meant in effect he was the god of the warrior aristocracy rather than of the peasants—though he was also a god of fertility, and the last sheaf of wheat at the harvest was left for his horse. Odin was possibly originally a historical person, chief of a powerful raven clan, early becoming a god of winds and nocturnal storms; his most ancient appearance was as a continental German raging storm giant called Wode who assembled the souls of the dead. Gradually replaced Thor (the peasants' god) as head of the pantheon—though Thor, representing order, remained more popular than

Odin, who represented primarily war and violence. His magical number was nine—the nights and days he endured initiation on Yggdrassill in his quest for knowledge. Known as Alfadhir ("All-Father"), and by dozens of other names—from Herjan ("War God") and Svafnir ("Luller to Sleep or Dreams") to Gagnrath ("Giving Good Counsel") and Drauga Drottin ("Lord of Ghosts"). Envisaged as tall, gray-bearded, wearing a dark blue cloak, and with only one eye, the other socket being covered by a broad hat or by the cloak as a hood. He lived in Valhalla attended by the Valkyries and his two ravens, Hugin and Munin, who kept him informed on events on Earth—though he visited Earth at will. Leader of the Wild Hunt, in which he rode across the night sky with a pack of red-eyed hounds, souls of the dead. He had an eight-legged horse, Sleipnir; a spear, Gungnir; a magic ring, Draupnir; and two attendant wolves, Freki and Geri. His wife was Freya (Frigg). He is consumed by the Fenris-wolf at Ragnarok. Identified with the German Wotan (earlier Wodanaz), the Dutch Wodan, and the Anglo-Saxon Woden, and by the Romans with Mercury (also a *psychopompos*, or conductor of the dead).

PAN: ("All, Everything," or possibly "Pasturer") Greek. God of all nature, the woods, and shepherds. Portrayed as goat-footed and horned. Originally from Arcadia, as was Hermes, said to be his father. According to tradition, his worship spread beyond Arcadia when he gave the Athenians victory over the Persians at Marathon in exchange for honoring him. After the victory, Athens built a temple for him on the Acropolis, and his cult spread throughout Greece. He then acquired a variety of parents. He was said to be the son by Hermes of Dryope, whose father's flocks Hermes tended; or of Hermes by Penelope, wife of Odysseus; or of Penelope by all her suitors in Odysseus's absence; or of Thimbris or Callisto by Zeus. Another named mother was Amalthea, the Cretan goat goddess who suckled the infant Zeus. The Romans identified him with Faunus, and he tended to merge with the ithyphallic Priapus (also said to be his son). His loves were many, quite apart from his constant pursuit of the anonymous nymphs of his own woodlands. Caves were often dedicated to Pan and a nymph. Nymphs were very much his female counterparts, often memories of primordial local goddesses, wild beings quite unlike the coy damsels of Victorian art. Beyond his pastoral and musical nature, Pan shared with his father Hermes the gift of wisdom and prophecy—seeming to personify the concept of wisdom through oneness with nature. His physical appearance supports this—from his goat-feet in touch with the ground, through his fertile loins, to his intelligent and music-making head. One story told by

Plutarch used to be quoted as confirmation of Christianity's victory over paganism. A sailor called Thamus, passing the Echinades Islands, heard a voice calling three times: "When you are arrived at Palodes, . . . make it known that the great God Pan is dead."[3] It is far more likely that what Thamus really heard was the ritual lamentation over the annual death of the vegetation god Tammuz, mourned as the "All-Great," in Greek *pammegas*, "Great Pan."

VELS/VELES/VOLOS/VELNIAS: Latvian, Lithuanian, and Slavic. God of death and the underworld, and of woodlands and hidden treasures. An evil god of night, darkness, and destructive magic, opposite of Dievas, god of the shining sky. Both of them created the world—Dievas the light and beautiful aspects and creatures, Veles/Velnias the dark and cruel ones. Strangely perhaps, while wheat and rye belonged to Dievas, barley, buckwheat, and all root vegetables belonged to Veles/Velnias. Equally strangely, Veles/Velnias was a God of contracts, music, water, and stones; a seer; and connected with cattle and prosperity. Envisaged as one-eyed, horned, and cloven-footed. Notorious for lusting after women. A famous example was a young woman who was picking mushrooms in the forest; when it began to rain in torrents, she took off her clothes and put them in her *kraitis* (hope chest) and stood naked under a tree till the rain stopped; then she put her dry clothes back on and went back to picking mushrooms. Velnias spotted her, and was curious to know how she was dry when everything else was soaked. She told him she had a secret technique to prevent rain from falling on her. She agreed to tell him, if he would tell her all his own magical arts. His curiosity overcame him, and he agreed, telling her all his arts of magic and healing. Then she told him her own simple "secret." He was furious, and flew away screaming that he had been tricked. The woman became the first witch, and passed her knowledge on to others; thus was witchcraft born. Since Christianity made him simply demonic, it may well be that originally the two contrasting gods represented a natural polarity rather than a confrontation—Dievas personifying light, consciousness, promise, and the reward of good deeds, and Veles/Velnias the mysterious otherworld, the unconscious, warning, and the punishment of bad deeds.

NOTES

1   Stewart Farrar. *The Witches' Goddess.*
2   Stewart Farrar. *The Witches' God.* 184.
3   Changes per Plutarch. *Plutarch's Morals.* Translated from the Greek by Several Hands. Corrected and Revised by William W. Goodwin, with an Introduction by Ralph Waldo Emerson. 5 Volumes. (Boston: Little, Brown, and Co., 1878).

Appendix C

Correspondence
Tables

The Seven Planetary Correspondences

Planet:	Sun	Moon	Mars	Mercury	Jupiter	Venus	Saturn
Element:	Spirit	Ether	Fire	Air	Mind	Water	Earth
Magical tool:	altar	cauldron	sword	wand	staff/stang	chalice	pentacle
Chakra:	crown	throat	solar plexus	heart	third eye	sacral	root
Realm:	Gwynfyd/ Asaheimr	Annwn/ Helheimr	Finias/ Muspellheimr	Gorias/ Jotunheimr	Abred/ Midgardhr	Munas/ Vanaheimr	Falias/ Niflheimr
Colors:	gold/yellow *white/gold/silver	white/silver *blue	red *yellow	orange *green/turquoise	blue/purple *indigo/purple	green *orange	black *red
God/Goddesses:	Apollo, Baldur, Mabon	Diana, Hecate, Selene	Aries, Lugh, Tiuw	Anubis, Hermes, Odin	Thor, Taranus, Zeus	Aphrodite, Freya, Isis	Norns, Morrigan
Day of week:	Sunday	Monday	Tuesday	Wednesday	Thursday	Friday	Saturday
Tree: (Ogham):	birch (Beith)	willow (Saille)	holly (Tinne)	ash (Nuin)	oak (dur)	apple (quert)	alder (fearn)
Runes:	Sigel	Lagu	Tyr	Eoh	Thorn	Gifu	Nied
Tarot:	The Sun	The Moon	The Chariot	The Hermit	The Emperor	The Empress	Death
Sephiroth:	Tiphareth	Yesod	Geburah	Hod	Chesed	Netzach	Binah
Attributions:	joy, success, advancement, growth, natural power, healing, light	inspiration, psychic skills, emotions, secrets, cycles	strength, struggle, conflict, anger, aggression	communications, intelligence, creativity, science, trickery	leadership, politics, power, honor, responsibility, wealth, business	love, harmony, attraction, pleasure, sexuality	obstacles, limitations, time, death

*　Chakra color used for opening/closing.

The Four Elemental Correspondences

Element:	Air *(To know)*	Fire *(To will)*	Water *(To dare)*	Earth *(To be silent)*
Cardinal point:	east	south	west	north
Time of day:	dawn (sunrise)	midday	dusk (sunset)	midnight
Magical tool:	wand	sword	chalice	pentacle
Season/ Solar festival:	spring equinox	summer solstice	autumn equinox	winter solstice
Fire festival:	Beltane	Lughnasadh	Samhain	Imbolg
Archetype:	Sage/Wizard	Warrior	Maiden	Mother
Planet:	Mercury	Mars	Venus	Saturn
Colors:	blue/yellow	red	sea-green/blue	green/brown/black
Moon phase:	waxing	full	waning	new/dark
Attributions:	the mind, knowledge, learning, memory	energy, will, life, cleansing and purification	emotions, feelings, courage, intuition and the unconscious mind	physicality, growth, nature, material gain, birth, death

Appendix D

Contacts and Useful Addresses

Organizations

The Pagan Federation:
BM Box 7097
London WC1N 3XX
England

Website: https://www.paganfed.org

E-mail: info@paganfederation.co.uk

Covenant of the Goddess:
PO Box 1226
Berkeley, CA 94701
USA

Website: http://www.cog.org/

E-mail: juliagrace03598@gmail.com
(Correspondence Officer)

Church of All Worlds:
PO Box 1359
Nebo, NC 28761
USA

Website: http://www.caw.org/
E-mail: caw@caw.org
Pagan Awareness Network:
PO Box 30
Casula Mall, NSW 2170
Australia

Website: https://www.paganawareness.net.au/
E-mail: committee@paganawareness.net.au

Websites

Janet Farrar and Gavin Bone:

Facebook: www.facebook.com/gavin.bone
E-mail: jsfarrar@eircom.net

The Witches' Voice:

Facebook: www.facebook.com/TheWitchesVoiceInc

E-mail: witchvox@witchvox.com

Magazines and Periodicals

Pagan Dawn:
Website: https://www.paganfed.org/shop/Pagan-Dawn-Subscription-p83283454

Witches & Pagans:
BBI Media
PO Box 687
Forest Grove, OR 97116
USA

Website: https://witchesandpagans.com

Witchcraft Magazine(Australia):
PO Box 7244
Kariong, NSW 2250
Australia

Website: https://www.whitemagic.com.au/wcraft/

Bibliography

Adler, Margot. *Drawing Down the Moon: Witches, Druids, Goddess Worshippers and Other Pagans in America Today*. New York: Penguin Group, 2006. First published 1979 by Beacon Press.

Ashe, Geoffrey. *The Finger and the Moon*. London: Heinemann, 1973.

Baldwin, Christina. *Calling the Circle: the First and Future Culture*. Bantam, 1998.

——. *The Seven Whispers: Listening to the Voice of Spirit*. New World Library, 2002.

Bates, Brian. *The Way of Wyrd*. London: Arrow Books, 1987.

Blavatsky, H. P. *The Secret Doctrine*. Los Angeles: The Theosophy Society, 1964.

Bleakley, Alan. *Fruits of the Moon Tree*. London: Gateway Books, 1984.

Bord, Janet and Colin. *Earth Rites*. London: Granada Publishing, 1982.

Buckland, Raymond. *Buckland's Book of Saxon Witchcraft*. 30th anniv. ed. Red Wheel/ Weiser, 2005. First published 1974 as *The Tree: The Complete Book of Saxon Witchcraft*.

——. *Buckland's Complete Book of Witchcraft*. St. Paul, MN: Llewellyn Publications, 1986, rev. 2002.

——. *The Witch Book*. St. Paul, MN: Llewellyn Publications, 2002.

Burland, C. A. *The Magical Arts*. London: Arthur Barker, 1966.

Butler, W. E. *The Magician: His Training and Work*. London: Aquarian Press, 1959.

Campbell, Joseph. *The Hero With a Thousand Faces*. Princeton University Press, 1990.

Crowley, Aleister. *Magick*. London: Routledge, and Kegan Paul, 1986.

——. *Moonchild*. New York: Samuel Weiser, 1970.

——. *777*. New York: Samuel Weiser, 1970.

Crowley, Vivianne. *Wicca: The Old Religion in the New Age*. Wellingborough: Aquarian Press, 1989.

Curott, Phyllis. *Witchcrafting*. New York: Broadway Books, 2001.

Curries, Ian. *You Cannot Die*. Shaftesbury, England: Element Books Ltd., 1978.

Deren, Maya. *The Voodoo Gods*. London: Thames and Hudson, 1953.

Drury, Nevill. *The Elements of Shamanism*. England: Element Books Ltd.: Shaftesbury, 1989.

Eliade, Mircea. *Shamanism: Archaic Techniques of Ecstasy*. New Jersey: Princeton University Press, 1972.

Ennemoser, Joseph. *The History of Magic*. Vol. One. New York: University Books Inc., 1970.

Farrar, Janet and Stewart. "Dictionary of World Deities" (unpublished manuscript).
——. *Eight Sabbats for Witches*. London: Robert Hales, 1981.
——. *Spells and How They Work*. London: Robert Hales, 1990.
——. *A Witches' Bible: The Complete Witches' Handbook*. Phoenix Publishing, 1996, 2002.
——. *The Witches' God*. London: Robert Hales, 1989.
——. *The Witches' Goddess*. London: Robert Hales, 1987.
——. *The Witches' Way*. London: Robert Hales, 1984.
Farrar, Janet and Stewart, and Gavin Bone. *The Healing Craft*. Custer, WA: Phoenix Publications, 2000.
——. *The Pagan Path*. Custer, WA: Phoenix Publications, 1995.
Farrar, Janet and Stewart, and Gavin Bone and Glenn Taylor. *The Complete Dictionary of European Gods and Goddesses*. Chieveley, Berks: Capall Bann Publishing, 2000.
Fitch, Ed. *A Book of Pagan Rituals*. York Beach, ME: Samuel Weiser, 1974.
Fitch, Ed., and Janina Renee. *Magical Rites from the Crystal Well*. St. Paul, MN: Llewellyn Publications, 1984.
Fortune, Dion. *The Mystical Qabalah*. London: Ernest Benn Ltd., 1972.
——. *Psychic Self Defence*. York Beach, ME: Samuel Weiser, 1982.
——. *Sane Occultism*. Wellingborough: Aquarian Press, 1987.
——. *The Sea Priestess*. London: Aquarian Press, 1957.
Frazer, J. G. *The Golden Bough*. London: MacMillan Press Ltd., 1974.
Gardner, Gerald B. *High Magic's Aid*. London: Michael Houghton, 1949.
Gilchrist, Cherry. *The Circle of Nine*. London: Arkana, 1991.
Graves, Robert. *The White Goddess*. London: Faber and Faber Limited, 1961.
Griffyn, Sally. *Wiccan Wisdomkeepers: Modern-day Witches Speak on Environmentalism, Feminism, Motherhood, Wiccan Lore, and More*. Boston, MA: Red Wheel/Weiser, 2002.
Grimassi, Raven. *The Encyclopedia of Wicca and Witchcraft*. St. Paul, MN: Llewellyn Publications, 2000.
——. *The Wiccan Mysteries*. St. Paul, MN: Llewellyn Publications, 1997.
——. *The Witches' Craft*. Llewellyn Publications, St. Paul, MN, 2002.
Guiley, Rosemary Ellen. *The Encyclopedia of Witches and Witchcraft*. New York: Facts on File, 1989.
Gundarsson, Kveldulf. *Teutonic Magic*. St. Paul, MN: Llewellyn Publications, 1990.
Halevi, Z'ev ben Shimon. *Tree of Life: An Introduction to the Cabala*. London: Rider and Company, 1972.
Hall, C. S., and V.J. Nordby. *A Primer of Jungian Psychology*. New York: Mentor Books, 1973.
Hampden-Turner, Charles. *Maps of the Mind*. London: Mitchell Beazley, 1981.
Haralambos, M. *Sociology: Themes and Perspectives*. Slough: University Tutorial Press, 1980.
Harner, Michael. *The Way of the Shaman*. New York: Harper and Row, 1980.
Heinlein, Robert A. *Stranger in a Strange Land*. Putnam/Ace Trade, 1987–2005.
Heselton, Philip. *Wiccan Roots*. Capall Bann Publishing, November 2001.
Hollander, Lee M., trans. *The Poetic Edda*. Austin: Texas University Press, 1962.
Hope, Murry. *Practical Celtic Magic*. Wellingborough: The Aquarian Press, 1987.

Houston, Phillip. *Wiccan Roots*. Chieveley, Berks: Capall Bann Publishing, 2000.

Hurston, Zora Neale. *Tell My Horse: Voodoo and Life in Haiti and Jamaica*. New York: Harpy & Row, 1990.

Hutton, Ronald. *The Triumph of the Moon*. Oxford University Press, 1999.

Jacobi, Jolande, and Ralph Manheim and C. J. Jung. *The Psychology of C. G. Jung*. London: Routledge and Kegan Paul, 1962.

Johns, June. *King of the Witches: The World of Alex Sanders*. London: Peter Davies, 1969.

Jones, Evan John, and Doreen Valiente (foreword). *Witchcraft: A Tradition Renewed*. Custer, WA, Phoenix Publications, 1989.

Jordan, Michael. *Witches: An Encyclopedia of Paganism And Magic*. London: Kyle Cathie Limited, 1996.

Judith, Anodea. *The Truth About Chakras*. St. Paul, MN: Llewellyn Publications, 1994.

——. *Wheels of Life*. St. Paul, MN: Llewellyn Publications, 1994.

Jung, Carl Gustav. *The Collected Works of C. G. Jung*, vol. 9, part 1, "Archetypes of the Collective Unsconscious." London: Routledge and Kegan Paul, 1959, 1968.

——. *Four Archetypes*. London: Routledge, 1972.

——. *Synchronicity: An Acausal Connecting Principle*. London: Routledge and Kegan Paul, 1955.

Kelly, Aidan. *Crafting the Art of Magic: A History of Modern Witchcraft: 1939 – 1964*. St. Paul, MN: Llewellyn Publications, 1991.

King, Frances. *Ritual Magic in England: 1887 to the Present Day*. London: Neville Spearman, 1970.

King, Frances, and Stephen Skinner. *Techniques of High Magic: A Manual of Self Initiation*. London: The C.W. Daniel Company, 1974.

Lady Sheba. *The Book of Shadows*. St. Paul, MN: Llewellyn Publications, 1971.

Larousse World Mythology. Secaucus, NJ: Chartwell Books Inc., 1973.

Leadbetter, C. W. *The Chakras: A Monograph*. Eighth reprint. Adyar: The Theosphical Publishing House, 1969.

Leland, Charles Godfrey. *Aradia, or the Gospel of the Witches*. London: The C.W. Daniel Company, 1974.

Murray, Margaret. *The Witch Cult in Western Europe*. Oxford University Press, 1921.

Neumann, Erich. *The Great Mother*. London: Routledge and Kegan Paul, 1963.

Niemark, Philiph John. *The Way of the Orisa*. San Francisco: Harper-Collins, 1993.

Pagels, Elaine. *The Gnostic Gospels*. London, Wiedenfeld and Nicolson, 1979.

Patrick, Richard. *All Colour Book of Greek Mythology*. London, Octopus Books, 1972.

Pennick, Nigel. *Runic Astrology*. Wellingborough, Aquarian Press, 1990.

Perowne, Stewart. *Roman Mythology*. London: Hamlyn, 1969.

Pinsent, John. *Greek Mythology*. London: Hamlyn, 1969.

Powell, A. E. *The Astral Body*. London: The Theosophical Publishing House, 1927.

——. *The Etheric Double*. London: The Theosophical Publishing House, 1925.

——. *The Mental Body*. London: The Theosophical Publishing House, 1927.

Reed, Ellen Cannon. *The Heart of Wicca*. York Beach, ME: Red Wheel/Samuel Weiser, 2000.

Roose-Evans, James. *Passages of the Soul*. Shaftesbury, England: Element Books Ltd., 1994.

St. Clair, David. *Drum and Candle*. London: Macdonald, 1971.

Starhawk. *Dreaming the Dark: Magic, Sex and Politics*. New York: Beacon Press, 1982.

——. *The Spiral Dance: A Rebirth of the Ancient Religion of the Great Goddess*. San Francisco: Harper and Row, 1979.

Sun Bear and Wabun. *The Medicine Wheel*. New York: Prentice Hall Press, 1986.

Valiente, Doreen. *An ABC of Witchcraft, Past and Present*. London: Robert Hale,1973.

——.*The Rebirth of Witchcraft*. London: Robert Hale, 1989.

——. *Witchcraft for Tomorrow*. London: Robert Hale, 1978.

Whitton, Dr. J., and J. Fisher. *Life Between Life*. London: Grafton Books, 1986.

Witt, R. E. *Isis in the Graeco-Roman World*. London: Thames and Hudson, 1971.

Wolfe, Amber. *In the Shadow of the Shaman*. St. Paul, MN: Llewellyn Publications, 1988.

Index

A

ABC of Witchcraft, An, 77, 218, 224, 226
Adler, Fred and Martha, 95
Aegeus, 49
Aesculapius, 172, 190
Africa, 1, 7, 67, 102
African, 6–8, 67
Ahriman, 4
Air (see *elements*), 81, 97–98, 100, 106, 113,
    115, 117, 120, 124, 126, 128, 140, 144,
    146–147, 203–204, 206, 208, 211–213, 218,
    221, 236–237; Guardian of, 126, 128, 212;
    Realm of, 120, 208
Ajna, 140–141, 181
Akashic Records, 120
Alban Arthan, 159
Alban Hefed, 158
alchemy, 131
All-Father (see *Odin*), 62, 66, 113, 233
altar, 99, 129, 175, 203, 218
America, 17, 27, 172
Anahata, 140
Anderson, Cora, 18; Victor, 18, 56
Androgeos, 49
Anglo-Saxons, 62, 159
anima/animus, 46, 48–55, 119, 122, 152, 182
Animal Farm, 37
animism, 38, 65
Anubis, 52–53, 123, 134
Aphrodite, 175, 231
Apollo, 155–156, 224
apostolic succession (see *lineage*), 18, 29
Aquarian Tabernacle Church, 102, 171
Aradia, 62, 87–88, 174, 223–224
Aradia, or the Gospel of the Witches, 11, 13,
    34, 177
Archbishop of Canterbury (see *Williams,
    Dr. Owen*), 64

Ariadne, 49
Artemis, 5–6, 73, 224
Artemis/Isis, cult of, 5–6
Arwen, 48–49, 54, 99
Ásatrú, 62, 114–115
Asia Minor, 5
astral body, 141
astral double, 85, 129, 147, 221
astral plane(s), 52, 119, 145, 147, 178
Astral Realm(s), 85, 119–122, 124, 129, 208,
    215
    lower astral, 120
Assyro-Babylonia, 5, 58–59, 114, 229
athame, 146, 202–204, 218
Athens, 49, 233
Atropos, 166–167
Audumla, 70
Augustus, Emperor, 173
aura, 144–147, 180–182, 203
    and chakras, 146–147, 182; colors, 144;
    of Deity, 180–182; and energy work,
    89, 133, 138–139; etheric, 136, 143–145;
    mental/emotional, 143, 145, 180;
    spiritual, 143, 145–146
Australia, 2, 65, 102, 113–114, 163, 239–240

B

bard, 44, 49, 54, 64, 113, 173, 225
Baron Samedi, 8, 178
Bast, 61
banishing
    Celtic cross, 205–206; pentacle/
    pentagram, 202, 205–206; quarters, 208;
    ritual stance, 206–207
Beltane, 50, 158, 161–162, 166, 237
Bealtaine, 158–159
Besant-Scott, Annie, 11
Bible, the, 9, 25, 103

Binah, 37
Black Rod (see *summoner*), 84
blatting, 75
Bluestar Coven/tradition, 27
Boann, 62, 70, 174
Book of Shadows, 12–13, 16, 25–26, 31, 82, 84, 89, 91, 93–94, 102–103, 105, 163, 200–202, 218
Borda, Paul, 61
Bríd, 157, 165, 174, 177, 205
Bridget, 157
Brigantia, 165
Brother Aurelius, 11
Buckland, Raymond, 17, 24, 34, 36, 78
Budapest, Z., 18
Buffy the Vampire Slayer, 20

C
Cabala, 38, 63, 106, 111, 177
caduceus, 134, 156, 212, 231
calendar, 114, 161–162, 175
cauldron, 203, 218, 225–226, 230
Cerridwen's, 218, 225–226; Dagda's, 203, 218; Gundestrup, 230
Cernunnos, 62–63, 73–74, 87, 123, 160, 230–231
centers/chakras, 182
    brow, 141, 148; colors, 236; crown, 134, 150; gall bladder, 139; heart, 140, 148–150, 181, 203, 205–206, 212; liver, 139; minor, 136, 148; opening and closing, 142–144, 151; petals, 137, 139–141, 152; root, 137–139, 142, 149, 151–152, 181, 184, 205, 208, 211–212; sacral, 142–143 146, 181, 207, 214; solar plexus, 137, 139, 181, 206, 213, 236, spinning, 136, 142–144, 151; spleen, 139; stomach, 139; throat, 136, 140, 144, 146–147, 150, 181
chalice, 88, 202, 214, 237
Christianity, 3–9, 20, 25, 71, 92, 112, 157–158, 189, 226, 234
Circles, 28, 82, 84–85, 104, 196–197
    festival, 84; full moon (also see *Esbats*), 84; training, 85, 196
Civil War, English, 9
cloaks, 88–89
Clotho, 166–167
Cochrane, Robert, 14–15, 218
collective unconscious, 52, 70, 85–86, 112, 121, 123, 125, 221
correspondences, 68, 97, 116, 163, 201–202, 209, 236–237
Council of Elders (Alexandrian), 24
Covenant of the Goddess, the, 102, 238
Coven Priestess, 83, 189, 195–198
cows (as deities), 70
Crete, 7, 49
Cronus, 166–167
Crowther, Arnold and Patricia, 13–14, 16, 56
Cult Danger Evaluation Frame, 198

cults, 3–4, 23, 86–87, 197
Curott, Phyllis, 24
cyber coven, 20, 105
cyber Witch, 20
Cyntefyn, 158

D
death, 3, 8, 42, 50–51, 53, 58, 73–74, 92, 100, 109, 120–123, 145–146, 154, 156, 159–160, 162, 165–169, 210, 214, 221, 234
dedication, 35, 56, 81, 86, 88, 90, 98–99, 101, 176–177
degree system (see *initiation*), 12, 35–37, 46, 78, 81, 96–98, 100
deities, 8, 42, 49, 54, 60–75, 87–88, 121, 160, 165–166, 173–177, 180, 205, 223–224, 236; ancestral, 8, 42, 62, 170, 173–174; genius loci, 174; primal, 166, 174
Demeter, 50, 59
devas, 68
Diana, 5–6, 11
divination, 25, 90, 102, 155, 218, 228
Diwali (Hindu Festival of Lights), 68–69
doctrine, 5, 13, 19, 24, 28, 30–31, 35, 38, 40, 42, 65, 67, 97, 134, 171
dogma, 23, 26–29, 37, 52, 57–58, 63, 89, 100, 108–109, 114, 132, 134, 163, 180, 195–196, 200
Dowth, 160
Drawing Down the Moon, 8, 32, 38, 66–67, 107, 119, 155, 175, 177-185
Druid, 64, 121, 225, 230
Druidism, 64, 112–113, 119, 121
dualism, 5
duotheism, 36–38, 66, 71

E
Earth (see *elements*), 38, 75, 81, 86, 97–101, 103–104, 106–107, 110, 112–113, 117, 119, 120, 124, 126, 130, 138–139, 144, 146–147, 157, 163–164, 188, 204, 206, 208–213, 218, 221, 223, 227, 229, 236–237; Guardian of, 126, 211; Realm of, 120, 208, 211
East Anglia, 9, 12
Easter, 157, 159–160
Eostre, 157
ego, 38, 41, 46–49, 51–52, 54, 57, 65, 70, 78–79, 83, 99, 119, 122, 141, 176, 183, 187
Elegguá, 68
elements
    Air, 81, 97–98, 100, 106, 113, 115, 117, 120, 124, 126, 128, 140, 144, 146–147, 203–204, 206, 208, 211–213, 218, 221, 236–237; *Earth*, 38, 75, 81, 86, 97–101, 103–104, 106–107, 110, 112–113, 117, 119, 120, 124, 126, 130, 138–139, 144, 146–147, 157, 163–164, 188, 204, 206, 208–213, 218, 221, 223, 227, 229, 236–237; *Fire*, 81, 84, 97–100, 108, 113, 115, 117, 120, 124, 126, 137, 139, 144, 146–147, 161–163, 165,

173, 202, 204, 208, 212–213, 218, 221,
236–237; *Water*, 49, 73, 81, 97–99, 101,
113–115, 117, 118, 120–121, 124, 127, 139,
144, 146–147, 165, 181, 204, 207–208,
214, 218, 221, 224, 236–237
enchantress, 4
endocrine glands, 137, 139, 141
entity: gestalt (see *coven mind*), 90
environmentalism, 19
Ephesus, 5–6, 224
     Council of, 5
Erik the Viking, 72
Esbat(s), 82, 84–85, 104, 156
Ether, 98, 136, 140, 144, 146–147, 181, 203,
236
etheric body/double, 140, 144–146
etheric energy, 146–147, 150, 205
etheric level, 140
Europe, 3, 5, 7–9, 11, 25, 45, 53, 58, 62,
67–69, 72, 75, 77, 90, 111–113, 115, 132,
134, 154–156, 161, 166, 171–173, 179–180,
186, 224
evolution, 23, 27–29, 40–41, 43, 46, 106, 113,
164

F
fairy folk, 62, 68
fairy tree, 6
Feri Tradition, 18
family: extended, 77, 91, 189; nuclear, 77,
189
Farrar, Stewart, 16–17, 19, 21, 25, 27, 32, 54,
62–63, 72, 78, 81, 94, 98, 106, 156, 163,
177, 187, 198
Fellowship of Crotona, 11–12, 18, 33–34,
45–46
feminism, 18–20, 39
festivals (see *Sabbats*), 6, 28, 50, 68–69, 77,
82, 84, 108, 156, 159–164, 189, 191, 201,
226–228; agricultural, 161; fire, 50, 84,
161–165; folk, 156; Pagan, 28, 68, 189; of
light, 69; seasonal, 163, 201; solar, 84,
156, 159–160, 228
Fire (see *elements*), 81, 84, 97–100, 108, 113,
115, 117, 120, 124, 126, 137, 139, 144,
146–147, 161–163, 165, 173; 202, 204,
208, 212–213, 218, 221, 236–237
     Guardian of, 126, 213; Realm of, 120,
208
Fitch, Ed, 94–95
Fortune, Dion, 37, 42, 128–129
Freud, Sigmund, 47–48, 107, 112, 119, 165
Frey, 55, 74, 113, 230–231
Freya, 55, 57, 61–62, 172–175, 226–227, 230,
233, 236
Frost, Gavin, 170

G
Ganesh/Ganesha, 60, 68, 72
Gardner, Gerald , 10–19, 21, 23–26, 30–35,
37, 45–46, 52, 64, 76–77, 80–81, 103, 196
Germany, 9, 11, 56
gestalt, 89
Gestalt theory, 85–85
Ghede (also see *Baron Samedi*), 8
God, 37, 42, 51, 63, 65, 141, 152, 172, 184–
185, 203, 230–234, 236
Goddess, 5–6, 13, 24, 29, 37, 42, 44, 48, 50,
51, 53, 57, 61, 63, 65, 70, 73–74, 79, 83,
116, 119, 141, 157–160, 162, 166, 168–169,
172, 177–179, 184–185, 203, 223–230, 236
Golden Bough, The, 163
Gowdie, Isobel, 34
Graves, Robert, 63
Great Windsor Park/Forest, 74, 231
Grimassi, Raven, 4, 7, 21, 34, 185
grimoire(s), 26, 33, 218
grounding, 90–91, 120, 128, 139, 151, 181,
202, 211–214
guardian(s)
     elemental, 124, 128, 206, 209, 218; of the
     mysteries, 53, 119–120, 123, 134, 218;
     underworld, 50, 53, 73, 119, 123, 166,
     218, 234
guide
     astral, 122–124, 129, 215, 218;
     underworld, 53, 123, 127, 215, 217–218

H
Haiti, 7
Hansen, John, 95
Hathor, 70
Hecate, 63, 119, 227–228, 231, 236
Hekate, 63, 66, 130
Hermes, 53, 123, 134, 156, 167, 231, 233, 236
Hermes Trismegistus, 53, 134, 156, 167, 212
Herne, 73–74, 160, 228, 230–232
Herne, John, 74
Herodias, 223, 226, 228–229
Hierarchy of Needs, The (see *Malsow,
Abraham*), 29, 96–97
high priest, 57, 77–80, 83, 91, 95, 101
high priestess, 12, 14, 21, 26, 57, 77–80, 83,
101
Hill of the Witch (Slieve na Callaighe), 62,
159–160
Hinduism, 58, 67–72, 132, 187, 189
Hocma, 37
holy days, 6
holy wells, 90
Holly King, 63, 158, 163
Hollywood, 20
Homo sapiens, 1
homosexuality, 48, 55
Hopkins, Mathew (Witchfinder General), 9
Horne, Fiona, 24
Horus, 166

houngan, 67
Hunt, the, 160
hypericum (St.-John's-wort), 164
hypnotic regression, 153, 178–179

I
id, 46–47, 49, 52, 57, 99, 118, 123–124, 215
Ifa, 7
indulgences, 9
initiation
   first degree, 31, 35, 51, 54, 84, 88, 93,
      98–101, 106, 218; ritual, 54–59; second
      degree, 30, 35, 50–51, 57, 80, 84, 98–99,
      101, 104, 108, 176; self-, 18, 42; spiritual,
      54–59, 221; sexual, 194; third degree, 51,
      98, 100–101, 103, 187
Indians: Conibo, 52; Jivari, 52
Internet, the, 20, 33, 102–103, 105, 190, 192
Ireland, 6–8, 10, 62–63, 88, 90–91, 102, 106,
      113–114, 159, 225, 230
Irminsul, 114, 117
Ishtar, 5, 59
Isis, 5–6 45, 50–51, 59, 73, 123, 129, 236
Italy, 7, 10, 223, 230
Italian, 3–4, 11, 15, 62, 224

J
James I, King (Sixth of Scotland), 9
Jesus (see *Christ, Jesus*), 7, 71
jewelry, 88, 176–177, 227
Jivarí (Indians), 52
Jung, Carl Gustav, 46–48, 59, 69–71, 85, 107–
      108, 110, 112, 119, 121, 141, 172, 179, 185
Jung, Fritz and Wren, 24
Jungian, 48, 54, 72, 99, 107–108, 112–113,
      119, 121

K
Karnayna, 62
Kelly, Tony, 95
Keres, 166
Kether, 37, 141, 185
King of the Witches, The, 21, 91, 187
Knowth, 160
Koran, the, 25, 75
Kore, 50, 59

L
Lachesis, 166–167
Lammas (Loaf Mass), 158, 161
Legba (Elegguá), 68
Leland, Charles Godfrey, 11, 13, 34, 177, 223
Liber Umbrarum, 201
lineage, 16–18, 27, 29–31, 37, 39, 42, 57, 191
Live and Let Die, 8
loa, 8, 67–68, 178–179
Loki (see also the *Shadow*), 48, 176
Lugh, 7, 205, 236
Lughnasadh (see *Lammas*), 7, 50, 158–159,
      161–162, 237

Luther, Martin, 9

M
Mabon, 50, 158–160, 168, 236
Macbeth, 66, 73, 166, 228
Maddalena, 11, 223
Madonna, 7, 116
maiden, 73, 84, 124, 207
Maiden (Goddess), 63, 73, 166, 168, 214, 237
magic
   black, 133; Cabalistic, 12, 52, 112;
      ceremonial, 39, 94, 106; high, 12–13,
      106, 131, 136, 152, 177; ritual, 12, 35,
      39–40, 43, 52, 65, 94, 111–112, 177, 218
mambo, 67
Manipura (solar plexus center), 139
Martello, Leo, 56
Maslow, Abraham, 29, 96–97, 100
May Day, 158
maypole, 158
meditation, 104, 137, 183, 208
megalithic sites, 90, 113
mind (see *coven mind*): gestalt, 86, 129
Minos, King, 49
Minotaur, 49–50
misogyny, 3
Mithraic, 4
Mithraism, 4–6
Modranacht (see also *Yule/winter solstice*),
      159
Moerae, the, 166
Morrigan, 49, 61, 236
monotheism, 54, 65–66
Muladhara, 138, 142, 181
Murray, Margaret, 11
mysteries, the, 2–3, 33–34, 42, 44–54, 73,
      99–100, 107, 109, 117, 119–120, 123,
      133–134, 141, 152, 156–157, 163–169, 176,
      198, 209–210, 218, 221
mystery tradition, 33, 42, 52, 67, 98, 107
myth, 4, 7, 11, 46, 49–51, 53–55, 59–60, 70,
      74–75, 87, 110, 112–114, 119, 121, 124,
      132, 134, 166, 173, 183, 203, 218, 225, 230
mythology, 4, 48–49, 63, 66, 75, 112, 114,
      119, 124, 132, 167, 169, 173, 175–176,
      226, 231

N
Native American, 65, 91, 128
New Forest, 10–11, 34
New Orleans, 7
New Zealand, 113, 163
Norns, 166, 236

O
Oak King, 63, 158–159, 163
occultism, 37, 48, 134, 136
   Western Tradition of, 37, 134, 136
Odin, 48, 53, 60–61, 66, 74–75, 107, 113, 123,
      166, 173, 226–227, 232–233, 236

Odinism, 62
Ordo Templi Orientis (OTO), 13, 31, 34–35, 128, 134
orisha, 67, 174–175
Osiris, 45, 48, 50–51
Ostara (see also *Imbolg*), 50, 157, 159–160
Ouija board, 189
owl, 4, 228
    screech (see also *striga, strix*), 4

P
Panagia Theotokos, 5
Pagan Federation, The, 58, 192, 238
Pagan Path, The, 198
Pagan Way, the, 27, 94–95
pujas, 68
Pasiphäe, Queen, 49
Paxson, Diana, 180
Pele, 174
Pendderwen, Gwydion, 110
pentacle, 88, 202, 208, 210, 236, 237
pentagram, 51, 98–100, 104, 130, 146–147, 204–206, 210
    banishing, 205; inverted/reversed, 51, 99; invoking, 130, 204; ritual, 100, 104, 130, 146, 204–206
personal unconscious, 112, 119, 221, 228
pharmakis, 4
Pickingill, George, 12
Poetic Prose, The, 114, 169, 179
Prose Edda, The, 66
polytheism, 36, 38, 54, 187
Portugal, 10
power
    animal (see *guide, underworld*), 52, 119, 122–123, 172, 217; -from-within, 132; -over, 132–133; tides, 84, 157, 164–166, 202
prophesy, 155, 178–179
Protestant, 7–10, 18
Protestantism, 9–10
    Reformation, 6
psychopompos, 52–53, 99, 119, 123, 156, 167, 231, 233
Ptah, 45
Pythoness of Delphi, 155

R
rapid eye movement (REM), 85, 145, 182
Realm(s)
    Astral, 85, 119–122, 124, 129, 208, 215; elemental, 113–115, 117, 119–122, 124, 205, 221; of Experience, 118–121, 123–124, 215; of Air, 120, 208; of the Ancestors, 53, 119, 121, 123–124; of Earth, 120, 208, 211; of the Divine, 121; of Fire, 120, 208; Underworld(s), 218; of Water, 118, 120, 208
rebellion, 10, 20, 37, 39, 132
    teenage, 189

rebirth, 3, 11, 50–51, 58, 109, 152–153, 162, 169, 203, 210, 214, 218
Rebirth of Witchcraft, The, 218
Reclaiming, 172
Rede, Wiccan, 27, 31, 34, 42, 93, 99
reincarnation, 51, 100, 121, 173, 187
relics, 9
religion, 4–8, 19, 21–23, 25, 28, 31, 34, 38, 41, 45, 54, 58, 63–72, 156, 169–170, 178, 186–187, 189
ritual stances, 207
River Boyne, 62, 113, 174
Roberts, Susan, 95
robes, 82, 88–89, 176–177
Robin Hood, 74, 223
Robin of Sherwood, 74
Roman Catholicism, 6–7, 9–10, 73, 158
Roman culture, 5, 72
Roman Empire, 4, 112
Roman god, goddess, 5, 53, 63, 224, 226, 228–233
    Diana, 5, 63, 224, 226, 228–229; Faunus/Priapus, 233; Mercury, 53, 231, 233
Roman officers, 4–5
Roman magic/paganism, 4, 18, 200
Romans, 46, 173, 229–230, 233
Roodmas, 158
Rosicrucianism, 45–46
Rosicrucians (group), 11–12
Rosicrucian theatre, 11, 45–46
runes, 53, 56, 75, 131, 166, 236
Russian, 6

S
Sabrina the Teenage Witch, 20
sacred sites, 87, 91
Sahasrara (crown center), 141
Samhain, 50, 62, 158–159, 161–162, 188, 230, 237
Sami-Lappish, 65
saints, 6–9, 159, 161–162, 165
    Bridget/Brighid, 157, 159; John, 229; Martha, 7; Michael, 159; Nicholas, 159; Stephen, 159
Sanders, Alex, 15–21, 23–24, 26, 32, 62, 75, 77, 94, 100, 106, 180, 187
Santeria, 8, 67–68, 72, 174–175
Satan (see also *Yahweh, Shadow*), 48, 66
Satanism, 12, 74, 186
science fiction (sci-fi), 35, 132, 154
Score, John, 95–96
seasonal affective disorder (SAD), 164
Seax-Wica, 17–18, 35, 56, 63, 78–79, 106, 188, 202
Seidr, 114, 154, 179–180
Seith, 55, 154–155, 178–180
Selene, 5, 229–230, 236
secrets, 12, 18, 26, 29–30, 32–34, 42, 53, 82, 87, 89, 93, 103, 129, 197, 221, 228, 234

secrecy, 28–30, 32–34, 42, 82, 89, 93, 103,
    129, 197, 221
sephira (see *Cabala*), 37
sex, 2, 28, 47–48, 54–55, 72, 118, 132, 139,
    142, 158, 174, 177–178, 194–195, 220,
    227, 236
sexism, 2
Shadow, 46, 48–51, 53–54, 57, 99, 108, 112,
    119–120, 123–124, 141, 176, 179, 214
Shaktiism (see *Tantra*), 132
shamanism, 1–3, 40, 46, 52–53, 62, 106–108,
    123, 128, 169, 183, 185
    modern, 52, 108, 169, 185
shrine(s), 69, 99, 175
Shinto, 58, 67, 173, 189
Shiva, 60, 68
Skadi, 226–227, 230
Skuld, 166–167
skyclad, 89, 194
Slieve na Callaighe, 62, 159–160
sorcery, 107, 131–152, 203, 223–224
Spain, 10
Spiral Dance, The, 18–19, 132, 209
Spirit, 38–39, 41–42, 98–99, 131, 136, 141,
    145, 147, 202, 206, 210, 236
spirituality, 10, 19, 23, 30, 33, 38, 40–41,
    44–59, 67, 107, 109, 153, 164–166, 171–
    172, 187–188, 196, 198
staff, 75, 155–156, 191, 203, 206, 212, 236
stag, 1–2, 123, 226, 231
stang, 203, 218, 236
Starhawk, 18–19, 24, 56, 107, 132–133, 172,
    209
Star Wars, 132
statues, 6–7, 69, 129, 141
Stranger in a Strange Land, 35
strega, 4, 11, 223–224, 228
Strega (tradition), 4, 15, 34, 40
striga, 4
strigare, 4
strix, 4
Sturluson, Snorri, 66
Styx (river), 121
summoner, 84
supernatural, 4, 64, 132, 187
Svadhistana (sacred center), 139
sword, 80, 120, 146, 202, 206, 212–213, 218,
    231, 236–237
synchronicity, 172, 185

T

Taliesin, 14–15, 113, 225
Tantra, 132
Taoism, 42, 132–133, 187
Tarot, 105, 155, 171, 189, 236
teenagers, 20, 189
temples, 6, 46, 69, 128–129, 226
    astral, 129; Hindu, 69; moon, 129
Time Machine, The, 154
Tir Bo Thuinn, 114

Tir Nan Og, 114
Themis, 166
Thor, 176, 232, 236
Tlachta/Tlachtga, 62, 230
Torah, the, 25
Tradition: Alexandrian, 17, 24, 27, 50, 78,
    89, 94, 99–100, 130, 177; Dianic, 18;
    Gardnerian, 17, 28, 50, 78, 87, 89,
    99–100, 130, 177
training, 17, 19, 22, 27, 29–31, 41, 43, 58,
    77–79, 82–85, 92–110, 190–192, 196,
    199–218
trance, 52, 67, 79, 85, 113–114, 153–155,
    177–183
*Tree, The: The Complete Book of Saxon
    Witchcraft* (see *Buckland, Raymond*),
    17, 34
tribal, 2–3, 13, 15, 39, 45, 52–53, 68, 109, 173
    magical worker/practice/witchcraft/
    shamanism, 2–3, 15, 39, 45, 52–53
tribalism, 189
Triple Goddess, 63, 73–74, 166, 225, 227

U
U.K., 43, 95
United Kingdom, 9–10, 19, 24, 28, 94, 190,
    238–239
unconscious mind, 49, 113, 125, 237
underworld, 46, 50, 53, 73–74, 85, 108,
    112–115, 119–124, 127, 166, 168–169, 176,
    179–180, 208, 214–215, 218, 227–228, 234
    deities, 74, 115, 227, 234; guardians, 218;
    guide, 53, 123–124, 127, 215–217
United States (see also *America*), 7, 15, 17,
    19–20, 23, 28, 52, 77, 91, 94, 171, 180,
    186, 190
Updike, John (see *Witches of Eastwick,
    The*), 20
Urd, 53, 166–167
U.S., 19, 22, 27, 75, 229

V
Valiente, Doreen, 11, 13–14, 18–19, 21, 25–
    26, 32–33, 44, 56, 64, 76, 80, 91, 93, 104,
    110, 177, 179, 187, 218, 224, 226
vampire, 4, 189
Verdandi, 166–167
Vietnam War, 19
Vishnu, 68
Vishuddhi (throat center), 140
vitki, 4, 131
Vodoun, 7–8, 40, 67–69, 71–72, 178–179

W
Walpurgis Night, 158
wand, 88, 182, 202, 211–212, 218, 236–237
Water (see *elements*), 49, 73, 81, 97–99, 101,
    113–115, 117, 118, 120–121, 124, 127, 139,
    144, 146–147, 165, 181, 204, 207–208,
    214, 218, 221, 224, 236–237

Guardian of, 127; Realm of, 118, 120–
   121, 208
Way of the Shaman, The, 52, 185
Wertheimer, Max (see *Gestalt theory*), 85–86
White Goddess, The, 63, 73, 163
Wicca
   Alexandrian, 16–19, 24, 26–27, 83, 93,
   108; Gardnerian, 14–19, 26, 28–33, 37,
   42, 50, 63, 78–81, 83, 87, 89, 93, 95,
   99–100, 108, 111, 113, 129–130, 163, 177,
   179, 184, 194, 202
Wiccan Rede, 27, 31, 34, 42, 93, 99
Wiccan Roots, 11, 21
Wiccans, 20, 28–31, 42, 58, 65, 171
Wiccan, The (magazine), 188
wicca/wicce, 3–4
Willow (see *Buffy the Vampire Slayer*), 20
Wilson, Joe, 95
witch/witches/witchcraft
   Alexandrian, 83; definition of, 40;
   Gardnerian, 17, 31, 83; hereditary,
   2, 4, 6, 8–12, 14–16, 18, 24, 33–35, 77;
   traditions, 10, 15–18, 24–27, 30, 37–39,
   41, 50, 52, 58, 61, 69, 73, 83, 87, 89, 93,
   99–100, 102, 108, 112, 130, 132, 134, 177,
   179, 192, 208, 222; village, 2–3, 6, 35, 45,
   74, 76, 92–93, 107, 115
Witchcraft for Tomorrow, 11, 18, 218
witches' mark, 88
Witches of Eastwick, The, 20
Witches' Voice, The, 24, 43, 192, 239
Witches' Way, The, 18, 25, 163, 177
Woden (also see *Odin*), 54, 75, 123, 233
world tree (see *Yggdrassil*), 53, 114–115, 117,
   119, 166
wounded healer syndrome, 189–190
Wyrd, 53, 133, 166–168

Y
Yahweh, 48
Yggdrassil (see *world tree*), 53, 114–117, 166,
   233
yoga, 137, 139, 142